INVASION OF LAOS, 1971

Invasion of Laos, 1971

Lam Son 719

Robert D. Sander

University of Oklahoma Press : Norman

Library of Congress Cataloging-in-Publication Data

Sander, Robert D., 1946–
Invasion of Laos, 1971 : Lam Son 719 / Robert D. Sander.
  pages   cm
Includes bibliographical references and index.
ISBN 978-0-8061-4437-5 (hardcover : alk. paper) 1. Operation Lam Son 719, 1971.
I. Title.
DS557.8.L3S26 2014
959.704'342   dc23
2013024356

The paper in this book meets the guidelines for permanence and durability of the
Committee on Production Guidelines for Book Longevity of the Council on Library
Resources, Inc. ∞

1 2 3 4 5 6 7 8 9 10

Contents

ILLUSTRATIONS

PREFACE

FOR YEARS I HAVE HARBORED A SENSE that I fought in a lost battle of a lost war. In 1971 I was a helicopter pilot in Operation Lam Son 719, a South Vietnamese Army Corps attempt, supported by U.S. air power, to sever the Ho Chi Minh Trail. It was the culmination of a ten-year effort to halt infiltration of North Vietnamese forces into South Vietnam. As a junior captain I certainly had little day-to-day knowledge of the battle plan or its progress and little influence over the operation's outcome. What I did know when it was over was that many of my fellow aviators, all helicopter pilots, had been shot down, killed, or wounded in what seemed a failed operation. This book is not an autobiography. It is an effort to trace South Vietnam's battle against infiltration from the Communists in the north, to consider the national policies and directives restricting military efforts, and to chronicle Operation Lam Son 719, the final chapter in the anti-infiltration battle.

Lam Son 719 was a bloody affair. Although historical sources contain varying casualty counts, the South Vietnamese force, the Army of the Republic of Vietnam (ARVN) 1st Corps, appears to have suffered more than 7,500 casualties, and the Communist forces approximately 13,000.[1] It is difficult to determine the number of soldiers each side committed to the battle. The South Vietnamese had approximately 17,000 troops available for the operation, but not all of these soldiers were in the area of operations at any given time. As for the Communists, reinforcements were rushed to the area of operations as the forces in contact were depleted, so a casualty rate is difficult to determine. While the overall U.S. casualties were low as compared to that of other epic battles, the casualties were confined primarily to aircrews, and within this smaller subset of the military community, they took on greater emotional significance. U.S. Army helicopter crews endured incomparably higher losses during this two-month operation in heavily defended airspace than during any other period of the Vietnam War.

Years after the war, having retired after twenty-five years of service, I mentioned Lam Son 719 to a friend who is also a Vietnam veteran. To my surprise, he had never heard of Lam Son 719. I knew that U.S. participation was limited primarily to air support, but I was mystified by his reply, especially since Gen. Creighton Abrams once said Lam Son 719 may have been the only decisive battle of the war.[2] Soon I began searching bookstores and libraries and collecting and reading Vietnam War histories. I found references to Lam Son 719, but few sources treated the topic with more than a brief overview, and some contained errors. Very few published accounts provide perspective on the events as they transpired on the ground in Laos. American advisors were prohibited from crossing the border with the South Vietnamese units they supported, and the only U.S. servicemen on the ground were aircrews that were shot down.

The two books that do delve into Lam Son (Tom Marshall's *The Price of Exit* and Keith Nolan's *Into Laos*) are both superb. Marshal presents the relatively narrow view from the helicopter cockpit, and Nolan provides a wider perspective. Books by Lt. Gen. Phillip Davidson (*Vietnam at War*), Stanley Karnow (*Vietnam: A History*), Gen. Bruce Palmer (*The 25-Year War*), and a host of other volumes by authors such as Lewis Sorley, Henry Kissinger, and Lt. Gen. Dave R. Palmer, as well as histories compiled by the army, air force, navy, and marines include brief discussions. One clear point that all of these authors make is that the operation, the timing, and the limitation of U.S. participation were all driven by U.S. foreign policy, not military necessity. Yet at least three questions evade detailed explanation in these accounts: Why was an operation of such importance launched at a time when U.S. combat power in Vietnam was declining? Who planned the operation? And why did it fail? With the publication in late 2010 of the volume of the

U.S. State Department's *Foreign Relations of the United States* that covers Vietnam from July of 1970 to January of 1972, details of the political decisions that shaped Lam Son 719 began to emerge. I found many answers buried in these previously classified files.

This historical document series published by the State Department, *Foreign Relations of the United States* (*FRUS*), became my premier source for research of U.S. foreign policy. To better understand the evolution U.S. policy decisions I began my research with the Kennedy administration. I examined eighteen *FRUS* volumes, each consisting of a thousand or more pages, and supplemented these references with the writings of prominent figures who participated in political decisions, such as Henry Kissinger and Alexander Haig. As my chronological examination of foreign policy approached February 1971 and the onset of Operation Lam Son 719, military documents became my primary references.

Other primary sources for this history of Lam Son 719 included *Lam Son 719*, a monograph by South Vietnamese Maj. Gen. Nguyen Duy Hinh, published by the U.S. Army Center for Military History; a previously classified U.S. Air Force document, *Lam Son 719*, written during and immediately after the operation; the U.S. 101st Airborne Division's after action review of Lam Son 719; the 101st Aviation Group's operations staff duty log; a 101st Aviation Group's weekly narrative summary; the XXIV Corps after action review of Lam Son 719; and interviews with veterans. Although all of these sources offer valuable insights, each has limitations, and the sources do not always agree. I also consulted Merle Pribbenow's translation of the North Vietnamese history of the war, *Victory in Vietnam*. The actions of South Vietnam's President Nguyen Van Thieu had a profound impact on the outcome of Lam Son 719, and it is an unfortunate fact that all relevant documents from the Republic of Vietnam apparently disappeared when Saigon fell to the Communists. The historical document collection of Mike Sloniker, a historian for the Vietnam Helicopter Pilots Association as well as a fellow army aviator and friend since college, was of immeasurable assistance.

General Hinh's monograph provides a macro view of the South Vietnamese Army's actions, but offers little narrative detail of the U.S. air effort. While General Hinh was a member of the 1st ARVN Division during Lam Son 719, his regiment was not deployed to Laos. During the operation there were conflicts between the ARVN corps commander, the Vietnamese Marine commanders, and the ARVN Airborne Division. Hinh's description of these command issues conflicts with those of other observers. The CHECO report is the account of the U.S. Air Force, and at times conflicts with Hinh's description of the operation. It also provides a parochial view of a dispute between the U.S. Air Force and Army discussed in the last chapter of this book.

The 101st Airborne Division's after action report *Airmobile Operations in Support of Operation Lam Son 719* is an excellent source for raw statistical data and provides detailed descriptions of operating procedures, the enemy situation, and logistical references. The 101st Aviation Group's operations duty log is a superb, if myopic, chronological record of U.S. Army aviation events as they were reported to the group tactical operations center (TOC). The document consists of over four hundred pages of Department of the Army Form 1594, each page authenticated and signed by the operations officer. The U.S. XXIV Corps shared responsibility for command and control of the allied force with the ARVN 1st Corps—an arrangement that violated the military principle of unity of command and contributed to the failure of the operation. U.S. ground forces, including the advisors to the South Vietnamese forces, were prohibited from crossing the Laotian border. But still, the senior advisors assigned to the XXIV Corps headquarters were in constant radio contact with their South Vietnamese counterparts as they flew over the battle area and participated in daily briefings conducted in the command posts in Vietnam. However, input from the senior advisors is conspicuously absent from the XXIV Corps' after action report of the operation, leaving the historical record incomplete.

I have included in this book a number of maps and simplified graphic depictions of the Ho Chi Minh Trail and Communist base areas. The trail and the base areas evolved over time, and few historical sources agree on exact locations. Many questions remain, but I hope that relevant documents, particularly documents and decisions originating with the government of South Vietnam, may still exist and eventually come to light.

The Vietnam War—like the Korean War and all the wars that have followed—was a limited war with limited objectives, so it is often difficult to assign such definitive terms as victory and defeat.

Invasion of Laos, 1971

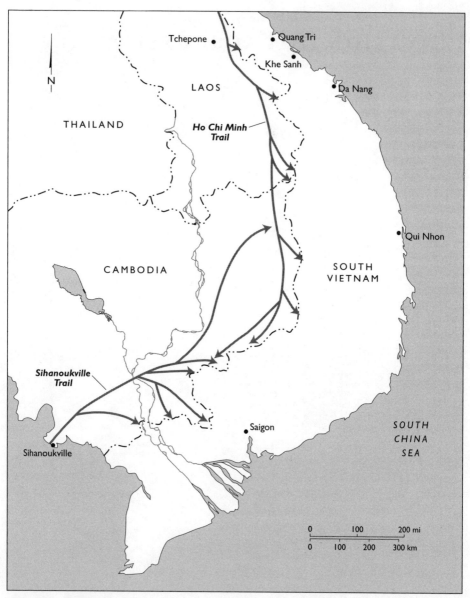

Map 1. The Ho Chi Minh Trail. Drawn by Bill Nelson. Copyright © 2014 by The University of Oklahoma Press.

INTRODUCTION

THE WAR IN VIETNAM CONSISTED of three prolonged battles: a battle against insurgency, a battle to win the population's loyalty (known as the Pacification Program), and a battle against infiltration. *Invasion of Laos, 1971* is a historical account of Operation Lam Son 719, the decisive battle in the effort to shut down Communist infiltration into South Vietnam via the Ho Chi Minh Trail. Tchepone is a small Laotian city near the western end of Route 9, a historic but primitive trade route extending from the southern Laotian panhandle, through the Annamite Mountains, to the South Vietnamese coast a few kilometers south of the demilitarized zone (DMZ). Between Tchepone and the Vietnamese border, Route 9 follows a geographic corridor that intersected the principle infiltration route from North Vietnam, the legendary Ho Chi Minh Trail. For the North Vietnamese it was a natural infiltration route into South Vietnam, and for the Americans and South Vietnamese it seemed the logical point of attack.

The war to seal the western borders of South Vietnam spanned eleven years, from 1961 to 1972. As the war in Vietnam progressed, a secret war occurred simultaneously in Laos. The decisive battle of this Laotian war was a bloody forty-two-day operation in which South Vietnamese forces, supported by U.S. air assets, strove to cut off the Ho Chi Minh Trail by seizing Route 9 and the North Vietnamese Army's transportation hub at Tchepone. The code name for the operation was *Lam Son 719.*

3

From the earliest days of the Vietnam War, a vital element of American strategy consisted of halting the infiltration of Communist troops and supplies into South Vietnam, thus foiling North Vietnam's essential strategy. The 1954 Geneva Accords had established a demarcation line between North and South Vietnam along the Ben Hai River, located just south of the 17th parallel. At this point it was just forty-two miles from the Gulf of Tonkin to the Laotian border. This narrow strip was comparatively easy to monitor through outposts, patrols, and surveillance. But the Annamite Mountains that formed the border between Vietnam and Laos created a vulnerable border—nearly 1,000 miles of steep, rugged mountains covered by a dense primeval rain forest. As the insurgency in the South evolved, the North Vietnamese relied on a network of centuries-old footpaths and trails connecting the few villages in eastern Laos and western Vietnam—the same paths the Vietminh had used during the French Indochina War. Access to Laos, and Cambodia further south, provided the North Vietnamese with limitless opportunity to stage their forces in secure sanctuaries and infiltrate troops and supplies across South Vietnam's western border. In May 1959 the North Vietnamese Army (NVA) organized the 559th Transportation Group with the mission of expanding the trail network.[1]

The situation in Laos was chaotic. Prior to the 1954 Geneva Accords, France had granted self-rule to Laos under a constitutional monarchy. A unified government was never established, however, as a three-sided power struggle ensued with the North Vietnamese and Soviets providing assistance to the Communist faction, the Pathet Lao.

During the transition between their presidencies, Kennedy sought Eisenhower's assessment of the situation in Laos. Secretary of State Christian Herter, offering the administration's view, referred to Laos as the "cork in the bottle." Herter implied that if Laos fell, the Domino Theory would be set in motion, and any proposal that included Communists *in* the government would result in Communist *control* of that government and should be regarded "with great suspicion." Kennedy asked whether the United States should intervene if the government of Laos invoked the defense provisions of the Southeast Asia Treaty

4

Organization. Herter stated, and Eisenhower agreed, that in comparison to South Vietnam, the Laotian government forces were more vigorous in the struggle against Communism but could be improved with the assistance of the U.S. Military Assistance and Advisory Group (MAAG). Kennedy summarized in his notes, "I came away from that meeting feeling that the Eisenhower administration would support intervention—they felt it was preferable to a Communist success in Laos."[2] Kennedy ended up taking Eisenhower's advice; he dispatched a MAAG to Laos and began providing arms and military equipment to pro-Western forces.

Concerned that the situation in Laos could lead to a confrontation between the United States and the Soviet Union, the international community convened a conference in Geneva, Switzerland, in May 1961 to negotiate an accord that would declare Laos a neutral nation. The first step toward ending the civil war in Laos was to negotiate a cease-fire. Anticipating the outcome of the conference, the North Vietnamese promptly stepped up their military operations to seize as much Laotian terrain as possible before a cease-fire agreement was signed, repeating a tactic that had served them well during the conclusion of the French Indochina War. A combined force of the North Vietnamese Army's 325th Division and Laotian Communist insurgents, the Pathet Lao, staged an attack along Route 9, seizing that highway from Tchepone to the village of Ban Dong (midway between Tchepone and the border of South Vietnam) on 11 April 1961.[3] A cease-fire agreement between the Pathet Lao and the Royal Laotian Forces was reached one month later on 12 May 1961. But the cease-fire agreement did not end Communist efforts to gain the upper hand in Laos. Immediately after the North captured Tchepone, Ban Dong, and Muong Phine (the last, a village located at a key road intersection on Route 9 southwest of Tchepone), the 559th Group shifted its strategic transportation route to the western side of the Annamite Mountain Range in Laos, and NVA engineers began building roads through the mountain passes between North Vietnam and Laos.[4] The pending Geneva Accords would declare Laos neutral, after which it would provide sanctuary for the northern army's strategic transportation route. In the meantime the Soviets supplemented delivery of supplies to the Communists with transport aircraft landing at the Tchepone airfield and parachute drops of supplies at Muong Phine. By March 1961 the Soviets brought in 2,400 tons by air and another 1,000 tons by truck. It was not long until NVA-constructed roads supported motorized transport as far south as Tchepone.

On 3 May 1961 deputy secretary of defense Roswell Gilpatric, anticipating ratification of the accords, wrote President Kennedy saying that the Geneva conference would, like the 1954 Geneva Accords, likely result in the appointment of an International Control Commission, and that over the past two years the Vietcong had stepped up their attacks to the point that the decisive battle to determine the fate of South Vietnam was approaching. He expected the Communists to use the process of international negotiation as a cover for continued subversive activities. He also pointed out that if the accords were ratified, the North Vietnamese would become the gatekeepers of the three principal passes through the Annamite mountains: the Nape Pass, the Mu Gia Pass, and the pass that controls the road from Quang Tri to Savannakhet in Southern Laos, "an invasion route that would outflank the most important defensive terrain [the DMZ] in the northern area of South Vietnam."[5] The last-named pass, controlling the road (Route 9) from Quang Tri to Savannakhet, passes through Tchepone. Thus, Tchepone was at the intersection of the major trails, waterways, and the few roads in the area. And more important, it had an airfield.

On 11 May President Kennedy took another step toward American involvement in the war when he approved National Security Action Memorandum (NSAM) 52 and directed that four hundred U.S. Special Forces advisors be deployed to Vietnam.[6] Five months later he ordered guerilla ground action, including the use of U.S. advisors if necessary, against Communist aerial resupply missions in the Tchepone area.[7] However, the raid was put on hold pending the outcome of the Geneva conference.

International pressure ruled out unilateral intervention, and President Kennedy decided to use this diplomatic route to neutralize Laos and separate the issue of Laos from the larger issue of Vietnam.[8] Fourteen nations, including the United States and North Vietnam, signed the 1962 Geneva Accords, which declared that Laos was to be politically neutral and was not to enter into any military alliance; Laos would not allow foreign military forces to use or occupy its territory, and would not recognize any military alliance or coalition. All foreign troops, paramilitary forces, and foreign military personnel were to be removed from Laos in the "shortest possible time," and the accords provided for an International Control Commission (ICC) to monitor compliance. Kennedy's decision to use diplomacy instead of overt military force was monumental and ultimately decided the outcome of the Vietnam War. The ICC was impotent; the North Vietnamese ignored the agreement and had unrestricted access to the infiltration routes while the hands of American military commanders were tied by a policy that prohibited overt military action in Laos.

The United States promptly withdrew its Military Assistance and Advisory Group, but the North Vietnamese paid little heed to their agreement to withdraw and left a force of 7,000 NVA soldiers in Laos. The ICC was composed of representatives from Poland (a Communist country), Canada (a Western democracy), and India (a neutral country), and as international events unfolded, it became clear that India was in the Soviet orbit. The ICC had neither the inclination nor resources to ensure compliance with the accords. The government of Laos was powerless to prevent continued North Vietnamese occupation and construction of the Ho Chi Minh Trail.

Although U.S. reconnaissance flights over Laos continued, so did North Vietnamese expansion of the Ho Chi Minh Trail, and the infiltration of soldiers and matériel escalated. Admiral Harry Felt, commander in chief of U.S. Pacific forces, told President Kennedy that Phoumi Nosavan, the leader of the right-wing Laotian faction, needed heavier equipment than the United States was providing. President Kennedy remarked that the United States could fly supplies into Laos, but that certain planes would have to be flown by "civilianized" active duty U.S. Air Force (USAF) pilots.[9] Both Prime Minister Souvanna Phouma and the United States were intent on maintaining the appearance of abiding by the 1962 accords, even as Phouma asked for U.S. military assistance in 1963. Therefore, the United States extended aid, but could never establish a military commission, which was prohibited under the accords. Together, the American diplomatic mission and the CIA meticulously coordinated military support with the government of Laos. Thus was born the secret war in Laos that would go on for the following twelve years. The situation was a curious arrangement. Once the United States commenced its secret, diplomatically restrained bombing of the Ho Chi Minh Trail, the North Vietnamese made no complaints, but they continued to deny the presence of their troops in Laos as well as South Vietnam.

As the Ho Chi Minh Trail extended southward through neutral territory, the terrain offered numerous off-ramps that would allow the Communists to turn east and enter South Vietnam. South Vietnamese forces, accompanied by U.S. Special Forces soldiers, attempted to patrol infiltration routes along South Vietnam's border, but it was a futile effort. The scope of the problem far exceeded the resources available. The terrain of the border region made it all but impossible to seal off infiltration. On 20 March 1963 Undersecretary of State for Far Eastern Affairs Averill Harriman received a memorandum from William Jorden, his special assistant for political affairs who had been briefed by intelligence officials and recently made tour of the region in question. His memorandum described an impossible situation: the pace of infiltration was accelerating, and increasingly lethal weapons supplied by the Communist bloc were flowing across the borders of Cambodia and Laos. Sealing off the western borders of South Vietnam was impossible because the region was mile after mile of steep mountains covered by impenetrable forest and there were far too few troops to patrol the region.[10] But cross-border infiltration was only one of the problems facing the Kennedy administration.

The head of South Vietnam's government was Ngo Dinh Diem, a devout Catholic who had risen to power after the 1954 Geneva Accords partitioned Vietnam.[11] After defeating his rivals, he consolidated control of the government in an oligarchy composed of his immediate family. His brother, Ngo Dinh Nhu, the head of the secret police, exerted growing influence in his role as Special Counselor to Diem. Two attempted coups against Diem, in 1960 and 1962, by disgruntled military officers had strengthened Diem's conviction that senior military leaders should be selected not on the basis of competency, but by their personal fidelity to him. As an additional defense against coups, the military chain of command was purposely muddled so that no one commander in any region could have absolute authority.[12] Given these circumstances, the battle against the insurgency made little or no progress, despite U.S. aid.

By 1963 infiltration and insurgency were accelerating and the Pacification Program was floundering. After protests and demonstrations erupted, Diem, convinced by his brother that Buddhist organizations had been infiltrated by Communists and were responsible for the unrest, launched a campaign of repression against the Buddhist, the majority religion of Vietnam. All diplomatic efforts to convince Diem to separate himself from Nhu and end the anti-Buddhist campaign failed. Rumors of a coup plot surfaced on 21 August 1963 and were confirmed four days later when Brig. Gen. Nguyen Khanh told CIA agent Lucien Conein that he and other generals were determined to stop taking orders from the Nhu family, who were now allegedly plotting to move toward neutrality and reconciliation with North Vietnam.[13] Khanh asked if the United States would support an army takeover of the government.[14]

President Kennedy sent Secretary of Defense Robert McNamara and former Chairman of the Joint Chiefs of Staff Maxwell Taylor to Vietnam to assess the situation. When they returned, they reported that the military campaign against the insurgency was progressing but that opposition to Diem was growing. They speculated that continued repression by Diem could reverse the favorable military trend, but that Diem's previous rejection of U.S. pleas for moderation made it unlikely that he would change.[15] As to the prospect of a coup, McNamara and Taylor recommended that no initiative should be taken to encourage a change in government: "Our policy should be to seek urgently to identify and build contacts with an alternative leadership if and when it appears." The report also included a variety of recommendations and possible courses of action. One of these was to start a phased withdrawal of American advisors from Vietnam. Kennedy accepted this recommendation and directed implementation of plans to withdraw 1,000 U.S. military personnel prior to the end of 1963.[16] The administration provided tacit support for the coup and made plans to grant asylum to Diem.[17]

The conspirators launched their coup on 1 November and by the night of 2 November and both Diem and Nhu were arrested, and much to Kennedy's dismay, murdered.[18] President Kennedy was assassinated on 22 November 1963, eighteen days after Diem's death, and Vice President Lyndon Johnson was sworn in as president. Johnson set aside all plans for U.S. withdrawal and set the nation on a course toward a protracted and increasingly unpopular war.

The Ho Chi Minh Trail was still a primitive network of roads and footpaths, but by late 1963 increasing numbers of NVA cadre and more sophisticated weapons were arriving in South Vietnam. The North Vietnamese road network now extended from the Annamite Mountain passes to points south of Tchepone where the cargo was shifted to porters, cargo bicycles, and pack animals. But these were not all-weather roads, and the annual monsoon season slowed the southward flow of men and matériel southward.

Lyndon Johnson turned to a strategy of graduated response to convince the North Vietnamese to end their infiltration of South Vietnam. Meanwhile, the North Vietnamese continued their efforts to extend their roads well past Tchepone and across the border to neutral Cambodia. According to Gen. Vo Nguyen Giap, the architect of the North Vietnamese Army, by the time the South Vietnamese government collapsed in 1975, North Vietnam's infiltration route totaled over 12,400 miles of trails, roads and footpaths. Not all of the roads and trails were operational at the same time; some segments were abandoned and replaced with new roads and trails offering greater concealment and improved mobility. In addition, the North Vietnamese built an eight hundred-mile communications network to coordinate movement over the supply route, and a petroleum pipeline system that ran from the Chinese border to near Saigon.[19]

In the meantime, the new South Vietnamese government, headed by Gen. Duong Van "Big" Minh and his revolutionary council of twelve generals, was paralyzed by ineptitude. They constantly bickered during meetings, which Minh frequently avoided in order to play tennis and attend to his orchids and exotic birds.[20] The ineptitude of the new South Vietnamese political leadership in no way lessened Lyndon Johnson's determination to continue the policy of containing Communist expansion.

Chapter 1

Johnson's War

During Lyndon Johnson's five years in office, America's role in Southeast Asia evolved from military assistance and covert participation in the Vietnam War to commitment of more than 500,000 American troops and a secret war in Laos. Bound by a pretense of honoring the 1962 Geneva Accords and the faux neutrality of Cambodia, Johnson refused to authorize overt actions against the Ho Chi Minh Trail. The eastern border areas of Cambodia and Laos provided a safe haven for the North Vietnamese Army and Vietcong forces where they could withdraw when threatened and stage their attacks on allied forces at the time and place of their choosing.

On 23 November 1963, the day following Kennedy's death, Secretary of State Dean Rusk provided newly sworn-in President Johnson with a report that summarized the situation in Vietnam. The report cast an optimistic outlook on the future stating that, since Diem's demise, the outlook for progress was much improved: the new government had the enthusiastic support of the urban population and recognized the need to win the support of the peasants; officers in South Vietnam's notoriously politicized armed forces were now being chosen on the basis of merit; and the United States was withdrawing 1,000 of its 16,500 military forces from Vietnam.[1] Unfortunately, Rusk's claims of progress were soon proven wrong.

President Johnson met with the National Security Council two days after Kennedy's assassination. During this meeting Director of Central

Intelligence John McCone contradicted Rusk's optimistic appraisal with the CIA's more pessimistic and accurate estimate of the situation in Vietnam. The CIA had noted an increase in Vietcong activity since the first of November, and the level of message traffic on the Vietcong military and political networks might reflect preparations for further sustained guerrilla pressures. McCone stated that the military junta was having considerable trouble in completing the political organization of the government and was receiving little, if any, help from the civilian leadership. He concluded by stating that his agency could not give a particularly optimistic appraisal of the future. McCone wrote in his notes of the meeting that "Johnson definitely feels that we place too much emphasis on social reforms; he has very little tolerance with our spending so much time being 'do-gooders'; and he has no tolerance whatsoever with bickering and quarreling of the type that has gone on in South Vietnam."[2] Director McCone also commented that President Johnson's "tone" contrasted with that of President Kennedy: whereas Kennedy was willing to entertain discussions of opposing views and build consensus, it would soon become clear that Johnson was an authoritarian, unwilling to tolerate any discussion of views contrary to his own.

Lyndon Johnson's policy on the war was issued two days later. National Security Action Memorandum 273 stated that the United States was committed to assisting the South Vietnamese in their contest "against the externally directed and supported Communist conspiracy." Paragraph seven of the memorandum directed that planning should include increased levels of covert actions "resulting in damage to North Vietnam," and that all planning should include the "plausibility of denial." The directive for covert activities led to the formulation of Operation Plan (OPLAN) 34A, a concept that was developed at the headquarters of the Commander in Chief, Pacific command (CINCPAC), in 1963 and expanded at McNamara's direction by the CIA and the Military Assistance Command, Vietnam (MACV), in 1964. OPLAN 34A included more than 2,000 proposed covert activities, including reconnaissance, psychological warfare, sabotage, and small-scale raids in and on the coast of North Vietnam.[3]

By early January 1964 the situation in Vietnam was in a downward spiral. A junta led by Gen. Duong Van Minh replaced President Diem. Then, on 30 January 1964 Minh and his junta were ousted in a successful coup by one of their co-conspirators in the coup of Diem, Gen. Nguyen Khanh. In the meantime, the Communist insurgents were gaining on the battlefield. By August covert OPLAN 34A raids were hitting the North Vietnamese coast. These raids led to the Tonkin Gulf incident, U.S. retaliatory air strikes, and a congressional resolution giving President Johnson open-ended authority for military operations. Despite this authority, Johnson continued to avoid overt military activity.

Lyndon Johnson, running as the "peace candidate," defeated Barry Goldwater by a landslide margin in the 1964 presidential elections. The United States was still not "at war" in Vietnam since the acknowledged military presence was still limited to an advisory role. But the covert war was expanding. The Tonkin Gulf incident led to ineffective limited retaliatory air strikes as the Communist forces struck back against increasing American military presence. The pace of infiltration continued to increase as well. By the end of the year complete battalions of the North Vietnamese Army (NVA) were making the trek down the rapidly expanding Ho Chi Minh Trail and entering South Vietnam. One regiment of the NVA's 325th Division had crossed the Cambodian border and entered the central highlands of South Vietnam, and the two remaining regiments of the division were on their way.[4]

During the 1964 strategy discussions, Westmoreland consistently argued that border control operations into Laos would benefit the counterinsurgency campaign more than attacks against North Vietnam.[5] Westmoreland recognized that the only way to seal South Vietnam's eight hundred-mile western border was to shut down the infiltration routes. However, the administration rejected his logic and continued to follow the policy of aid and assistance to the South Vietnamese government and covert OPLAN 34A operations. By early 1965 Communist momentum was threatening to push the United States out of Vietnam. On 7 February the Vietcong attacked the U.S. air bases at Pleiku and Camp Holloway in the western highlands, destroying several aircraft and inflicting eighty-five casualties. Johnson ordered immediate retaliation, and launched carrier-based Operation Flaming Dart. Three days later the Vietcong struck again, this time on the enlisted barracks at Qui Nhon, killing twenty-three American soldiers and wounding another twenty-one. Again, Johnson ordered limited retaliatory airstrikes on North Vietnam. On 13 February President Johnson ordered a "program of measured and limited air action" against selected targets in North Vietnam. The code name for the operation was Rolling Thunder.[6]

Secretary of Defense Robert McNamara provided the strategy for Rolling Thunder that fit Johnson's needs: that is, a "graduated response." Under this strategy, in theory, small increments of increasing military force would signal U.S. resolve to the North Vietnamese, who would then end infiltration and cease their efforts to reunite Vietnam under a Communist government by force. Mindful of the catastrophic entry of the Chinese Communists in the Korean War, these increments were intended to pose no overt threat to Communist China or the Soviet Union and to minimize the risk of Chinese or Soviet intervention. At the same time, the incremental application of force was designed to maintain the support of the political Right while being small enough to avoid alienating the political Left. Johnson took the middle road, a road that would take the nation into a long, bloody war with little hope of victory.

Rolling Thunder was originally intended to be an eight-week program; it quickly expanded to twelve weeks, but it ultimately continued until late 1968, with periodic pauses intended to advance negotiations. Johnson, driven by fears that the war would widen to a land war with China, and all too familiar with how Gen. Douglas McArthur had brought the nation to the brink of nuclear war in Korea, was determined to maintain personal control over the operation.

President Johnson, assisted by Secretary of Defense Robert McNamara, personally assumed the task of selecting targets. Strikes on targets in and around Hanoi and Hiaphong (the latter a major point of entry for military supplies and equipment from the Soviet Union) were rarely authorized. The airfields housing the Soviet-built MIG fighters were off-limits, as were (for a period of time) the surface-to-air (SAM) missile sites, for fear of killing Chinese and Soviet technicians and advisors.[7] Johnson and McNamara then determined the number of strike aircraft, the date and time that each target was to be struck, the type and amount of ordnance used on each target, and in many cases, the direction of attack. President Johnson is alleged to have bragged, "They can't even bomb an outhouse without my approval."[8]

The majority of Johnson's advisors endorsed the concept of bombing North Vietnam to force an end to their infiltration of South Vietnam. The major difference of opinions dealt only with the scope of the proposed operation. The exception was Undersecretary George Ball who had never been an advocate of U.S. military intervention in Vietnam. Ball argued that the proposed air offensive would be ineffective.[9] While Ball's cabinet position as undersecretary of state for economic and agricultural affairs would seem to undermine his qualifications to make such an assessment, Ball was uniquely qualified. During the latter part of World War II Ball had been a member of a board of experts assembled to produce an assessment of the bombing of Germany. During the French Indochina War he had served as counsel to the French embassy and had great insight into the war. In November 1961 he met with President Kennedy to discuss an unrelated matter, but the discussion eventually turned to Vietnam. Ball stated that he was opposed to committing American forces to Vietnam because it would be a tragic error. Once it started there would be no end: "Within five years we'll have three hundred thousand men in the paddies and jungles and we will never find them again. . . . Vietnam is the worst possible terrain both from a physical and a political point of view." Kennedy's reply was, "George you are crazier than hell. That's just not going to happen."[10]

The graduated response strategy provided the North Vietnamese the time and opportunity to disperse critical assets and assemble an effective air defense system. As time went on, North Vietnamese prisons became populated with downed American pilots and aircrews. Rolling Thunder entailed a dramatic increase in the number of aircraft required to support air operations. In 1964 the Vietcong had scored a major victory when a successful rocket-and-mortar attack on the Bien Hoa Airfield, located twelve miles north of Saigon, destroyed four B-57 bombers and damaged fifteen others. The first U.S. ground combat forces, the 9th U.S. Marine Expeditionary Brigade, was deployed to Da Nang on 8 March 1965 to protect the airbase and the USAF squadrons stationed there. The North Vietnamese failed to react to the signal Rolling Thunder was designed to transmit, so in late March the target list was refined to transmit a stronger signal. On 6 April yet another small increment was added to the graduated response when the president approved a change of mission for all marine battalions deployed to Vietnam. The mission for the marines at Da Nang changed from passive defense of the airbase to active counterguerilla operations.[11]

Director of Central Intelligence John McCone had reservations about the wisdom of changing the mission for U.S. ground forces. On 2 April he sent a memorandum outlining his reservations to secretaries Rusk and McNamara, National Security Advisor McGeorge Bundy, and the U.S. ambassador to South Vietnam, Gen. Maxwell Taylor. McCone stated that he believed the decision to change the marines' mission was correct only if Rolling Thunder targets were less restrained. His reports stated that the air strikes had not caused a change in North Vietnam's policy of directing the Vietcong insurgency and infiltration, and he doubted that the new changes in target selection would accomplish anything more than hardening the attitude of the North Vietnamese. He believed that under these conditions, the United States "can expect requirements for an ever-increasing commitment of U.S. personnel without materially improving the chances of victory." He concluded that if the mission of the marines was going to change, then the ground rules for airstrikes against targets in North Vietnam must also change.[12]

Director McCone reiterated his conclusions to President Johnson during a National Security Council meeting later that day. Johnson listened to McCone's appraisal without comment, and a copy of the memorandum was included in the president's reading file. McCone continued to insist that the graduated response strategy was failing, and Rusk and McNamara continued to hold the line for graduated response.

Still convinced that President Johnson had not had an opportunity to read a copy of the memorandum, McCone composed a detailed letter to President Johnson repeating his assessment. On 28 April he met with President Johnson yet again. The president listened stoically, accepted his letter, and set it aside. McCone resigned that same day.[13]

The landing of the marines at Da Nang was followed by the arrival of the army's 173rd Airborne Brigade at the Bien Hoa Air Base near Saigon on 3 May. President Johnson approved a request from General Westmoreland for forty-four additional combat battalions. The 1st Infantry Division arrived at Lie Khe, north of Saigon. The 25th Infantry Division deployed to an area northwest of Saigon, and the 4th Infantry Division was sent to Pleiku. The 1st Cavalry Division, reorganized as an airmobile division, deployed to An Khe in the central highlands. The South Korean government sent the 9th Republic of Korea (ROK) Division, which was assigned an area of operations around Tuy Hoa.

The Cambodian government, led by Prince Norodom Sihanouk, severed diplomatic relations with the United States on 3 May 1965, claiming America was responsible for air attacks by the South Vietnamese Air Force that allegedly killed Cambodian citizens. In order to avoid further international attention, President Johnson issued orders prohibiting any action, including aerial reconnaissance, across the Cambodian border. North Vietnamese infiltration into the Cambodian border area increased immediately.

In late 1965 infiltration of North Vietnamese forces increased to the point that, in their estimation, they had sufficient forces to move from a war of insurgency and guerilla warfare to a war of movement by conventional forces. The NVA's 324th Division moved southward, through the Laotian panhandle into northwest Cambodia, to a position west of Pleiku, to engage U.S. and ARVN forces in an apparent attempt to drive to the coastal lowlands in Quang Ngai Province to bisect South Vietnam south of Da Nang. The U.S. 1st Cavalry Division intercepted the NVA 66th Regiment and elements of the 33rd NVA Regiment near the Cambodian border during the bloody battle of the Ia Drang Valley from 14 to 18 November 1965. The NVA was forced to retreat across the Cambodian border after taking severe losses. The battle demonstrated an aspect of the war that would remain constant: when confronted by a superior force, the NVA would retreat back into safe havens west of the South Vietnamese border, and U.S. policy would honor this sanctuary.

Following the battle in the Ia Drang Valley, Secretary of Defense McNamara sent a memorandum to President Johnson summarizing the situation in South Vietnam. It stated that Prime Minister Nguyen Cao Ky estimated that his government controlled no more than 25 percent of the population. The Vietcong Army was expanding, and with increasing infiltration of NVA battalions, the combined Communist forces had the potential capability of expanding by sixteen battalions per month. McNamara estimated that even with the current level of sea and air interdiction, the NVA would be able to infiltrate more than two hundred tons of matériel per day, more than enough to support the combined Communist forces. McNamara recommended that additional U.S. battalions be deployed to Vietnam, bringing the total to seventy-four by the end of 1966. He stated that, combined with USAF squadrons, combat support units, and additional advisors, the proposed increase would bring the total U.S. strength in Vietnam to more than 400,000, and that 200,000 additional deployments might be required in 1967. In addition to the troop increases, McNamara recommended a slow expansion of the bombing campaign over North Vietnam, but that both the troop increase and the incrementally intensified bombing campaign should be delayed until after a three-to-four-week bombing halt. McNamara stated that this strategy would not guarantee success and that the number of U.S. killed-in-action could be expected to reach 1,000 per month. McNamara indicated that Ambassador Lodge, Generals Westmoreland and Wheeler, and Admiral Sharp (commander in chief of U.S. Pacific forces), all concurred with the "prolonged course of action," but that "General Wheeler and Admiral Sharp would intensify the bombing of the north more quickly."[14] In truth, the Joint Chiefs of Staff had serious reservations, but their views rarely made it past McNamara, the gatekeeper to Johnson's office.[15]

The Joint Chiefs took the extraordinary step of requesting an audience with the president so that they could present an alternative strategy. No one except the Joint Chiefs and the president were expected to be in the room, but the White House military office failed to provide an easel for the briefing map, and Lt. Col. Charles Cooper was directed to remain in the room to hold the map. The Chairman of the Joint Chiefs, Gen. Earle Wheeler, opened the briefing presenting a plan that called for sustained B-52 bombing of Hanoi and mining of North Vietnam's ports, a plan similar to the one the U.S. would use in 1973 to bring the North Vietnamese to their knees. It was a bold plan designed to use U.S. superiority in air and sea power in order to preclude protracted land warfare.

When General Wheeler concluded the briefing and asked President Johnson if he had any questions, Johnson turned to the chief of staff of the army and the commandant of the marine corps and asked if they agreed with the plan. After they indicated agreement, Johnson exploded. He screamed obscenities, cursed, and ridiculed them for coming to his office with their "military advice." After disparaging their abilities, he added that he did expect their help and that he was not going to allow some "military idiots" to talk him into World War III. He ended the conference by shouting "Get the hell out of my office!" In the opinion of Charles Cooper, it was apparent that McNamara had set up the chiefs of staff.[16]

The U.S. troop level soared during the next two years, but Johnson never allowed U.S. ground forces to pursue the enemy across the border or take a decisive action to cut the infiltration routes in Laos and Cambodia. Nor would he make full use of American sea and air power to isolate North Vietnam from its sources of supplies from the Soviet Union and China. Lyndon Johnson was a man consumed by his fear of intervention by the Soviets or Chinese, but also of the political consequences of withdrawal. But he was not afraid to travel a path that Robert McNamara accurately predicted could take the lives of 1,000 American fighting men every month: by May 1965 U.S. aircraft were flying an average of 1,500 combat air sorties per month in Laos.[17] And the pace of infiltration continued to increase.

In late 1966 Westmoreland's staff completed plans for an assortment of major cross-border campaigns. Operation Plan Full Cry called
for a multi-divisional force to drive into Laos along Route 9, while his
airmobile division, the 1st Cavalry, landed on the Bolovens Plateau
further south and drove north, destroying enemy matériel and installations until they linked up with the forces along Route 9.[18] In a vari-
ation of the plan the 1st Cavalry Division was to establish an airhead
on the Bolovens Plateau and then attack north and west to reach the
Mekong; the 3rd Marine Division was to attack along Route 9 to capture Tchepone, while the U.S. 4th Infantry Division attacked westward
from Pleiku and an ARVN division attacked westward from the A Shau
Valley.[19] The plan called for a significant increase in troop strength, and
when it became apparent that President Johnson would not approve
additional deployments, Westmoreland turned to two smaller, but
less decisive, proposals for South Vietnamese cross-border operations
during 1967. The U.S. ambassador to Laos, William Sullivan, opposed
each of these plans on the grounds that the Laotian government would
never approve an incursion on Laotian territory, and if an incursion
should occur, the prime minister of Laos, Souvanna Phouma, who was
thus far cooperative with clandestine U.S. operations, would probably
resign.[20] The plans were rejected.

A small portion of one plan survived. Operation York 2 called for
an ARVN brigade to attack into Base Area 607 in Laos, which was
adjacent to the A Shau Valley in South Vietnam and an amphibious
landing north of the DMZ.[21] In addition, the U.S. 1st Cavalry Division would be moved to Khe Sanh and conduct an airmobile attack
into the enemy's rear. On 27 November the Joint Chiefs sent a memorandum to Secretary of Defense McNamara stating that they had
examined the plans and that York 2 "has merit and appears militarily
necessary."[22] The idea of an amphibious assault was quickly discarded
when Secretaries Rusk and McNamara recommended against it. One
portion of the plan temporarily survived when Secretaries McNamara
and Rusk agreed to the ARVN raid into Base Area 607, and the president granted approval during a 5 December meeting.[23] However, the

events of early 1968 and the Communists' Tet Offensive overcame execution of this plan.

In late 1967 Westmorland anticipated that the 1968 elections could result in a new administration and a change to policies that would permit operations in Laos. He directed the United States Army, Vietnam (USARV), staff to begin work on a new plan for interdicting the Ho Chi Minh Trail with a cross-border attack. Two plans were developed—El Paso 1 and El Paso 2.[24] While there were differences in the two plans, they both contained one of the central themes of OPLAN Full Cry: an attack westward from Khe Sanh along Route 9 to Tchepone.

Col. John M. Collins served as the chief of the USARV campaign planning group. In 1997 Colonel Collins briefly described one of the versions of El Paso in an article entitled "Going to Tchepone" in the National Defense University's publication *Joint Forces Quarterly*. The article provides a detailed description for the initial assault force that included an ARVN airborne division, a U.S. Army airmobile division, a U.S. infantry division, and "substantial combat and logistical support." The attack would extend well past Tchepone to the village of Muong Phine, southwest of Tchepone, in order to prevent the North Vietnamese from simply moving their infiltration routes further west in Laos.[25]

The concept of operations called for the ARVN airborne division to make a parachute assault on Muong Phine, while U.S. airmobile brigades seized Tchepone, Ban Dong, and the airfield at Ban Houei Sane on Route 9. Simultaneously, U.S. tanks and infantry would attack westward from Khe Sanh along Route 9 and link up as soon as possible. The priority tasks of the army's engineers included the conversion of Route 9 to a double-lane primary supply route and rehabilitation of the airfields at Tchepone and Ban Houei Sane.[26]

Geography dictated the proposed landing zones for airmobile operations. Each of the selected landing zones contained abandoned, bombed-out airfields. In their current state of repair they were useless for fixed-wing aircraft, but more than suitable for use as helicopter landing zones, and large enough to accommodate the simultaneous landing of five or more helicopters, ensuring a rapid buildup of ground combat strength upon arrival. The south side of the Xepon River was purposely not selected for proposed landing zones. The terrain rose sharply up an escarpment to a rugged plateau that was blanketed with double- and triple-canopied rain forest. Any landing zone (LZ) on the south side would have to be constructed in advance of an airmobile landing; the element of surprise would be lost, and the landing zone would be a single-ship LZ, requiring a daisy chain of lift helicopters to disgorge their passengers one at a time, extending the amount of time required to build up ground combat power and increase aircraft exposure to enemy fire as they approached the LZ in single file.

El Paso was conceived as corps-sized operation. While Collins does not provide a detailed troop list, it can be assumed that the "substantial combat and logistical support" normally associated with corps operations would include as a minimum a corps artillery headquarters with two or more subordinate field artillery groups (with each group consisting of two to four artillery battalions), an engineer brigade to supplement the engineer battalions of the three divisions, a corps support command (with transportation, maintenance, and quartermaster battalions), and an armored cavalry regiment. Although not specifically addressed by Collins, forces would also have to be allocated to secure the DMZ and to protect Route 9 in South Vietnam.[27] El Paso required engineering and logistical support efforts exceeding all previous operations during the Vietnam War.

The monsoon weather pattern was considered an important factor in timing El Paso. The Ho Chi Minh Trail operated at maximum capacity during the dry seasons, but traffic came to a near-halt during the wet seasons. If, at the onset of the dry season, the allied forces could sever the trail, they could shut off Communist supplies for a total of eighteen months (the dry season plus the previous wet season and the following wet season). The regional weather patterns are complicated by the fact that the Annamite Mountains separate the proposed area of operations into two separate but overlapping patterns. Air support of the operation was critical to success and the attack had to be timed to take maximum advantage of clear skies and dry weather, which would facilitate overland movement. After a review of the metrological history for the proposed area of operations, October was deemed the best time to launch the attack.[28]

President Johnson rejected this plan as well. On 18 December 1967 he dictated a memorandum for record: "As for the movement of U.S. forces across the frontiers of South Vietnam, I am inclined to be extremely reserved unless a powerful case can be made. There are two reasons: the political risks involved, and the diversion of forces from pressure on the VC [Vietcong] and from all other dimensions of pacification. But I believe it would be unwise to announce a policy that would deny these options."[29] Anticipating a change of administration in the coming 1968 presidential elections, and with Johnson's decision on cross-border operations being less than absolute, the USARV staff continued work on OPLAN El Paso. But a major Communist offensive put an end to all hopes of a cross-border attack.

THE TET OFFENSIVE

While Westmoreland's staff planned for operations in Laos, the North Vietnamese set in motion their plan for a major offensive in South Vietnam. They executed the first phase of their plan in early 1967 with a series of attacks against U.S. strongpoints along the borders of South Vietnam designed to draw U.S. forces away from South Vietnam's population centers. In February the North Vietnamese struck at Con Thien, a USMC position on the DMZ, and stiff combat continued in and around Con Thien throughout the rest of 1967. The next Communist target was Song Be, a small town located near the Cambodian Border on the northwest approach to Saigon. Two days after attacking Song Be, the NVA hit the nearby village of Loc Ninh. The NVA next targeted Ben Het, an allied strongpoint defended by 250 Americans and 750 Montagnards, located eight miles from the tri-border intersection of Cambodia, Laos, and South Vietnam. The final border battle in 1967 was by far the bloodiest.

In November four regiments of the NVA attacked a battalion of the U.S. 4th Infantry Division at Dak To, located farther north in the tri-border area. Westmoreland immediately sent in a total of nine U.S. battalions and six ARVN battalions to reinforce the vastly outnumbered battalion. It was a bloody, hard-fought battle, but in the end the surviving Communists retreated back across the border to sanctuary.

A captured NVA document revealed North Vietnam's intent to annihilate a major U.S. unit in order to force Westmoreland to deploy as many additional troops as possible to the western highlands.[30] While the document did not disclose why the North Vietnamese wanted to lure U.S. forces to the border regions, it was apparent that it must be the prelude to a major offensive. However, there was no indication of when or where this Communist offensive would occur. In November there were clear indications that the North Vietnamese were posturing troops for an attack on the USMC brigade at Khe Sanh, the proposed launch point for Operation Plan El Paso and the western anchor for U.S. forces defending the DMZ.

By early January 1968 the situation for the marine garrison at Khe Sanh was becoming precarious. Elements of as many as four NVA divisions were converging on the 6,000 marines. The NVA cut off Route 9 east of Khe Sanh, isolating the defenders from their only ground supply route. Some analysts perceived the NVA intentions as an effort to inflict a defeat on the U.S. forces at Khe Sanh that would parallel the defeat of the French at Dienbienphu.[31]

The Joint Chiefs of Staff discussed two possible courses of action. The first was to withdraw the marines from Khe Sanh. The second was to preempt the NVA attack on that city with a U.S. attack into Laos as outlined in OPLAN El Paso. The Chairman of the Joint Chiefs of Staff, Gen. Earle Wheeler, addressed the issue with General Westmoreland, whose reply was that he favored neither of these two options. Instead, he intended to defend at Khe Sanh because he considered it a critical position. Khe Sanh anchored the western end of the defenses along the DMZ. Westmoreland supported his position with three major points. First, the preemptive assault would have to be launched in the near future to be effective. There was inadequate time for preparing logistical and assembling the attack force. Second, the Northeast Monsoon season was approaching, which would limit air operations, and the current airlift capabilities were not adequate to support the anticipated operations in Laos and the rest of the theater of operations. Third, Westmoreland had new source of intelligence: unattended ground sensors, planted along trails and roads, that detected and reported enemy movement.[32]

In 1966 Secretary of Defense McNamara ordered the construction of an electronic "fence" along the DMZ from the coast of South Vietnam and across Laos. Part of that effort was part of Operation Igloo White. Air-dropped electronic sensors were implanted along the infiltration routes in the Laotian panhandle. The available technology came from the navy's antisubmarine warfare forces. A specialized squadron, VO-67 (a visual observation squadron), was organized, equipped with twelve specially modified P2V-5 "Neptune" aircraft, and trained to seed the Ho Chi Minh Trail with variants of antisubmarine sensors.[33] The squadron was organized in February 1967 at Alameda Naval Air Station and deployed to Nakhom Phanom (NKP), Thailand, in November 1967. Assisted by USAF forward air controllers who guided the Neptunes over the myriad of trails and coordinated air cover, VO-67 began the process of seeding sensors along the infiltration routes.

Originally designed in 1950 for maritime reconnaissance and antisubmarine warfare, the Neptune was slightly less than seventy-eight feet long and had a wingspan of one hundred feet. It was powered by two radial engines and had a maximum airspeed of 313 miles per hour and a cruising airspeed of just 174 miles per hour. The Neptune was a slow, lumbering target as it flew down the heavily defended trail dropping sensors. The Neptune was never the aircraft of choice for this mission; it was simply the only choice that was immediately available. As soon as F-4 fighter-bombers were modified to drop the sensors, VO-67 was disbanded. The surviving members were sworn to secrecy and reassigned.[34] While VO-67's life span was relatively short, the sensor program continued until the end of U.S. involvement.

Two types of sensors were used to detect and track enemy troop and truck movements. The acoustic sensor was deployed at a low level, and it was equipped with a small parachute to slow its decent and suspend the sensor in the jungle canopy. The second type of sensor, the Air Delivered Seismic Detection sensor (ASID), was deployed from a higher altitude and was designed to penetrate the soil and leave its camouflaged antenna above ground.

Operation Igloo White consisted of three parts: planting sensors, orbiting aircraft to relay the signal, and recording at the infiltration surveillance center at NKP (completed by Task Force Alpha). The sensor signals were too weak to reach NKP directly, so aircraft orbited the trail twenty-four hours a day, monitoring the sensors and relaying the information to Task Force Alpha. The sensors were deployed in strings, and by recording the time of activation for each sensor, Task Force Alpha could estimate the number of trucks in the convoy and the direction and speed of movement. While the system was successful in the defense of Khe Sanh, early attempts to conduct air strikes on the Ho Chi Minh Trail based solely on Task Force Alpha data failed. The system was limited by the accuracy of sensor emplacement and false activations, and the target locations supplied by Task Force Alpha assumed that the convoy would continue movement at a given rate of speed along a previously identified road segment. The NVA became aware of the sensors and, while not having a complete knowledge of the system, became adept at building bypasses that avoided the projected target areas. While the system produced useful intelligence, forward air controllers had to locate and mark the targets.[35] But perhaps the greatest limitation was that before a trail segment could be seeded with sensors, the trail had to be detected, and many were not.[36]

In late January 1968, as the threat to the USMC garrison at Khe Sanh continued to develop, VO-67 was given the mission of seeding the approaches to Khe Sanh as part of Westmoreland's Operation Niagara—a plan to defend the combat base with a deluge of air strikes when the NVA was detected. The plan was successful. Although the actual outcome of the Tet offensive was a resounding defeat of the

Communists, the public perception promoted by the press was just the opposite, and opposition to the war increased.[37]

Planning for OPLAN El Paso was completed in March 1968, but the plan was dead on arrival. Johnson, shocked and demoralized by the Tet Offensive and the reaction of the American press, refused to consider a cross-border operation. Ironically, when General Westmoreland had forces available for a major cross-border operation to cut the Ho Chi Minh Trail, the political environment in the United States would not permit it.[38] Gen. Creighton Abrams replaced General Westmoreland as the Military Assistance Command Vietnam (MACV) commanding general, and the combat base at Khe Sanh was abandoned. The death of Operation El Paso can be summed up by Westmoreland's statement to Creighton Abrams in March 1968: "I'd like to go to Tchepone, but I haven't got the tickets."[39]

During a televised broadcast on 31 March 1968, President Johnson announced that he would not seek reelection for a second term. During the same broadcast, he announced a unilateral halt to the bombing of North Vietnam above the 20th parallel, a line 207 miles north of the DMZ and 70 miles south of the North Vietnamese capital at Hanoi, as a gesture of goodwill and an effort to bring the North Vietnamese to the negotiating table. The North Vietnamese were not willing to enter formal talks unless there was a total cessation of bombing. The negotiations stalled when the North Vietnamese demanded that the bombing halt be specifically worded as "unconditional," and the United States demanded a reciprocal agreement that the North Vietnamese would cease their offensive actions. On 3 October President Johnson met with Cyrus Vance a member of the U.S. delegation to the Paris Peace Talks. Johnson conceded that the North Vietnamese could announce the bombing halt as unconditional if they chose, but the United States would make no such announcement. In return, the U.S. negotiating team pressed for a private agreement on three specific points: the government of South Vietnam must be represented in the negotiations, Hanoi must honor the DMZ, and South Vietnam's population centers must not be attacked.[40]

Armed with President Johnson's guidance, the U.S. delegation led by Ambassador-at-Large Averell Harriman resumed negotiations with the North Vietnamese, but the Communist delegation refused to publicly agree to the three conditions, as it would be contrary to their position that the bombing halt would be "unconditional." Unexpected resistance on the part South Vietnamese President Thieu overshadowed the debate over conditions. It was obvious that any peace agreement would have to include the sovereign government of South Vietnam. But the North Vietnamese insisted that the National Liberation Front (NLF), the governmental arm of the insurgency in South Vietnam, be included in the talks and that the talks be characterized as a four-party negotiation. Thieu was adamantly opposed to recognizing the NLF, and without Thieu's agreement there was no way the meaningful talks could go forward. The situation was further complicated by the 1968 presidential elections. President Johnson became convinced that someone in the Nixon campaign had advised Thieu to hold his ground because he would get better conditions from Nixon, assuming Nixon won the election. In the rush to conclude an agreement with the North Vietnamese prior to the election, Johnson allowed the agreement to go forward without a specific acknowledgement of the three conditions, which would later be referred to as "the facts of life," as well as an agreement on the part of the South Vietnamese government.[41]

The bombing halt was announced on 31 October 1968, two days before the presidential elections. Ending the bombing of North Vietnam freed up air sorties for use elsewhere in the theater of operations, and President Johnson ordered intensified attacks against the enemy in South Vietnam and the infiltration routes in Laos.[42] The air war over Laos intensified. Operation Commando Hunt, an air interdiction effort of the Ho Chi Minh Trail, was initiated on 11 November 1968 and continued until 29 March 1972.[43] The U.S. flew 12,803 sorties against targets in Laos in November 1968, which was nearly a 300 percent increase over the November 1967 total of 4,399 sorties.[44] As policy makers continued reject a cross-border attack by ground forces, the

USAF forward air controllers working over the Ho Chi Minh Trail were immediately saturated with strike aircraft looking for targets. The South Vietnamese government refused to send a delegation to Paris until late December and negotiations did not begin until January 1968.

Chapter 2

THE TRUCK HUNTERS

AS A PRELUDE TO THE 1962 GENEVA ACCORDS, the royal Laotian government and the Pathet Lao signed a cease-fire agreement on 3 May 1961. The fighting subsided, but it did not end. After the cease-fire, and prior to signing of the Geneva Accords, the Pathet Lao and the North Vietnamese continued to press royal Laotian forces back from positions along the Laos-Vietnam border with raids and combat patrols. Meanwhile, the Royal Laotian Army attempted to defend areas that had been under their control as of the 3 May cease-fire—or to retake them if lost—but took no aggressive action to capture additional areas. During this time, prior to the signing of the accords, there was a distinct buildup of Communist forces in the southern Laotian panhandle that possibly indicated their intent to gain control of the panhandle in order to infiltrate South Vietnam.[1]

After the accords were signed, the Pathet Lao refused to allow the International Control Commission (the body created to assure compliance by all parties) access to areas under their control, and North Vietnam refused to withdraw its army. In a reciprocal move, the U.S. government continued to provide covert aid to Gen. Vang Pao's guerilla army and Le Kong's neutralist forces. By the spring of 1963 the opposing forces were postured for a resumption of hostilities on the Plain of Jars in central Laos.

From 1960 to 1963 American military operations along the Ho Chi Minh Trail in Laos were generally confined to aerial photoreconnaissance, and patrolling was limited to U.S.-trained Laotian tribesmen and South

Vietnamese border patrols. Given the difficulty of the terrain and the natural concealment afforded by the forest canopy, the extent of infiltration was difficult to ascertain. Intelligence analysts correctly concluded that the Laotian panhandle was a conduit for a significant amount of North Vietnamese matériel and manpower arriving in South Vietnam.

In 1963 the Laotian government received covert military assistance from the United States in the form of small arms, mortars, howitzers, and a few obsolete aircraft, all of it delivered by Air America, an airline passenger and freight company covertly owned by the CIA. Under the direction of the U.S. embassy, the CIA also managed military aid programs and took steps to strengthen irregular forces in the non-communist area of Laos. On 19 June 1963 President Kennedy authorized actions designed to gradually increase pressure on the Communists in Laos, but because the Geneva Accords prohibited the United States from providing direct military aid or sending military advisors or training teams to Laos, the T-6 and T-28 aircraft and other matériel were shipped to Thailand. At the request of Laotian prime minister Souvanna Phouma, Operation Water Pump deployed Detachment 6, 1st Air Commando Wing, to Ubon, Thailand, in April 1964 to provide on-the-job training assistance and forward air controllers to the Royal Laotian Air Force.[2]

In addition to providing covert aid to Laos, the United States periodically flew reconnaissance missions over Laos. When two reconnaissance aircraft were shot down over Laos in early June 1964, Secretary of Defense McNamara urged President Johnson to retaliate to preclude North Vietnam from believing that the United States "talked tough, but acted weak." Johnson approved a retaliatory strike.[3] Although the news of the lost aircraft and the retaliatory strike were announced to the public, a secret air war expanded over Laos. President Johnson ordered the reconnaissance flights to continue, but with armed escorts. On 14 December 1964 the United States, with the approval of the Laotian government, launched a limited air interdiction campaign against the infiltration routes called Operation Barrel Roll.[4] It was part of the overall strategy of graduated response and intended to dissuade the North Vietnamese from continuing to support the insurgency in South Vietnam.

The Laotian panhandle was a difficult environment for air operations. Steep forested mountains were frequently enshrouded by rain and fog, and the earliest maps of the area were crude by any standard, creating an obvious problem of target acquisition. McNamara queried the services about their capabilities to locate enemy vehicles at night using aircraft equipped with infrared sensors. The air force believed that it could develop a night target-acquisition system using its four infrared-equipped B-57s stationed in Thailand and South Vietnam in conjunction with improved navigational aids. The army had the infrared-equipped OV-1 Mohawk, a twin engine turboprop Grumman aircraft fielded in 1961. And the navy had its A-6A Intruder, an aircraft specifically designed for night armed-reconnaissance, which was scheduled to enter the inventory in the spring of 1965.[5]

At the direction of MACV, the army conducted a test of the Mohawk's night acquisition capability in southern Laos and produced high-quality infrared photography. But little came of the results. The air force was more concerned with an unwarranted intrusion into what it considered to be its the role and mission.[6] The question of night operations was temporarily dropped after CINCPAC, Admiral Sharp, stated that night operations would only complement day operations.[7] While Sharp's comment may have been correct in 1964, the truth changed in 1965.

The U.S. ambassador to Laos, William Sullivan, sent a message to the Department of State describing the difficulty in finding the North Vietnamese infiltration routes. Sullivan had spent 19 June 1965 with the Royal Laotian Air Force commander, Gen. Thao Ma, whose pilots had flown hundreds of sorties over the Laotian panhandle searching for the infiltration routes and had been able to flush out truck convoys and destroy several trucks. Ma flew Sullivan in a helicopter out to the area where U.S. jet reconnaissance aircraft could find no sign of a road. They overflew the area at low altitude, and in all but a few small areas the road was totally concealed. Then Ma's pilot landed and Ma and Sullivan drove jeeps down to a portion of the route that Laotian forces had managed to wrest temporarily from the Communists. Even in the rainy season it was a thoroughly passable road that could accommodate a 4x4 truck, but it was almost totally obscured from view by the forest canopy and a meticulously constructed trellis.[8] It was apparent that fast-moving, high-flying jet reconnaissance aircraft were not up to the task.

On 10 December 1965 the CIA reported that the Communists had expanded and improved their supply routes and that the NVA convoys now moved almost exclusively at night.[9] In the meantime, the air force and army launched a joint operation. MACV Studies and Operation Group (MACVSOG) reconnaissance teams made a shallow penetration of the Laotian border in search of NVA supplies and trucks, while the air force stood by with strike aircraft. The mission was successful and made more successful by a forward air controller (FAC) who piloted a small, slow moving, observation aircraft and was able to identify and mark additional targets for the strike aircraft. The success of the mission led to a new operations plan, Tiger Hound, which would use FACs to locate and mark the targets, and a C-130 airborne command-and-control center to direct strike aircraft to the target. The area of operations was the eastern half of the Laotian panhandle, an area that encompassed most, though not all, of the infiltration routes, but avoided the more heavily populated western half, which included Route 23, one of the principle infiltration routes.

The concept of using an FAC to locate and mark targets for attack aircraft was not new. FAC organizations had evolved during World War II, but were disbanded after the war only to be reinvented during the Korean War, and again disbanded. Between the Korean War and Vietnam, the air force, apparently believing that an FAC would be not needed in future conflicts, directed its attention to development and procurement of high-performance jet aircraft designed to penetrate Soviet air defenses and win the air superiority battle. As a result, when the war in Vietnam started, the only aircraft available to the air force that was capable of flying low and slow enough for pilots to search for trucks on the concealed trails was the aging O-1 "Birddog," a light-weight aircraft devoid of armor protection for the crew and other critical aircraft components. FACs were organized in tactical air support squadrons (TASS), which were stationed through South Vietnam. A covert organization of FACs calling themselves the Ravens was stationed in Laos. As President Kennedy had predicted in 1961, Raven pilots were "civilianized"; that is, they were stripped of their military identity and were flying unmarked aircraft.[10] These slow-moving, propeller-driven aircraft were precisely what was needed to seek out the hidden enemy supply routes. Under ideal circumstances pilots selected for the forward air control mission were experienced fighter pilots, well versed in air-to-ground attack. But as the Vietnam War progressed, the demand for FACs increased to the point that B-52 pilots from the Strategic Air Commander as well as transport pilots were trained and assigned as FACs.

Figure 1. O-1 Birddog. Photograph provided by the Air Force Museums and History Office.

The 20th TASS, stationed in Da Nang, supported Operation Tiger Hound. The squadron established a forward operating base at Khe Sanh in northwest South Vietnam, adjacent to the Tiger Hound area of operations. One month after its arrival it deployed Capt. Benn Witterman with a detachment of six pilots, five aircraft, and thirteen support personnel from Da Nang Air Base to the Royal Thai Air Force Base at Nakhom Phanom, Thailand, to conduct visual reconnaissance on the Communist supply lines in the Laotian panhandle.[11] Twelve more pilots and ten additional aircraft arrived during the first week of April 1966. In addition to seeking out targets during the nights, the FACs flew continuous daylight missions collecting all visible clues as to the location of the multitude of roads, trails, and storage areas and slowly began mapping out some of the infiltration routes. In June General Westmoreland reported that FAC saturation of the Laotian panhandle was paying rich dividends as the FACs' familiarity with the enemy's logistical system and pattern of activity increased.[12]

Witterman's detachment remained at Nakhom Phanom and was designated the 23rd TASS flying under the call sign "Nail." Nakhom Phanom (nicknamed NKP and sometimes "naked fanny" by the American pilots) was located eight miles west of the Mekong River, which formed the boundary between Laos and Thailand. It was northwest of Tchepone and southwest of the Mu Gia Pass on the Laos–North Vietnam border. Both of these major infiltration sites were well within range.

The air force recognized the deficiencies of the O-1 aircraft and began the process of design and procurement for a replacement, the OV-10. But because of the immediate need for an upgraded FAC aircraft, the air force purchased an off-the-shelf aircraft, the Cessna "Super Skymaster," as an interim solution. The modified Skymaster, designated as the O-2, was a twin-engine aircraft with the engines installed in line. The front engine powered a "puller" propeller and the rear engine powered the "pusher" propeller. The O-2 had greater mission time and airspeed and was more heavily armed than the O-1. Although designed to be capable of sustaining single-engine flight, the additional weight of armament and radios combined with high-density altitude made it almost impossible to stay airborne with a single engine. Walter Want, an FAC assigned to the 23rd TASS, wryly observed, "if you lost an engine in the O-2, the second engine would get you to the scene of the crash."[13]

In February 1967 the FACs were flying O-1 Birddogs and O-2s. Daylight missions were flown single-pilot, without the benefit of a copilot. Normally the trip to the objective area required about forty-five minutes to an hour. After spending an hour reconnoitering and directing strike aircraft and an hour return flight, there was about a thirty-minute fuel reserve left for contingencies such as tactical emergencies and weather variations. The primary navigation equipment was a magnetic compass and a map. When the pilot found a target he contacted the airborne command-and-control center (ABCCC) and requested strike aircraft. The ABCCC would issue a fragmentary (frag) order, diverting strike aircraft to the target. Once the strike aircraft arrived, the FAC provided the target description, location, and all known antiaircraft gun locations to the strike aircraft and marked the target. Once the strike aircraft identified the target, the FAC cleared the strike aircraft to hit the target and stood by to conduct a post-strike bomb-damage assessment.

Figure 2. O-2 Skymaster. Photograph provided by the Air Force Museums and History Office.

Night missions were flown in a blacked-out O-2 with a crew of two pilots.[14] One pilot flew while the other hung out the window searching for targets with a starlight scope.[15] The night missions were usually flown as hunter-killer teams: the FAC was the hunter and the killer was usually an A-26 holding in an orbit a safe distance away. In order to maintain vertical separation and avoid a mid-air collision, the blacked out O-2 had a shrouded red navigation light installed on the top of the fuselage. The pilots marked targets with rockets, flares, or phosphorus logs dropped from the wing stores.[16]

The A-26 was a modified twin-engine World War II light bomber, painted black for night operations and equipped with eight .50-caliber machine guns in the nose, as well as wing-mounted guns and racks for bombs and flares. An A-26 squadron with the call sign "Nimrod," which had covertly deployed to South Vietnam in 1961, arrived at NKP in 1966. The A-26 possessed awesome firepower, but as NVA air defenses improved, the vintage aircraft proved vulnerable to ground fire. Like other World War II–era aircraft, it was no longer in production and every loss was irreplaceable. The remaining A-26s were withdrawn in 1969.

The OV-10 "Bronco" was the first aircraft designed specifically as an FAC aircraft. As opposed to the O-1, which offered little more ballistic protection than a Solo cup, the crew had armored seats, and the aircraft was equipped with self-sealing fuel tanks. It was also much more powerful and heavily armed. With the centerline fuel tank installed, the OV-10 had a range of 1,200 miles, over twice that of the O-1. The external stores racks on the wings provided a wide selection of possible armaments configurations, but with the centerline fuel tank installed, the most common configuration was two seven-shot rocket pods, each loaded with smoke rockets, and two M-60 machine guns.[17] During the later years of the war, some OV-10s were also equipped with laser designators to guide precision munitions.

Aircrews had to comply with a bewildering array of constantly changing restrictions imposed by higher authorities to minimize the risk of civilian casualties and to prevent widening the war.[18] Rules of engagement (ROE) agreed upon by CINCPAC, MACV, and the American embassy in Laos, and further supplemented by restrictions ordered by the 7th Air Force, stated what was permitted or forbidden during the air war over Laos. Laos was divided up into seven sectors, and while there were rules that applied to all sectors, some rules applied only to specific sectors. In the sectors delineated as armed reconnaissance areas, U.S. aircraft could strike targets of opportunity outside of a village provided it was within two hundred yards of a motorable road or trail and the target had been validated by the Royal Laotian Air Force, or in an alternative case, if approval was granted by an air attaché and fire had been received from the target. In some areas air strikes were prohibited unless an FAC was present. In other areas, air strikes could be conducted, but only if the pilot could confirm his position using radar or a tactical air navigation system (TACAN). Overflight of Laotian cities was prohibited, and aircraft had to remain clear of some of these cities by as far as twenty-five nautical miles.[19]

Figure 3. OV-10 Bronco. Photograph provided by the Air Force Museums and History Office.

Such ROE were directive in nature, and violations had serious consequences. Because the ROE changed periodically, every pilot was responsible for keeping abreast of changes. All of these rules were intended to prevent civilian casualties and accidental strikes against friendly ground forces. The Communists understood these rules and used the restrictions to their advantage.

Reports of a growing enemy supply capability followed every report of progress in the war against trucks. Despite a tremendous number of truck kills reported between 1966 and 1968, the CIA reported that the enemy's capability to infiltrate troops and supplies into the northern part of South Vietnam would increase because of an intensive NVA effort to construct supply routes with limited all-weather capability.[20] During the wet season, the throughput capacity of the roads leading into the A Shau Valley was estimated to be only 15 percent lower than during the dry season. Such all-weather capabilities would give the NVA the ability to increase deliveries by fifty tons per day.[21]

As the war progressed, so did American technological efforts to find and destroy trucks concealed beneath the forest canopy. In addition to the sensors from Operation Igloo White, U.S. forces also developed and deployed starlight scopes, radar, infrared scopes (designed to detect the heat of truck engines), low-light television systems, and a "Black Crow" system (that could detect the electrical emissions of vehicle ignition systems). But each of these systems had inherent limitations and could not offset the NVA advantages of cover and concealment afforded by the terrain and weather.

In an attempt to increase the ratio of truck kills to sightings, the U.S. Air Force utilized increasingly lethal weapons systems and munitions. The most lethal of these was the fixed-wing gunship. As figure 4 demonstrates, the weapons were installed on the port side of the aircraft. When a target was sighted, the pilot would bank left and execute a pylon turn around the target. He could keep his weapons on the target as long as he remained in the turn, making multiple circles if necessary.

The first aircraft modified for this mission was the World War II vintage C-47 armed with three 7.62mm mini-guns. Later, C-119s were modified and 20mm Gatling guns were added to the arsenal. By the time the AC-130 gunship was fielded, the armament included 40mm Bofors guns, and a limited number of AC-130s were outfitted 105mm howitzers.[22]

As the lethality of aerial weapons systems increased, so did the lethality and numbers of NVA antiaircraft systems, and the large, slow-moving gunships were forced away from critical areas of the trail. But FACs controlling fighter-bombers remained.[23] FACs also played a critical role in the ground war on the infiltration routes as the communications outlet and the guardian angels of the small, out-numbered, reconnaissance and road-watch teams that existed to find targets for the air arm and collect intelligence.

Figure 4. AC-130. Photograph provided by the Air Force Museums and History Office.

THE GROUND WAR ON THE TRAIL

While most air operations over the Ho Chi Minh Trail were of such magnitude that they could not be kept secret, all ground operations prior to Lam Son 719 were covert, deeply guarded secrets. Ground reconnaissance teams supplemented the air interdiction effort. The Studies and Observation Group (SOG), a thinly veiled moniker for Special Operations Group, was an outgrowth of National Security Action Memorandum (NSAM) 273 and President Johnson's directive to take covert actions against the North Vietnamese, and the resulting Operation Plan 34A. In early 1964 MACV and South Vietnamese forces jointly developed a series of plans for conducting ground reconnaissance and harassing and blocking enemy supply routes in the Laotian panhandle. The general concept of the plan was that air and ground reconnaissance would locate the targets, and a larger air or ground action would destroy or disrupt the target. Secretary of Defense McNamara embraced the idea and recommended presidential approval. President Johnson incorporated such incursions into Laos in NSAM 288; however, at the insistence of the ambassador to Laos, these incursions were limited to small-scale operations, and each of these operations required his approval.

MACV's first attempt to use South Vietnamese soldiers to reconnoiter the Ho Chi Minh Trail (code-named Operation Leaping Lena) was a complete failure. The concept was that the teams of ARVN soldiers, who had been put through a cram course at Nha Trang, South Vietnam, would be deployed by parachute. When it came time to deploy, the U.S. Special Forces soldiers that accompanied the ARVN soldiers to the drop zone, "practically had to force them on the aircraft at gun point."[24] Most were captured, and the few who returned brought back reports of roads and trails, but could not point out the location of what they had observed on a map. In August 1964 General Taylor, the ambassador to South Vietnam, reported that the capability for Leaping Lena operations was virtually nil as the result of "disaffection" of the trainees at Nha Trang.[25] Ground operations were stalled for the remainder of 1964 while MACV revised their plans and assembled reconnaissance teams made up of Civilian Irregular Defense Group (CIDG) volunteers and led by U.S. Special Forces soldiers.

During 1963 and 1964 the Pentagon controlled SOG operations , but in January 1965 they handed command of SOG over to MACV. The first sixteen members of SOG, handpicked Special Forces volunteers trained in Okinawa, supplied just enough men to lead five reconnaissance teams with one man remaining as a spare. Each team had three Special Forces members—an American leader, an assistant team leader, and a radio operator—and eight to nine Nung mercenaries. In an operation code named Shining Brass these small, highly trained teams were the first to cross the Laotian border to reconnoiter enemy supply lines and identify targets for air attack.[26] With Ambassador Sullivan responsible for coordinating all military activities in Laos and with SOG under the command of MACV in South Vietnam, conflicting interests were inevitable.

Ambassador Sullivan restricted the first Shining Brass operations to two small areas of operations along the South Vietnamese border. At first, Sullivan would not allow insertion by helicopter for fear of revealing American incursions into Laos, and the teams had enter Laos on foot. But when the SOG commander arranged for Vietnamese Air Force (VNAF) H-34 helicopters to support the insertions, he lifted those restrictions.[27] In June 1966 Sullivan temporarily expanded the area of operations to a zone of no deeper than twenty kilometers into Laos, exclluding a portion of the border around Route 9 where a Royal Laotian battalion was stationed. Souvanna Phouma had told him that he would not agree to the presence of U.S. ground forces, and Sullivan was concerned that U.S. participation in Shining Brass would be detected.

In December 1966 MACV submitted a request to have Sullivan's temporary expansion of the twenty-kilometer zone be made permanent. Sullivan disgreed. He stated that although the original ground rules prescribed avoiding both contact with the enemy and sabotage

and harassment tactics, the reconnaissance teams were burning isolated huts and small villages, destroying livestock and food caches,
capturing and killing enemy soldiers, and revealing their presence
by firing on suspected enemy personnel. He added that during the
month of October eight of the nine Shining Brass reconnaissance
teams required emergency extraction because of enemy attacks and
the helicopters used for both insertion and extraction often encountered enemy ground fire.[28] The issue was settled at the "highest level."
On 24 February 1967 a State Department telegram to the embassy in
Laos stated that the extension of Shing Brass activity was approved as
one of a series of steps to improve the defense against infiltration.[29]
Later in 1967 the Shining Brass code name was changed to "Prairie
Fire" after too many people learned the meaning of "Shining Brass."

Having won the first round in the effort to expand the area of
operations, MACV continued its efforts to expand the scale of its
covert operations in Laos during 1967. One of the plans submitted
by Westmoreland involved recruiting the Kha tribesmen indigeonous
to the Laotian panhandle as a guerilla force.[30] This effort put him in
competition with William Sullivan and the CIA, who were recruiting
the same tribesmen for their system of trail-watch parties. Sullivan
argued that Westmoreland's plan would accomplish little because
the NVA had set up a new logistics system in Cambodia that would
absorb the loss of the Ho Chi Minh Trail, and the majority of personnel
infiltrating into South Vietnam was entering from the DMZ. Sullivan
continued his objections by stating that the CIA-controlled forces in
the panhandle were, "on the point of take-off," about to conduct operations in the same territory that MACV wanted to take over. Then he
posted an appeal for aircraft dedicated to supporting his operations in
Laos, claiming that if the air force would "assign 50 propeller-driven
aircraft to work regularly with our assets in the Panhandle, we could
clean up those routes and dry up those base areas twelve months of
the year."[31]

Ambassador Sullivan was quick to tout the successes of his
road-watch teams. On 31 July 1967 the CIA sent a memorandum to

President Johnson reporting that the teams had expanded from intermittent coverage of a few spots to almost continuous coverage of all major trafficable routes running from North Vietnam through Laos to South Vietnam and that in addition to collecting intelligence, the teams were inflicting substantial damage to the NVA as their trucks transited Laos.[32] Later in November 1967 the embassy in Laos sent a message to the State Department claiming that the number of trucks damaged or destroyed in Laos was already more than six hundred for the month and that practically none of the dry-season cargo was getting as far south as Route 9. The message optimistically added that if the rate of truck-destruction continued, North Vietnam's truck inventory could be "wiped out" by the end of the year.[33] Sullivan's assessment was overly optimistic but could have been more realistic if all of the tributaries to the Ho Chi Minh trail were found. He believed that MACV was "nibbling away" at the restrictions he placed on operations in the panhandle and that the ultimate issue was whether Westmoreland or he would direct the operations of irregular forces in the panhandle.[34]

Sullivan's request for dedicated support clashed with the air force doctrine that the full effects of air power can only be achieved when centrally controlled and directed against the most vital part of the enemy.[35] The strength of this doctrine is that it preserves the mass of air power instead of parceling it out as piecemeal reinforcements. The weakness is that it adds response time, which is critical when attacking fleeting targets. The State Department refined Sullivan's request for additional air support stating that Sullivan believed that the air force generally gave him tactical air-strike support for targets in Laos only after requirements in Vietnam were satisfied. He was only asking that the 56th Air Commando Wing (ACW) at NKP be "dedicated" to Laos so that he had "first call" on some planes.[36]

Sullivan's statement that the NVA was taking "increasingly sophisticated countermeasures" against SOG reconnaissance teams is confirmed by SOG historian and former member John Plaster. NVA countermeasures began appearing in layers. The first layer was a system of landing zone watchers. There are few natural helicopter landing zones in the twenty-kilometer belt of the eastern Laotian panhandle, and it required little effort to position an observer where he could watch and report landings on one or more potential landing zones. The second layer was trail watchers. Although not conclusively proven, Plaster also believes that the NVA used radio direction-finding equipment to locate reconnaissance teams once they had landed. Next came NVA patrols, Route Protection battalions, and 12.7mm antiaircraft machine guns in mutually supporting positions surrounding the landing zones.[37] All of these layers were in place by the end of 1967. During 1968 the SOG reconnaissance team's casualties exceeded 100 percent of their authorized strength, many of which were Lao citizens who offered their services to fight the common enemy, the North Vietnamese Army.[38] One of the CIA's secret warriors, Sar Phouthasack, provided the following account.

The U.S. Military Assistance and Advisory Group had selected Sar Phouthasack in 1961 for specialized training in radio communications and parachute qualification. After graduation Sar was assigned to the Team Whiskey headquarters in military region 3, Laos. In 1963 Team Whiskey was ordered to move to Nakhom Phanom, Thailand, where it selected the location for and helped to build the American air base there. Sar returned to Laos to recruit, train, and support road-watch teams along the Ho Chi Minh Trail. He was promoted to 2nd lieutenant, and his duties expanded to recruiting and training the CIA's special guerilla units (SGU).

In 1964 Sar was selected for an exceptionally dangerous mission in which he parachuted deep behind enemy lines to restore communications for a covert team operating in North Vietnam. He spent nearly four months behind enemy lines and was ordered to work his way back though Mu Gia Pass on foot. Kha tribesmen guided him along the way. At approximately midnight, as he was crossing the pass on a high mountain overlooking the North Vietnamese road through the pass, he heard a convoy of trucks come to a stop in the valley floor. When dawn came, he asked one of his guides about the trucks.

The guide responded that the NVA frequently parked in a concealed area near the river and waited for the next night to come before they continued their journey into Laos. After Sar and his guide made their way down to a point where the parked trucks were visible, Sar was able to contact a Royal Laotian Air Force FAC with the call sign Jaguar. The FAC called for strike aircraft, and two F-105s returning from a mission in North Vietnam with unexpended bombs responded and hit the target. Sar's guide, under the guise of a local fisherman, entered the area and confirmed that fifteen to twenty trucks had been destroyed or heavily damaged.

Team Whiskey was ordered to move to Savannakhet, Laos, and set up a new communications station in 1965. In 1966 Sar was selected to conduct three more missions deep behind enemy lines where he served on road-watch teams calling in airstrikes on NVA trucks. He continued to work as a communications specialist and participate in numerous missions in northern and southern Laos. In late 1970 he accompanied an American advisor to the southern area of the panhandle to coordinate an attack by Group Mobil (GM) 30 in support of operation Lam Son 719 and remained with GM 30 to provide communications support.[39] In 1974 and 1975 Sar worked in the Laotian capital, Vientiane, where he coordinated the evacuation of Lao citizens fleeing Communist forces to refugee camps in Thailand before the Communists took over. Sar and his family escaped to Thailand in 1975 where he continued his service to the CIA, providing support for the resistance movement in Laos until February 1983 when he and his family moved to the United States.[40]

The stark difference between the manner in which the CIA's road-watch teams and the SOG recon teams operated may account for the success of Sar's teams. Sar revealed that his teams were inserted no closer than four days march to the target area. They used local guides and blended in with the population. The SOG teams rode a helicopter to work, a less than inconspicuous entry into the area.

Ambassador Sullivan sincerely believed that the SOG efforts in the panhandle were of little value and that he and the CIA were better equipped to deal with interdicting the NVA supply lines without upsetting the delicate diplomatic relationship with the Laotian government. He was openly contemptuous of SOG operations, stating that "the record of Shining Brass to date has not given much substance to the military justification," and that SOG operations would be more useful if they were conducted near or in the DMZ, or even in North Vietnam, rather than in Laos.[41] In a verbal jab at General Westmoreland, who was an Eagle Scout, Sullivan referred to Shining Brass as "essentially an Eagle Scout program devised by some extremely well motivated and brave young men."[42] It is difficult to argue with Sullivan's characterization of the soldiers of SOG as extremely well motivated and talented: they created havoc on the Ho Chi Minh Trail. By 1967 the NVA had 25,000 troops devoted to defending the trail against SOG operations.[43]

During the coming years Sullivan's statement that the NVA were developing a new supply route through Sihanoukville, a sea port on the southern tip of Cambodia, which could absorb the loss of NVA supply routes in the Laotian panhandle, was proven to be at least partially correct. However, the CIA apparently dismissed this claim and infiltration continued at an accelerated pace. After Richard Nixon became President in 1969, the war against infiltration continued, as did the debate over the effectiveness of air operations and irregular forces on the Ho Chi Minh Trail. It became apparent that stemming the flow of infiltration required overt cross-border operations by ground troops.

Chapter 3

NIXON'S WAR

WHEN LYNDON JOHNSON ANNOUNCED the 31 October agreement with North Vietnam (that all parties, to include the NLF and South Vietnam would convene peace talks in Paris), he also announced that all U.S. bombing north of the DMZ would be terminated. The North Vietnamese made no concessions. They stoically listened to Johnson's demand—that in return for cessation of the bombing they honor the DMZ and cease their attacks on South Vietnamese cities—but did not indicate that they accepted these conditions or the U.S. declaration that aerial reconnaissance flights would continue in the region immediately north of the DMZ. After suffering debilitating losses during their 1968 offensive, the Communists returned to their strategy of protracted warfare and continued to expand their infiltration routes into Laos and Cambodia.

Historically the tempo of combat in South Vietnam, as measured by U.S. casualties, followed the monsoon weather pattern. Communist offensives peaked during the January–June dry season and receded during the wet season that extended to the end of December.[1]

Militarily, little had changed when Richard Nixon took the presidential oath of office on 20 January 1969, and the Paris Peace Talks showed little hope of progress. The only significant difference was that Nixon was burdened with Johnson's bombing halt proclamation and deteriorating public and congressional support for the war.

On 1 February 1969 Nixon sent a memorandum to his assistant for national security affairs, Henry Kissinger, stating:

In reading the January 31 news report on the Paris negotiations, it seems vitally important to me at this time that we increase as much as we possibly can the military pressure on the enemy in South Vietnam. Will you convey this view to Wheeler [Chairman of the Joint Chiefs of Staff] and tell him I believe it is absolutely urgent if we are to make any kind of headway in Vietnam that we find new ways to increase the pressure militarily without going to the point that we break off negotiations. I do not like the suggestions that I see in virtually every news report that we anticipate a "Communist initiative in South Vietnam." I believe that if any initiative occurs it would be on our part and not theirs.[2]

Historically there had been sharp increase in Communist offensives and a corresponding increase in American casualties during the February–May "dry season." Therefore, U.S. forces anticipated renewed attacks in 1969. A combination of SOG trail-watchers and electronic sensors detected a large increase in traffic along Route 548 in the A Shau Valley and Route 922 located in the adjoining area of Laos.[3]

While the international borders of Laos and Cambodia frustrated efforts to deal with the Ho Chi Minh Trail, one important trail segment was located adjacent to the Laotian border, but within South Vietnam: the A Shau Valley. The A Shau Valley is located twenty-five miles west of Hue, the historic imperial capital city of Vietnam. It is a long, narrow valley running from the northwest to the southeast and flanked by towering, forested mountains on either side of the valley floor. Route 548, an important NVA supply line, ran down the valley floor (parallel to the Rao Lao River) and intersected with Route 547 leading to Hue. Dense thickets of thorny bamboo dotted the valley floor covered by elephant grass growing to a height in excess of five feet. It was a primeval environment. Caught between the northeast and southwest monsoons, the valley was typically enshrouded in mist and fog. Tropical thunderstorms and rains were frequent and heavy.

The NVA dominated the valley after the battle of A Shau in March 1966. Intelligence sources indicated that the North Vietnamese were preparing for a major attack across the DMZ. Three company-sized outposts were positioned along the infiltration route running down the valley floor and were given the missions of border surveillance and interdicting infiltration. During the first week in March 1966, captured enemy documents and information from defectors indicated that an attack by the NVA 325th Division was imminent. South Vietnamese troops occupied the outposts near the deserted villages of Ta Bat and A Loui, and a seventeen-man U.S. Special Forces detachment—accompanied by approximately 120 civilian irregular defense group (CIDG) soldiers—occupied an outpost near the village of A Shau. In March 1966 a large NVA force entered the valley, and patrols from the allied outposts were forced back to the confines of their fortified positions. The South Vietnamese forces at Ta Bat and A Loui withdrew, leaving the Special Forces and CIDG troops at A Shau to block the infiltration route. They sought reinforcements, but I Corps headquarters disapproved the request. However, on 7 March the 5th Special Forces group sent a mobile strike force company of 143 men, led by seven U.S. Special Forces soldiers, to reinforce the outpost.[4]

Patrols and night ambush parties failed to find the North Vietnamese on 7 and 8 March. The Communists began to probe the outer defenses at 1930 hours on the eighth. Early on 9 March NVA forces opened up with 82mm mortars damaging camp structures and causing fifty-seven casualties. Heavy ground fog rendered air strikes ineffective, and one inbound C-47 crashed after being hit by ground fire.

The Communists began firing mortars and 57mm recoilless rifles at 0400 hours on 10 March and destroyed the remaining buildings, silencing half of the crew-served weapons. The NVA launched heavy assaults across the runway at 0500 hours. The defense on the southeast corner collapsed, and the fighting surged into the camp. Survivors from the east and south wall defenses withdrew to positions near the communications bunker and the north wall at about 0830. Air strikes were brought in with good effect on the NVA forces occupying the breached walls and gathering east of the airstrip for another assault. Despite adverse weather and poor flying conditions, the 5th Special Forces group launched an airmobile operation to extract the allied forces. The defenders abandoned the camp and moved to a nearby landing zone to await extraction by a flight of sixteen H-34 helicopters accompanied by tactical air support. The Special Forces mobile strike force troops fought a rear guard action, while the survivors retreated to the landing zone. Intense enemy fire at the landing zone inflicted heavy casualties, and the CIDG troops panicked, trying to force their way into the aircraft. Two helicopters were destroyed by enemy fire, and some were unable to touch down due to the low ceiling. Only sixty-five allied soldiers escaped, and all seventeen Special Forces men were either killed or wounded.[5]

U.S. and South Vietnamese forces made no attempt to regain control of the valley until immediately after the 1968 Tet Offensive when the 1st Cavalry Division attempted an airmobile sweep into the valley during Operation Delaware. After modest initial success, the 1st Cavalry ran into heavy antiaircraft fire and torrential rains that brought the operation to a halt. Every U.S. effort to gain control of the valley failed. The best that could be accomplished was a sweep through the valley followed by immediate withdrawal. The Communists stubbornly defended against every effort. Because they had a firm grasp on the A Shau Valley, they turned it into a major supply base. Massive supply caches were concealed in bunkers and caves, and a network of roads, trails, hospitals, bivouacs and training areas were carefully camouflaged under the jungle canopy. The valley remained a Communist stronghold as well as a staging area for attacks into the foothills and coastal lowlands of northern Military Region I until the war ended. The Communist forces in the A Shau Valley were destined to play a major role in allied efforts to shut down the Tchepone corridor.

In January 1969 intelligence indicated that two NVA regiments were moving eastward through the A Shau Valley. The logical course of action was a sweep through the A Shau Valley to intercept the enemy and capture or destroy the supply caches in order to preempt attacks in the I Corps area. And that was the intent of Operation

Dewey Canyon, a fifty-six day operation that kicked off on 22 January 1969, two days after Nixon's inauguration.

The 9th Marine Regiment of the 3rd Marine Division, located at Vandergrift Combat Base, (a newly established combat base located along Route 9 east of the abandoned base at Khe Sanh) moved overland fifty kilometers south establishing artillery fire support bases as they moved into the A Shau Valley. The marines were within range of the NVA artillery in Laos as they hacked their way through the difficult terrain. After multiple engagements with the NVA and being subjected to enemy artillery fire, the marines reached a position in South Vietnam where they could observe the traffic along Route 922 in Laos. But they did not have authority to continue their attack across the border. The situation was reported to Maj. Gen. Raymond G. Davis, the 3rd Marine Division commanding general.

After he received the report, he authorized the 9th Regiment to conduct a raid into Laos to intercept and destroy the enemy along Route 922. While Laos was still officially considered neutral and he did not have presidential approval to cross the border, he claimed the right of a commander under the Geneva Convention to protect his force from imminent attack and notified Abrams of his intent somewhat after the fact. He received Abrams's support, and the first overt American incursion into Laos was underway. Companies E, F, and H from the 2nd Battalion, 9th Marine Regiment, crossed the Laotian border on 24 February and set up ambushes along Route 922. The marines continued a series of combat patrols and ambushes until they withdrew on 3 March. The enemy, not expecting an American force to cross the border, was caught by surprise.[6]

Dewey Canyon was a bloody affair for both sides of the combat. The marines claimed to have killed in excess of 1,617 NVA soldiers and wounded an unknown number. They captured or destroyed over five hundred tons of matériel, including several air defense guns and artillery pieces. But the marines also paid a price; of their 2,200-man force, 130 were killed in action and another 920 were wounded.[7]

While Dewey Canyon may have blunted the Communist offensive, it did not terminate it. The Communists launched their offensive on 22

February 1969. A combination of Vietcong main force units and NVA regular forces attacked 125 locations scattered around the country and shelled an additional four hundred targets with rockets and mortars. They centered most attacks on military targets near Saigon and, to a lesser extent, Da Nang. The heaviest fighting was around Saigon, but fights raged all over South Vietnam. Communist forces managed to penetrate the American supply depot at Long Binh near Saigon, and 1,140 servicemen were killed in action.[8] The concentration of attacks in the vicinity of Saigon was a clear indicator that the attacks—and the supplies for these attacks—were coming from Cambodian sanctuaries west of Saigon. As Abrams had indicated during President Johnson's 29 October 1968 meeting to discuss the bombing-halt proposal, Cambodia's "neutrality" was becoming a problem.[9]

Henry Kissinger, Secretary of Defense Laird, and the Chairman of the Joint Chiefs of Staff, Gen. Earle Wheeler, met on 30 January 1969 to discuss a "menu" of possible military options.[10] A contingency plan evolved for a phased B-52 bombing campaign, Operation Menu. Each phase of Operation Menu was given a code name, the first three designated as Operations Breakfast, Lunch, and Dinner.

On 22 February as President Nixon prepared for a scheduled trip to Europe, he received a briefing on the new Communist offensive. He directed Henry Kissinger to call the Soviet ambassador, Anatoly Dobrynin, and make it clear that the United States would retaliate if the North Vietnamese offensive continued.[11]

As he was en route to Brussels on 23 February, President Nixon called and ordered immediate execution of Operation Menu. Henry Kissinger, recommended a forty-eight hour postponement, because he felt that planning was incomplete, and Nixon agreed to the delay. Kissinger and his military assistant, Alexander Haig, immediately flew to Brussels to meet with Nixon, where they refined the plan. Bombing was restricted to within five miles of the South Vietnamese border. The bombing would not be announced, but if Cambodia protested the United States would acknowledge the attacks and invite the United Nations to inspect the base areas. Secretary Laird opposed the plan, and Kissinger recommended that the plan should not be executed while Nixon was on his European tour. The following day Nixon cancelled the plan.[12] Unable to strike across the borders of Laos and Cambodia, U.S. forces were locked into a defensive posture, and the Communists had the initiative, a situation that contradicted Nixon's 1 February statement asserting, "I believe that if any initiative occurs it would be on our part and not theirs."[13]

While President Nixon was completing his tour of Europe, Secretary Laird and Gen. Earle Wheeler consulted with General Abrams and Ambassador Bunker in Saigon. On the evening of 6 March, while Laird and Wheeler were still in Saigon, the Communists struck the city with eleven 122mm rockets.[14] President Nixon immediately ordered a strike on the Cambodian sanctuaries. The strike was scheduled for 9 March, but this time it was the secretary of state, William P. Rogers, who opposed the strike. Rogers based his dissent on three arguments: a strike on the Cambodian sanctuaries might erode public support for the war, retaliation stood only a fair chance of ending the rocket attacks on Saigon, and the strike would provide the North Vietnamese with an excuse for leaving the Paris Peace Talks.[15] Clearly frustrated, Nixon once more cancelled the air strike. According to Kissinger, "Nixon retracted his order a second time. But each time he marched up the hill and down again, his resentments and impatience increased."[16]

Saigon was hit with another rocket attack on 15 March. President Nixon immediately authorized the first phase of Operation Menu, Operation Breakfast. When he ordered the attack, Nixon specifically excluded the possibility of any further objections from Secretary Rogers, stating that Rogers was to be notified only after the point of no return.[17] The target was Base Area 358, the suspected location of the elusive Central Office for South Vietnam (COSVN), the headquarters for the insurgent Communist government. Neither North Vietnam nor Cambodia protested. They had fervently denied the presence of the Communist Army in Cambodia for years.

The day following the B-52 strike, Kissinger and Wheeler discussed the results. Wheeler was enthusiastic, stating, "the [secondary explosions]

were about 4 to 7 times the normal bomb burst, this was significant."
Kissinger suggested, "If they retaliate without any diplomatic screaming,
we are in the driver's seat. Psychologically the impact must have been
something." Wheeler mentioned that North Vietnamese MiGs had
been recalled to China, "and they are in a high state of alarm." Kissinger
responded, "Now they have to go back to the drawing board since they
didn't expect it to happen."[18]

The original plan was for a single B-52 raid, but on 15 April two
North Korean MiG 17s intercepted and shot down an American
EC-121, an unarmed propeller-driven intelligence collection aircraft,
ninety miles off the Korean coast over the Sea of Japan. The North
Koreans did not hesitate to take credit for the attack, claiming that the
EC-121 violated North Korean airspace. There was little doubt as to the
real location. Both U.S. and Soviet radar systems tracked the aircraft,
and Soviet Navy destroyers were the first surface vessels at the crash
site. The EC-121 carried a crew of thirty-one and all were lost.

A National Security Council meeting convened immediately, and
Nixon told his staff that he would meet force with force. He instructed
Secretary Laird to send the 7th Fleet to the Sea of Japan. As the discussion continued, Nixon found that his staff was divided on the issue of
retaliation: Laird and Rogers opposed retaliation, while his assistant for
national security affairs, Dr. Kissinger, was in favor. Approximately three
days later, Nixon inquired as to the location of the 7th Fleet and could
not get an answer from the Pentagon. Going outside normal channels,
Nixon discovered that Secretary Laird had never executed the order
to move the 7th Fleet. Instead, Laird ordered suspension of all EC-121
reconnaissance flights worldwide without informing the president.[19]
According to Alexander Haig, Nixon wanted to fire both Laird and Rogers but was restrained by the fact that Laird, a former congressman and
senator, had a large contingent of supporters in congress, and that by firing Laird, he would lose the support of Laird's former colleagues.[20] Nixon
was determined to not let Communist provocations go unanswered. In
a discussion with his White House chief of staff, Nixon stated that he
was determined to "make a positive move" but was not convinced that

"Korea was not the best time or place. . . . He knows that if we don't retaliate in Korea we'll have to find another similar incident in the next three or four weeks or go with Operation Lunch."[21] Nixon authorized Operation Lunch in May, and the air strikes on Cambodia continued on an intermittent basis until August.[22]

The Communist defeat during the 1968 Tet Offensive gave Cambodian prince Sihanouk pause to reconsider his position. He was an opportunist and constantly maneuvered to assure that he would be in the good graces of the eventual victor in the Vietnam War.[23] Sihanouk began making overtures to reestablish diplomatic relations with the United States. Even after news of the bombing was published, Sihanouk did not protest. During a May press conference he stated that he had not been informed of the raid; there were no Cambodian witnesses, no Cambodians were killed and no houses destroyed. He concluded his statement by saying, "There have been no Khmer [Cambodian] witnesses, so how can I protest? But this does not mean, and I emphasize this, that I will permit the violation by either side."[24]

In May the new administration completed the policy review that the president had ordered on his second day in office. Handing off more responsibility for ground combat to the South Vietnamese had been a campaign promise for both presidential candidates during the 1968 presidential elections, and it was inevitable that the new policy would include this item. How to accomplish the handoff of combat responsibilities to the South Vietnamese was a matter of debate within Nixon's inner circle, but another bloody battle in the A Shau Valley sealed the matter of timing.

The 101st Airborne Division reentered the valley in two operations during the spring of 1969, Massachusetts Striker entering from the south and Apache Snow entering from the north. The southern attack was successful in destroying several Communist supply caches, but the northern attack ran into a determined enemy on Hill 937, a prominent peak on the western side of the valley adjacent to the Laotian border. On 10 May 1969 one infantry company from the 3rd Battalion, 187th Infantry, was conducting a reconnaissance in force and working its way toward the crest when it encountered a line of well-camouflaged bunkers. Enemy fire forced the troopers to withdraw, and all subsequent attempts to maneuver against the enemy position failed. Air strikes and artillery were called in to soften up the position, but punishing enemy fire continued to push ground assaults back. Soon the entire battalion was committed to the effort to take the hill, but each time it defeated one line of field fortifications, it encountered another concentric line of bunkers just a few meters further up the hill. The battle continued for ten days as the brigade maneuvered other battalions to reinforce the effort. As airstrikes and artillery denuded the jungle canopy, it became clear that the battalion had encountered a major enemy force occupying a carefully constructed defensive position. The bunkers, capable of withstanding heavy bombardment, were interconnected by a series of communications trenches and tunnels. Each night, as the battle subsided, the NVA infiltrated reinforcements from the adjacent sanctuaries in Laos, sending infantry forces to attack U.S. troops in their night defensive positions or to set up ambushes for when U.S. forces attempted to continue the attack the following morning. After ten days of hard fighting and high casualties, the surviving NVA force, threatened by superior strength as other U.S. and South Vietnamese battalions that had converged on the mountain, was forced to abandon their positions and retreat back to Laos. It was a bloody retreat. The fleeing Communists were intercepted by ambushes. At some point in the battle an unknown G.I. scrawled out a sign and posted it along a trail leading up the mountain. The sign read "Hamburger Hill."[25]

Fifty-six U.S. soldiers were killed in action, and another 372 were severely wounded, the majority of the casualties sustained by the 3rd Battalion, 187th Infantry.[26] The domestic and political backlash in the United States was immediate. On the senate floor Edward Kennedy denounced the battle as "senseless and irresponsible." The furor only increased when U.S. forces abandoned the position a few days later. It would have been impossible to continue to hold the position; it could only be resupplied by air, and monsoon weather would have made that impossible. Moreover, it was only a few kilometers from Laos where the

NVA was free to position its artillery and mass their forces for attack. The domestic uproar over the battle and continuing protests over the bombing of Cambodia added fuel to the war protest movement.

When American ground troops were first committed to combat in Vietnam, it was understood that the U.S. ground combat role would end as soon as the South Vietnamese armed forces were trained, equipped, and capable of defending their own country. The Johnson administration began the process of strengthening the South Vietnamese Army, but had no specific plans to begin the process of handing off the responsibility for combat to the ARVN and starting the withdraw of U.S. troops from Vietnam. Immediately after taking office, the Nixon administration began studying reductions of American troops in order to bolster public support and to encourage the North Vietnamese to consider serious negotiations. In a news conference on 14 March 1969, Nixon announced that troop withdrawals could begin as soon as the South Vietnamese were capable of defending themselves, the North Vietnamese entered meaningful negotiations, and the level of enemy activity subsided.[27] Defense Secretary Laird labeled the process "Vietnamization" and became the driving force behinds its implementation. Following his 14 March speech, Nixon decided that the time had come and directed that a meeting with President Thieu be arranged.

On 7 June, the day prior to the meeting with Thieu, Nixon met with Kissinger and the military leaders and informed them of his decision to withdraw 25,000 troops. Kissinger noted that the others "accepted the decision with a heavy heart."[28] Nixon met with Thieu at Midway Island on 8 June and informed the South Vietnamese president that American troop strength would be reduced. In July General Abrams received a revised mission statement from Nixon which differed from the mission given to General Westmoreland in 1966. Vietnamization was now his number-one priority, followed by the pacification program and reducing the flow of supplies to the enemy.[29]

Secretaries Laird and Rogers immediately recommended additional withdrawals for the calendar year of 1969. Laird recommended a second increment, bringing the total to 50,000, and Rogers wanted to increase the increment to 85,000. The first point Rogers listed in his proposal was "for political impact in this country, North Vietnam, and Paris," the site of the peace talks.[30] While many American military leaders did not agree with the decision to start the troop withdrawals and limit American offensive operations, General Abrams saluted and followed orders. There was no North Vietnamese reaction. The negotiations did not move forward and their military operations continued unabated.

In retrospect, few disagree with the need for the Vietnamization Program. The issue was timing. An argument can be made that the announcement was premature, that allied forces had convincingly defeated the Communists during the preceding two years of combat, and that by staying the course and slowing the pace of handing the battle off to the South Vietnamese, military victory was within reach. The opposing argument is that the announcement was overdue. Regardless of which point of view one holds, there were other considerations. First, while Nixon's personal goal may have been to "win the war," deteriorating public support and mounting congressional criticism hamstrung him. Second, given the American policy of maintaining a small standing army supported by reserve and National Guard forces, and the decision not to call up significant numbers of reserve forces, the war in Vietnam exhausted the nation's ability to react to other contingencies. There were few forces available to react to the seizure of the USS *Pueblo* by North Korea in 1968 or the downing of the EC-121 in 1969. The U.S. forces deployed in Europe, South Korea, and stationed in the United States were hollow shells, little more than pools of manpower that could be used to supply the pipeline of individual replacements being deployed to Vietnam. When the Soviets invaded Czechoslovakia in 1968 and the U.S. considered participating in a NATO-led intervention, the largest body of troops considered available from the two U.S. Army corps stationed in Europe was a single brigade of approximately 5,000 men.[31]

The USMC's 3rd Division, stationed in northern Military Region 1, was the first major combat unit withdrawn. As the marines withdrew, the 101st Airborne Division spread out to cover the area of operation.

The 101st was now spread out from the DMZ to the Hai Van Pass just north of Da Nang. It was a huge area of responsibility that encompassed both the Quang Tri and Thau Thien provinces, two of the deadliest provinces in all of Vietnam.[32]

In October 1969 U.S. forces captured an enemy document that outlined Communist plans to force the United States to withdraw from Vietnam before Vietnamization could succeed. Although the document contained few specifics, it was clear and convincing evidence of the enemy's intentions; it forewarned President Nixon that he could expect no progress at the Paris Peace Talks and that he should be prepared for increased enemy attacks. Nixon met with the chiefs of staff and provided them with an overview of his thoughts, which proved to be a roadmap for his future decisions.

President Nixon reiterated that the public policy stance should be a continuation of Vietnamization, getting South Vietnamese forces into the fight and U.S. forces out. He emphasized to the chiefs that if U.S. forces left Vietnam without accomplishing their objective, it would encourage the Communists and discourage U.S. friends and allies worldwide.[33] He was convinced that Vietnamization would work given time, but that the missing ingredient was the support of public opinion. Nixon refused to rule out escalation and reminded the chiefs of the public outcry that followed the Tet Offensive, which should have alerted the chiefs of staff that Nixon was prepared to make preemptive strikes. His focus was not confined to Vietnam. He reminded the chiefs of the EC-121 incident and forewarned them that the next provocation by the North Koreans would result in "suitable retaliation." President Nixon did not call for a change of current strategy; the current efforts would continue for the next year, but he stated that if there was no progress, "we must act. We can not stand still."[34]

While Nixon made no mention of what actions he proposed in the absence of progress, a simple resumption of Rolling Thunder would have been of little value unless restrictions on the types and locations of targets were lifted. North Vietnam was essentially an agrarian nation with few manufacturing facilities capable of producing war matériel, and a renewal of bombing would lead to both a domestic and an international outcry. Restricted bombing, as Lyndon Johnson had learned, did little to reduce North Vietnam's capacity to wage war. However, mining Haiphong and Sihanoukville's harbors could be effective if coupled with the closure of roads and rail lines coming into North Vietnam from China. President Johnson had undoubtedly been aware that blockading North Vietnam and cutting off outside sources of supply would reduce North Vietnamese capabilities, but was restrained by fears that to do so could lead to a military confrontation with Communist China or the Soviet Union.

At the conclusion of the meeting, President Nixon stated that there was one option that he ruled out. The United States would not leave Vietnam because of public opinion. He stated that there was a chance Vietnamization could work, but that he needed the option to do more. He warned the chiefs to be prepared to strike back hard at any North Vietnamese offensive and not be confined by the previous policy of measured retaliation.[35]

Intervention by the Chinese or the Soviets was still a possibility that had to be considered, but President Nixon and Henry Kissinger were secretly taking steps to minimize the threat. After Joseph Stalin died in 1953, doctrinal disputes had divided the Soviet Union and the People's Republic of China, as each sought to be recognized as the leader of world Communism. The only issue that remotely united the two was U.S. involvement in Vietnam, as each competed with the other to bring North Vietnam into its sphere of influence, and the North Vietnamese used this situation to garner military aid from both nations. However, the Soviet-Sino split widened with a border dispute in 1969. The border dispute erupted into armed conflict on 2 March 1969 when Chinese forces fired on Soviet border guards patrolling Zhenbao, an island in the Ussuri River between the two nations. Approximately fifty Soviet soldiers were killed. A second armed clash occurred on 15 March when the Soviets retaliated.[36] Kissinger and Nixon were secretly sending out feelers through third-party nations soliciting rapprochement with the Chinese, the ultimate goal of which was to create a triangular relationship and further separate the two Communist giants.[37]

During 1969, President Nixon's first year in office, 9,414 U.S. troops were killed in action in Vietnam. An additional 55,390 were wounded, and 112 were listed as missing in action.[38] The Paris Peace Talks were stalled, and the North Vietnamese exploited the 1968 bombing halt to move reinforcements and supplies into the border sanctuaries. Nixon was ready to strike back and the developing situation in Cambodia provided the opportunity.

Chapter 4

1970
The Cambodian Incursion

THE OPERATION MENU BOMBINGS TARGETED the base areas that sat astride the Vietnam-Cambodia border west of Saigon, but as military wisdom dictates, the job is not done until you have boots on the ground—meaning that air power has its limitations. When President Nixon restricted air strikes to targets close to the border, the Communists simply pulled back further into Cambodia. And when the bombing halted in August 1969, they returned to their border sanctuaries, resuming their pattern of border attacks followed by retreats. The South Vietnamese, in keeping with the Vietnamization program, manned the border outposts. Civilian irregular defense group (CIDG) camps along the Vietnam-Cambodia border were subjected to constant mortar and rocket attacks. The enemy was a fleeting target in these operations, and response by air power was of little value. Military commanders lobbied for permission to clean out the border sanctuaries with ground forces. But Cambodia was still a "neutral" country and its leader, Norodom Sihanouk, continued to walk the diplomatic tightrope trying to balance his relations with both the United States and North Vietnam.

The North Vietnamese presence in Cambodia spawned subversive activities and gave rise to the Khmer Rouge, the Cambodian Communist insurgent organization. Sihanouk was obviously concerned about the increasing North Vietnamese influence, if for no other reason than the increasing opposition to the North Vietnamese in the lower levels of his government. In mid-March Sihanouk departed for a tour of Europe. While he was gone, the National Assembly convened and voted to depose Sihanouk, creating a new government, the Khmer Republic. Lon Nol, who controlled Cambodia's armed forces, became the prime minister on 18 March. The coup sparked feelings of nationalism and latent resentment to the North Vietnamese presence among the Cambodians.

Nixon's first response was to do nothing—to honor the neutrality of Cambodia and not become involved. But the North Vietnamese immediately turned on their reluctant host when the new Cambodian government shut down trade with the Communists and closed Sihanoukville, the port of entry for supplies flowing north along a road network known as the Sihanoukville Trail. The North Vietnamese began moving out of the sanctuaries they occupied along the Cambodia-Vietnam border and engaging the Cambodian Army in an effort to isolate the capital, Phnom Penh, and restore their supply source at Sihanoukville. Nixon authorized emergency actions to give the new Cambodian government financial support and supply the Cambodian Army with weapons and ammunition.[1]

A concurrent crisis arose in the secret war in Laos. Gen. Vang Pao's CIA-sponsored Hmong Army was in danger of being overrun by Communists in its stronghold at Long Tieng, and the government of Laos was appealing for support. The Washington Special Actions Group (WSAG) first considered the request on 19 March and found itself in a dilemma. The very nature of the secret war meant that any support had to be covert. In addition, weather over the target area precluded air reconnaissance, making it difficult to employ B-52 strikes without risking civilian casualties. The WSAG decided to increase tactical air strikes, but those faced the same limitations. The government of Laos requested that Thai battalions under U.S. control be sent in as reinforcements, but the WSAG was divided on this proposal: some feared that the troop movement could not be done covertly, while others argued that the Thai troops would not be sufficient to turn the tide of battle. The WSAG recommended that the problem should be solved through diplomatic channels, but the president immediately sent them back to the drawing board. He wanted a "hard option."[2] The WSAG continued to debate the issue during meetings conducted from 19 to 24 March. The State and Defense Departments were opposed to deploying the Thai battalion, while the Joint Chiefs and the CIA were in favor of it. On 25 March President Nixon told Henry Kissinger that he was not inclined to allow Laos to "go down the drain."[3] The first Thai battalion was sent in immediately. A second Thai battalion deployed on 15 April, and Nixon ordered maximum B-52 and tactical air support over Laos the following day.[4]

Meanwhile in Cambodia, Lon Nol appealed to his Asian neighbors for support.[5] Thailand agreed to release a battalion that had been involved in joint operations with the United States in Laos to assist Cambodia, and Indonesia assisted by providing small arms and ammunition. In the midst of this whirlwind of activity, the Laotian government, falling back against heavy pressure from the Pathet Lao and the North Vietnamese, requested that Cambodia, a nation incapable of defending itself, send forces to Laos. The fall of both Cambodia and Laos to the Communists would make holding South Vietnam impossible for the allied forces.

Military planners put together options for attacks into the border sanctuaries to clean out the base areas and destroy or capture the NVA's supply caches. The first plans included only South Vietnamese ground forces, supported by U.S. air and artillery, positioned in South Vietnam. A proposed U.S.-South Vietnamese joint operation soon replaced these plans. As General Westmoreland, the acting Chairman of the Joint Chiefs of Staff, pointed out to Secretary Laird, "The North Vietnamese and Viet Cong have taken a calculated risk in moving out of their base areas. Their logistic situation is becoming more strained. I believe we should move quickly to exploit their vulnerabilities."[6] General Haig, Kissinger's military assistant, reviewed the plans and, in a memorandum to Kissinger dated 3 April 1970, stated that the proposed operations could trigger an "all out" enemy offensive in I Corps. He advised that troop withdrawals should be delayed, adding that the operations would pose a threat that could force the NVA to turn and halt their advance toward Phnom Penh. In his view, the operation would devastate the enemy's logistical system, but there were not enough blocking forces to keep the NVA from fading deeper into Cambodia.[7]

Nixon knew that a cross-border operation would trigger a firestorm of protest, particularly if U.S. troops were involved. Secretary Rogers opposed crossing the border, and Secretary Laird opposed participation by U.S. ground forces. They both maintained that if U.S. forces were to cross the border, it should only be a shallow penetration.

President Nixon met with Henry Kissinger and CIA director Richard Helms on 16 April. Nixon directed Helms to "get the word out abroad, if not here at home, that the US was prepared to intervene militarily in the event Hanoi initiates direct attacks against Phnom Penh."[8] On 21 April Helms notified Kissinger that the CIA had taken several steps that gave the North Vietnamese leadership clear reason to believe that if Communist forces attacked Cambodia's capital, Phnom Penh, U.S. and South Vietnamese forces would hit them in the rear by attacking their Cambodian sanctuaries.[9]

Agent reports on 24 April confirmed that the North Vietnamese received the message. Helms's memorandum to Kissinger described the reaction of an unnamed Communist official who became extremely nervous after reading the written report and was unable to control his shaking legs and feet. The man stated that the National Liberation Front (NLF) had expected the United States to intervene in Cambodia, but not so soon. When the unnamed official was questioned about the presence of NVA and Vietcong forces in Cambodia, he acknowledged their presence, but stated, "It would be political suicide for us to admit it."[10] The Communists ignored the warning, and two days later President Nixon issued National Security Council Decision Memorandum 57, authorizing U.S. and South Vietnamese forces to conduct ground attacks into known Cambodian base areas up to a depth of thirty kilometers.

South Vietnamese armored cavalry and ranger units, operating without their U.S. advisors, struck across the border and uncovered large caches of enemy matériel.[11] On the morning of 29 April three additional South Vietnamese task forces, accompanied this time by their American advisors, launched Operation Toan Thang 42, attacking an area known as the Parrot's Beak due to the shape of the border where it jutted eastward from Cambodia toward Saigon. Two days later, elements of the U.S. 1st Cavalry Division, 25th Infantry Division, 3rd Brigade, 9th Infantry Division, 11th Armored Cavalry, and 3rd ARVN Airborne Brigade attacked a region north of the Parrot's Beak known as the Fish Hook. The U.S. 4th Infantry Division attacked from positions further north in II Corps four days later.[12]

The battle with the enemy's rear guard was finished by 3 May, a battle of such short duration that it provided no test of the ARVN's logistical support and staying power. While the operation continued for another sixty days, that time was consumed in searching for, destroying, or seizing enemy supply caches. Also, it was an allied operation in which American combat units joined, not solely a South Vietnamese campaign. Nor was it difficult: resistance was relatively light, and the Communist base areas were located on terrain not normally considered conducive to defense. The topography afforded multiple overland avenues of approach for pincer movements against the objective areas, located in salients where Cambodia's border jutted eastward, and was bounded by South Vietnamese territory on three sides. The primary defense of these Communist base areas rested on the presence of a line on the map—the Cambodian border. And the operation was supported by American firepower, controlled and coordinated by American field artillery forward observers, forward air controllers, and American advisors. The operation took place along South Vietnam's southern border, and there were no reinforcements immediately available for the Communists; the NVA simply did not have the tactical mobility to rush in reinforcements or run the gauntlet down the Ho Chi Minh Trail in Laos. The ground attack was preceded by B-52 strikes, fighter-bomber sorties, and a heavy field artillery preparation.[13] While there was resistance early in the operation, the NVA and Vietcong troops did not put up a fierce defense. They evacuated their base areas and faded westward beyond the 30-kilometer limit imposed by President Nixon.[14] The allies attacked in force on a broad front over terrain that favored mechanized forces. Resistance and allied casualties were lighter than many anticipated, and the enormous caches of weapons, ammunition, medical supplies, and rice the allies were able to secure exceeded expectations. The captured documents revealed that the volume of Communist arms and munitions flowing through the port of Sihanoukville far exceeded previous CIA estimates.

From the beginning, the Communists had exploited all possible means of infiltrating supplies to their forces in South Vietnam. While the overland trails flowing south from North Vietnam through Laos and Cambodia were almost exclusively the routes used for troop movements, not all of their supplies were transported via the Ho Chi Minh Trail. Significant amounts of matériel were also smuggled in through the coast of South Vietnam. In 1965 Operation Market Time, a navy and coast guard operation, reduced infiltration by sea to a trickle. However, Market Time was restricted to patrolling the beaches, inland waterways, and the territorial waters of South Vietnam. The North Vietnamese answer was to sail around South Vietnam's territorial waters and off-load their supplies at Sihanoukville, Cambodia, which became an important hub in the Communist supply system.[15]

U.S. intelligence agencies were aware of arms trafficking in Cambodia, but there was serious disagreement as to the extent of trade. The CIA maintained that the amount of arms and supplies coming up the Sihanoukville Trail was of little significance. But the MACV's intelligence staff insisted that Sihanoukville was the major point of entry. The debate emerged as early as 15 October 1968 when Marshall Wright, of the National Security Council staff, cited General Abrams's view that there had been a shift in the Communist supply system from Laos to Cambodia. Abrams stated that, because of the intensified air campaign on the Ho Chi Minh Trail, only about fifteen trucks per day were getting through Laos, and the Communists were relying on the Cambodian supply routes. The CIA's position was diametrically opposed to that of Abrams; it stated that the NVA was moving two-and-a-half times the tonnage down the northern trail than in 1967, and it could document truck traffic over the Ho Chi Minh Trail as far south as the Parrot's Beak in Cambodia. According to the CIA, the Laotian route was supplying all Communist forces in South Vietnam except for those in the southern part of IV Corps.[16]

General Westmoreland, who was now the army chief of staff, provided additional evidence of infiltration through Sihanoukville. Westmoreland met with General Prashat, the commander of the Royal Thai Army on 16 October 1968. Prashat disclosed that his agents in Phnom Penh and Sihanoukville had observed a regular flow of Chinese arms and ammunition through the port city, and that their report was confirmed by information he received from the Japanese embassy in Bangkok. He stated that the supplies were moved in boxes from merchant ships into a warehouse built by the Russians. From there the supplies were moved by trucks to storage points near the Vietnamese border, and then delivered to the NVA and Vietcong forces.[17]

General Wheeler addressed the issue with the commander in chief, Pacific, Adm. John McCain. McCain confirmed the military intelligence position, estimating that 60 percent of the enemy's external logistics flowed through Cambodia, and that truck traffic in Laos had provided only minimal quantities of supplies as far south as the tri-border area. McCain also noted that military intelligence had detected considerable expansion of storage and support facilities and road construction in areas of Cambodia under enemy control.[18]

The issue turned on the effectiveness of the air campaign in Laos, and the deputy secretary of defense, Paul Nitze, asked the secretary of the air force, Dr. Harold Brown, for his assessment, which was inconclusive. Brown stated that there might be fewer trucks operating in Laos as compared with the air force estimate for 1967. The number of truck sightings for 1968 was comparable with the number of sightings for 1967, but the number of forward air control and reconnaissance sorties had increased from 1,905 to 2,812, raising the possibility that the number of sightings could be a factor of increased surveillance and double counting. He stated that during 1968, a large percentage of truck sightings and kills occurred at night, and because of this, the bomb damage assessment was limited. He concluded by stating that looking strictly at truck kills for the past year, "we did not do so well," but if 7th Air Force estimates of the reduction in throughput were accurate, the air operation "should be judged successful."[19] The CIA's position prevailed. An extensive air campaign to close down the Ho Chi Minh Trail on the northern end continued, while little effort was made to stem the flow of supplies from the southern end.

Captured documents from Operation Toan Thang 42 and documents provided by Lon Nol revealed that as much as 70 percent of all Communist munitions in Cambodia were coming through the Sihanoukville connection. Nixon was perturbed. He characterized the intelligence failure as one of the worst records ever compiled by the intelligence community and that the individuals responsible for the failure should be fired.[20]

The CIA conducted an internal investigation and discovered that numerous indicators and reports from clandestine agents indicated the magnitude of munitions flow through Sihanoukville. The problem was that the body of evidence, much of which was based secondhand information, failed to meet the analysts' standards for absolute certainty and was not reported. Washington analysts lacked objectivity. Having espoused an erroneous position on Sihanoukville's role in the war effort earlier, they persisted in minimizing the steadily increasing mass of evidence that contradicted their original assessments.[21] An official North Vietnamese history says, "between 1966 and 1968 we shipped 21,400 tons of supplies through port of Sihanoukville and paid the [Cambodian] government $50 million U.S. dollars in port fees and transportation charges."[22] While the number of tons of supplies coming through the port may seem low, Cambodia's lucrative rice sales to the NVA dramatically reduced the total number of tons of supplies that had to be shipped from North Vietnam.

There is little doubt as to the magnitude of the CIA's Sihanoukville intelligence failure, but the failure cannot be attributed exclusively to the CIA. The contradicting military intelligence was documented and passed up the chain of command, where the national leadership may

have been guilty of "selective listening." Cambodia had severed diplomatic relations with the United States in 1965, and U.S. policy towards
that country was strictly "hands off." Cross-border patrols by SOG and
aerial reconnaissance were prohibited during the Johnson administration, so Sihanouk was handled with kid gloves. Any allegation of U.S.
incursion would have led to the international accusation that the U.S.
had extended the war into a neutral nation.

President Nixon met with Adm. John McCain on 29 April 1970, the
same date that South Vietnamese crossed the border into Cambodia.
During the meeting it became clear that the president wanted to do
more than just clean out border sanctuaries; he wanted to sever the Ho
Chi Minh Trail. McCain advised the president that that an operation of
this magnitude would require two to three divisions in the III and IV
Corps areas and approximately five divisions in I and II Corps, and in
his opinion, a combination of air strikes and irregular forces would be
more effective. Nixon "expressed high interest" in contingency plans for
the operation.[23] The combination of air strikes and irregular forces was
the same tactical formula used since the beginning of the war. What
was different was the intent: the president wanted to do more than just
interdict or disrupt the Communist supply line; he wanted to sever the
trail. When a president expresses "high interest" to one of his military
commanders it is tantamount to issuing an order. If there was any misunderstanding, the order was clarified a month later.

President Nixon met with his cabinet at the western White House
in San Clemente on 30 May 1970 to discuss the progress in Cambodia.
When the discussion turned to the topic of Vietnamization, Abrams,
encouraged by Laird, painted an overly optimistic appraisal of ARVN
capabilities. General Abrams stated that ARVN operations in Cambodia had progressed far better than expected. Abrams described
a competent South Vietnamese force that had gained a new sense of
confidence and enthusiasm. He had high praise for the ARVN airborne
division, stating that this was the first time that the division had conducted division-level operations, and it was now "capable of running
its own show." Nixon instructed Abrams to clean out the Cambodian

sanctuaries and granted Abrams the authority to continue to fly close air support and interdiction missions for the South Vietnamese in Cambodia. Nixon concluded his remarks to Abrams with an order to prepare plans for offensive operations in Laos: "I want to get the South Vietnamese to move offensively and at the same time keep our casualties low. Prepare plans which provide for offensive operations in Laos."[24]

General Abrams's enthusiasm for the apparent success of Vietnamization was not necessarily warranted. By all accounts he was a superb commander, but this error in judgment would have serious repercussions. The Cambodian incursion was not a demanding test of ARVN military competence. According to Lt. Gen. Phillip Davidson, who served as the MACV intelligence chief from 1967 to 1969, Lt. Gen. Do Cao Tri commanded the ARVN corps, and Tri was by far the most competent ARVN field commander. Tri had relied heavily on elite forces during his thrust into the Parrot's Beak—the rangers, airborne division, and the 2nd Armored Cavalry Squadron. When forced to use troops from the ARVN infantry divisions, he bypassed the politically appointed division commanders and formed task forces under the command of more competent lieutenant colonels and colonels. Support from the ARVN field artillery was practically nonexistent. The mechanized infantry and armor got off to a good start, but quickly lost momentum as their maintenance program—or more correctly put, their absence of a maintenance program—brought them to a halt with broken armored personnel carriers and tanks strewn along the routes of advance.[25]

The incursion into Cambodia added fuel to the protest movement, and the level of violence in protests intensified. On 1 May 1970 protesters at Kent State University torched the Reserve Officer Training Corps (ROTC) building. Ohio governor James A. Rhodes deployed national guard troops to quell the riots. On 4 May the guardsmen opened fire on the protesters, killing four and wounding eight. The actions at Kent State ignited more protests and strikes. More than four hundred universities were shut down, and nearly 100,000 protestors descended on the capital. The political repercussions were severe. Antiwar members of the House and Senate began attempts to limit Nixon's war-making prerogatives and legislate an end to the war.

Senators John Sherman Cooper and Frank Church attached an amendment to the Foreign Military Sales Act that would end funding of U.S. ground troops and advisors in Laos and Cambodia after 30 June 1970, ban air operations in Cambodian air space in support of Cambodian forces without specific congressional approval, and end American support of ARVN forces outside of South Vietnam. After a seven-week filibuster and six months of debate, the amendment passed the senate by a vote of fifty-eight to thirty-seven. President Nixon threatened to veto the bill if it came to his desk, but a veto was not necessary. The bill, in its current form, was defeated in the House of Representatives.[26] Once the bill had been defeated, Cooper and Church revised it softening some of its measures. The revised bill continued to allow the funding of cross-border operations by ARVN forces and U.S. air forces, but funding for cross-border operations by U.S. ground forces was prohibited. The new bill passed both houses of Congress on 22 December 1970. Nixon was adamantly opposed to the restriction on ground forces and advisors, but did not exercise his veto power. His political support was crumbling and the much more draconian McGovern-Hatfield bill was in the wings. If passed, it would require the end of U.S. military operations in Vietnam by 31 December 1970 and a complete withdrawal of American forces by the end of June 1971.

Another battle, Operation Texas Star, was brewing in northern Military Region I while world attention was focused on operations in Cambodia. Better known for the battle at Fire Support Base Ripcord, Texas Star was under the radar of the American press and public knowledge for years after the Vietnam War. It was not that the operation was classified; the 101st Airborne had imposed a press blackout after being burned by an increasingly antiwar press corps and congressional criticism a year earlier during the battle of Hamburger Hill, and even army reporters and photographers were excluded from the operational area.[27]

After the 101st Airborne withdrew from the A Shau Valley at the conclusion of Operation Apache Snow and the battle at Hamburger

Hill, the NVA reinforced and expanded its positions in the valley. By early 1970 it was apparent that the Communists were postured to strike eastward from the valley toward the coastal lowlands and population centers held by the South Vietnamese and U.S. forces. This had to be countered, but U.S. forces were limited to "protective reaction" operations and orders to minimize casualties. The 3rd Brigade was tasked with Texas Star, the purpose of which was to blunt the NVA's eastward movement and establish a string of fire support bases in the mountains east of the A Shau that would support a second operation, Chicago Peak, which involved a sweep through the A Shau Valley by the 1st ARVN Division.

Operation Texas Star was launched on 13 March 1970, but the 3rd Brigade encountered unexpected resistance when the 2nd Battalion, 506th Infantry, attempted to reopen fire support base Ripcord, located on high ground overlooking the valley floor.[28] Ripcord was the pivotal fire support base for the sweep through the valley. The assault force was extracted two days later, and airstrikes were called in to soften up the area. The second assault was conducted on 1 April. The enemy still held the crest of Ripcord. The 506th's infantry companies landed on adjacent slopes and, after a stiff fight, managed to gain control of the hilltop. Base construction began immediately. The 2nd Battalion controlled Ripcord, but the North Vietnamese held the surrounding mountain peaks, positions that enabled the enemy to bring observed fire on Ripcord. The battalion sent out combat and reconnaissance patrols in a series of attempts to dislodge the enemy, but most of these attempts failed. The battalion had landed in the midst of a regiment of the NVA's 324th Division, which was given the mission of crushing the American forces on Ripcord, while the NVA's 304th Division attacked the allied forces on the northern end of the A Shau Valley and southwest Quang Tri Province. The 304th was not able to gain much traction. The division's 9th Regiment was caught out in the open by the aerial scouts and gunships from the 101st's air cavalry squadron, whose Cobra gunships and minigun equipped OH-6 scout ships shredded the regiment as it moved through thick elephant grass.

Meanwhile, north of Ripcord, the 1st ARVN Division established Fire Support Base (FSB) Henderson in the mountains east of the north end of the valley, and U.S. forces occupied FSB Maureen at the southeast corner of the valley. NVA sappers penetrated the defenses at Henderson on the night 6 May. The ARVN battalion failed to prepare protective revetments for their artillery ammunition, and the sappers, armed with satchel charges, managed to hit the ammunition supply point, setting off a huge series of explosions that wrecked the fire support base. Sappers hit Maureen on the following night, but were turned back. After Maureen was hit, Maj. Gen. Hennessey, the commanding general of the 101st Airborne, decided that the division was overextended and cancelled the planned sweep through the valley. Contact around Ripcord intensified during the remainder of May and June. By the first of July Ripcord was under siege. For the next twenty-three days the defenders at Ripcord were subjected to a barrage of enemy mortar and recoilless rifle fire. Although the NVA certainly sustained a considerable number of casualties, air power and artillery could not silence the enemy gunners. Every resupply ship that landed at Ripcord was greeted with intense fire. The base took a crippling blow when a CH-47 with a sling load of artillery ammunition was shot down and it crashed into the 105mm howitzer battery. The battery, along with all the ammunition, was destroyed in a series of violent explosions. Shortly thereafter a security patrol operating outside the base discovered an NVA telephone line. They tapped the line, and the company's Vietnamese interpreter listened in on the NVA's communications. Enemy regiments, planning to overrun the base, surrounded Ripcord. Brig. Gen. Sidney B. Berry, the division's acting commander in Maj. Gen. John J. Hennessey's absence, made the decision to evacuate Ripcord.

The airmobile evacuation of Ripcord was an intense operation. Every inbound sortie had to weave its way through heavy fire, while all available artillery, air strikes, and Cobra gunships poured in suppressive fires. Almost without exception, every helicopter crew that came in to pick up a load had to either set down or hold in a low hover while absorbing multiple hits from enemy mortar, machinegun, and small arms fire, then fly their battle-damaged ships back to Camp Evans, Phu Bai, or Camp Eagle.[29] The Communists had once again successfully defended the A Shau Valley "warehouse."

While critics may question the decision to retain Ripcord after Chicago Peak was canceled or infinitely delayed, continued occupation of Ripcord provided a barrier to possible NVA plans to attack the coastal lowlands. It was a battlefield that absorbed considerable NVA strength and military stores. Operation Texas Star and the forced evacuation of FSB Ripcord should have imparted valuable lessons for the planners of Lam Son 719: The North Vietnamese were totally committed to the defense of their northern infiltration routes. They would not, as they had in Cambodia, fall back and allow the South Vietnamese to wreck their strategic supply route. Totally within the borders of South Vietnam where political considerations of cross-border operations posed no limitations on military action, the A Shau Valley was close enough to Laos for the Communists to flee to sanctuary when threatened with superior force and close enough to North Vietnam for the NVA to reinforce. The valley was a section of the Ho Chi Minh Trail that was impossible to shut down except on a temporary basis.

While the South Vietnamese and U.S. forces were cleaning out the Cambodian base area and severing the Communist supply line at Sihanoukville, the Communists were expanding their control over southern Laos, capturing the cities of Saravane and Attopeu, and the strategically important Boloven Plateau, giving them access to southbound Highway 13 in Laos. Controlling the western half of the panhandle provided the NVA with the opportunity to expand its trail network further west, and it provided greater protection from a possible incursion from South Vietnam. In an attempt to regain control of some of the territory, the CIA planned a major operation to regain lost territory: Operation Gauntlet.

The plans called for a large-scale offensive against the North Vietnamese route structure and enemy support elements in south Laos. An unusually complicated endeavor, Gauntlet required extensive preliminaries—including the capture and improvement of airstrips and an advance on Chavane—before some 1,500 troops could make the final thrust toward Muong Phine and Tchepone. Guerilla forces would conduct operations in four areas: in the vicinity of Ban Toumlan, along the Banghiang River from Saravane toward Chavane, and from Muong Phalane eastward to Tchepone. The Laotian Air Force and USAF AC-119 gunships stationed at Da Nang and the USAF squadrons at Nakhom Phanom, Thailand, would provide close air support. On 8 September 1970 a 1,500-man guerilla force landed on the eastern edge of the Boloven Plateau with the mission of recapturing the city of Chavane and the Chavane airstrip.[30] The guerilla force encountered stiff enemy resistance, and the operation resulted in only minimal disruption to NVA lines of communication. However, an associated operation produced results; Operation Tailwind was a MACVSOG operation designed for two purposes: to provide a reconnaissance in force and a diversionary attack in support of the Gauntlet guerilla force.[31] The Tailwind force was composed of a 120-man CIDG Company led by seventeen U.S. MACVSOG members; it was inserted on 11 September, three days after the Gauntlet insertion.

The company landed twenty miles deeper into Laos than any earlier SOG operation. For three days the Tailwind force, supported by gunships and tactical air, engaged the enemy in a fast-moving battle. It discovered and destroyed a major ammunition cache, captured a treasure trove of NVA documents detailing operations on the Ho Chi Minh Trail, and killed 428 of the enemy in a combination of air and ground action. Tailwind casualties were comparatively light: all seventeen U.S. soldiers and thirty-three CIDG soldiers were wounded, and three CIDG soldiers were killed.[32] Operation Tailwind had been brilliantly executed.

The SOG force raised such havoc in the enemy's rear that the enemy was forced to divert a major force to stop it. Moreover, once a vastly superior enemy force began to close on the SOG force, the company commander orchestrated a brilliant extraction operation. He kept his force moving, which prevented the NVA from encircling the landing zone with antiaircraft guns to destroy the incoming helicopters. He loaded each flight of helicopters with as many men as they could carry, then fought his way through the encircling NVA troops and moved to a different LZ when the flight returned to pick up another load. He was the last man to board a helicopter.[33] It was a tactic that would have served the ARVN well in the year to come.

The Cambodian incursion was a military victory for ARVN and U.S. forces. The southern point of entry for Communist supplies was severed. U.S. ground forces were withdrawn from Cambodia, and a combined South Vietnamese and Cambodian force had a tenuous hold on the border sanctuary area. With the loss of their southern point of entry, the Communists stepped up their efforts to expand and improve their infiltration and strategic supply routes in the Laotian panhandle. The North Vietnamese began moving large amounts of supplies southward in North Vietnam to areas that could support offensive operations farther south.[34]

President Nixon was determined to strike at the northern end of the Ho Chi Minh Trail, a move that would cut the Communist supply line, relieve NVA pressure in Cambodia, and buy time for the South Vietnamese to prepare to defend their nation while American forces withdrew from Vietnam. The path to victory in Vietnam lay in Laos, which secretary of state Herter had told president-elect Kennedy was the "cork in the bottle."[35]

By November 1970 planning was underway for a cross-border operation into the Laotian panhandle. Congressional restrictions on military funding, however, dictated that it would be an ARVN rather than a U.S. operation.

Chapter 5

Planning Lam Son 719

While Congress debated legislation designed to force the withdrawal of American forces from Vietnam, military planners moved ahead with the offensive operations in Laos that Nixon had ordered during his 30 May 1970 conference with General Abrams. These orders, paired with an overly optimistic assessment of Vietnamization and a last-minute restriction on U.S. ground forces and advisors, built the foundation for a plan to sever the northern Ho Chi Minh Trail, which would culminate in Operation Lam Son 719.

On 22 October 1970 Kissinger sent a memorandum to Nixon commenting on the CIA's latest assessment of North Vietnamese military intentions. He noted that the North Vietnamese had few immediate options for dramatic military action but were rapidly building their strength in Southern Laos. Kissinger acknowledged that the CIA had no clear indicator of North Vietnamese intentions, but speculated that much of the North Vietnamese effort was devoted to rebuilding and expanding their logistical system along the Ho Chi Minh Trail.[1] Although Admiral McCain had suggested interdicting the trail with irregular forces, Kissinger pointed out the difficulties in such a plan in his 30 October report to Nixon.[2] The reconnaissance in force and the failure of Operation Gauntlet both indicated a strong and determined NVA force in southern Laos and the Laotian panhandle. Thus, severing the northern end of the Ho Chi Minh Trail was going to require more than irregular forces and air power.

In early November CIA director Helms outlined for Nixon why Hanoi had rejected the president's latest peace offer, concluding that the North Vietnamese had suffered significant military setbacks as a result of operations in Cambodia and were unwilling to negotiate from a position of weakness. He anticipated a major North Vietnamese push from Laos during the upcoming dry season. In his summary of Helms's report Kissinger added, "In any event, it is clearly in our interest to prevent a large volume of supplies from moving through south Laos and to be prepared for a military push should the Communists attempt one."[3]

After the North Vietnamese rejection of Nixon's latest peace proposal at the Paris Peace Talks and the successful closure of Sihanoukville, severing the trail at the northern end became increasingly important to achieving a military victory. The North Vietnamese would then have to accept negotiations leading to a favorable outcome. The Laotian panhandle was the last critical link in the Ho Chi Minh Trail because its northern end had always been an infiltration route for Communist troops. Cutting off Communist supplies and reinforcements over that route in the coming year would provide additional time to complete the withdrawal of American forces under "victorious" circumstances. During that time South Vietnam could build its strength and perhaps force the North Vietnamese to accept a negotiated settlement. More important for the Nixon administration, successfully severing the trail would help ensure the president's reelection.

The situation represented an enemy vulnerability, but the window of opportunity to exploit this vulnerability was narrow. The National Security Council assessment indicated that, while the NVA would encounter greater difficulties if the trail was severed in Laos, the route was probably capable of providing sufficient supplies for the NVA in Cambodia.[4] Intelligence also revealed that the North Vietnamese were quickly intensifying their efforts to expand the trail's throughput capability. U.S. troop strength was in a downward spiral that, for political reasons, could not be reversed. This fact, combined with the cross-border limitations placed on American ground troops, meant that the operation would have to be conducted by the South Vietnamese. The availability of ARVN forces would last only as long as the allied forces held the upper hand in Cambodia. But there was mounting evidence that the Cambodian forces were incapable of successful operations against the Communists. Traditional animosities between the South Vietnamese and Cambodians prevented effective combined operations, and the North Vietnamese were intensifying their efforts to reestablish their supremacy in Cambodia. Planning for future military operations now became Nixon's priority, so he pressed for a strike at the northern end of the Ho Chi Minh Trail.

There was a shift in the traditional centers of power as Henry Kissinger, Nixon's national security advisor, absorbed some of the traditional roles of the secretary of state and secretary of defense. In the wake of the EC-121 incident, the president had directed Kissinger to establish a permanent subcommittee of the National Security Council in the event of a similar crisis. As early as 16 April 1969 it had become clear that Nixon and Kissinger did not trust Defense Secretary Laird to carry out their orders.[5] The subcommittee, dubbed the Washington special actions group or WSAG, provided a mechanism to bypass this problem. Kissinger convened its first meeting on 2 July 1969.[6]

Nixon's confidence in Secretary Laird and Secretary Rogers waned as they habitually opposed the bold strokes the president saw as necessary to win "peace with honor."[7] Dissatisfied with their performance, Nixon turned to Kissinger, and together they circumvented the problem. President Nixon signed National Security Decision Memorandum 57, which gave the WSAG implementation authority for the Cambodian incursion, bypassing Secretary Laird who later declared the action unconstitutional.[8]

As Kissinger's dominance grew, he increasingly bypassed Rogers by using back-channel messages and memorandums to ambassadors and bypassed Laird by directing inquiries directly to the members of the Joint Chiefs. Kissinger became Nixon's gatekeeper; all written communications to the president had to pass through Kissinger, who typically attached his opinion. On 22 February 1971 Secretary of State Rogers asked the White House chief of staff if there was any way he could have direct communication with the president without going through Kissinger.[9] There wasn't.

Kissinger's senior military assistant, Gen. Alexander Haig, began to take a direct role in reviewing and critiquing military plans formulated by the Joint Chiefs and the Department of Defense. Alexander Haig, a man Nixon once described as an "ambitious son of a bitch," had won the confidence of both Nixon and Kissinger and was in a position to influence the course of events. Still, Laird was not without power. In addition to his political clout in Congress, Laird had the power to set priorities in terms of manpower, acquisition of military supplies and equipment, regulation of draft quotas within the totals authorized by Congress, and coordination and review of military planning. It was in this convoluted environment that a monumental decision was made to undertake an invasion of the Laotian panhandle.

On 4 November Kissinger sent a memorandum to Rogers, Laird, and Helms relaying the president's order to develop contingency studies that would address likely enemy actions and recommend counteractions, both military and political. The studies were given a suspense date of no later than 20 November, and the plans were due by 1 December 1970.[10]

After the success of Operation Tailwind and the technical success of the Son Tay Raid—a superbly executed raid on a North Vietnamese prisoner-of-war camp that was unfortunately empty—enthusiasm was building for more determined actions, both across the border into North Vietnam and into the Laotian panhandle. When President Nixon and General Haig discussed Operation Tailwind during a 28 November telephone conversation, Haig commented that the South Vietnamese vice president, Nguyen Cao Ky, regretted that his air force had not been included in the operation.[11] Nixon embraced Ky's enthusiasm and directed Haig to "put out an order" to Abrams to have the South Vietnamese begin a monthly series of raids into North Vietnam and "blow up a power plant or something."[12] There is no evidence of any action resulting from Nixon's off-the-cuff order. If Haig put the order through Defense Department channels it is unlikely that it would have ever reached Abrams, given Laird's proclivity for selective compliance with Nixon's orders. MACVSOG cross-border operations were in progress, and there is little evidence of an increase in South Vietnamese raids.

Adm. John McCain, the commander in chief of the Pacific command (CINCPAC) and the commander directly above Abrams in the chain of command, sent the general a message containing a draft concept for an invasion of Laos on 10 November 1970 and requested that Abrams begin planning for a "major ARVN ground operation into the Laos Panhandle." Abrams complied with McCain's request. On 8 December McCain sent Abrams another message authorizing him to include in the planning Gen. Cao Van Vien, the chairman of South Vietnam's Joint General Staff (JGS). Later in December Kissinger sent Haig to Vietnam to consult with Abrams concerning the plausibility of military options for further operations against infiltration along the Ho Chi Minh Trail in either Cambodia or Laos.

On 11 December the WSAG discussed contingency plans for operations in Cambodia and Laos. The WSAG concluded that the South Vietnamese plan for an operation in the "Fish Hook" area of the Cambodian border and in the Chup rubber plantation was adequate for continuing operations against the southern infiltration routes. Turning their attention to Laos and the northern infiltration routes, the WSAG considered two candidate plans. The first plan called for an attack along the Route 9 corridor leading to Tchepone. A second proposal was an operation extending along Route 19 in South Vietnam, crossing the frontier, and cutting the Ho Chi Minh Trail near Attopeu along the northern Cambodian border. General Westmoreland, representing the Joint Chiefs in the absence of Admiral Moorer, favored the second option; he stated that if large-scale operations were conducted in Southern Laos, the balance of forces would heavily favor the enemy.[13]

In the meantime General Haig was in Saigon conferring with General Abrams, who rejected Westmoreland's Route 19 plan.[14] However, Haig returned to Washington with a recommendation, supported by General Vien, President Thieu, and General Abrams, for a plan developed largely as a result of Vietnamese initiate. The plan, codenamed

Lam Son 719, called for an invasion of Laos. On the surface the plan for Lam Son 719 had a striking resemblance to a previously scrapped operations plan, OPLAN El Paso, which Westmoreland had proposed for execution in 1968, a point in time when U.S. forces in Vietnam exceeded 540,000 and would make the main attack.

Kissinger and Admiral Moorer met at the White House on 22 December 1970 to discuss the plan as well as the strategy for obtaining the concurrence of the Secretaries of State and Defense. After Moorer described the four phases of the operation, Kissinger asked if it would result in the destruction of significant enemy stockpiles. Moorer answered in the affirmative and went on to explain that General Abrams selected the Tchepone area because it contains so many lucrative targets. When Moorer explained that the operation could commence in early February, immediately following the Tet holiday, Kissinger's replied, "The earlier the better. The only chance we have is to initiate bold moves against the enemy." Admiral Moorer agreed, noting that because of budget problems and planned troop withdrawals, the United States had only until the following spring to take such initiatives. He also noted that G. McMurtrie Godly, the U.S. ambassador to Laos, had forwarded a similar plan to U. Alexis Johnson, the undersecretary of state for political affairs, in early December, and Johnson had dismissed the plan as "preposterous."[15] The U.S. Ambassador to South Vietnam, Ellsworth Bunker, also favored the plan and noted that it was very similar to one that he had brought back to Washington several years ago (in OPLAN EL Paso). With Abrams's optimistic assessment of Vietnamization—a view that was also accepted by the South Vietnamese—and Nixon's insistence on a strike in Laos, the stage was set for Operation Lam Son 719.

President Nixon met with Henry Kissinger, Melvin Laird, newly appointed Chairman of the Joint Chiefs Admiral Moorer, and CIA director Richard Helms on 18 January to discuss the impending operation. Secretary Laird and Admiral Moorer opened the discussion with an overview of the operation: The plan was designed to capture the logistics center at Tchepone through a combined airmobile operation to seize the airfield and a ground linkup along Route 9. The ARVN's airborne division would conduct the airmobile operation, and the 1st ARVN Division would be in overall command of the ground linkup.

During Phase 1 the U.S. 1st Brigade, 5th Mechanized Infantry Division, would open Route 9 from Dong Ha to the Laotian Border. The airfield and combat base at Khe Sanh, abandoned since the conclusion of the 1968 Tet Offensive, would serve as the base of operations for the invasion. Phase 1 would also include a deception plan involving the use of code names from previous operations in the A Shau Valley. Hopefully the enemy would assume the operation was headed for the A Shau Valley when messages with these code names were intercepted.

Admiral Moorer went on to describe U.S. support. Heavy artillery positioned along the Laotian border would support the ARVN attack, and U.S. forces would provide helicopter and tactical air support, including B-52 strikes. All agreed that the ARVN forces would face a tough fight in Laos, but Kissinger commented that "if the enemy stood and fought it would be to our advantage and that it could set the enemy timetable back as much as a year."[16]

Secretary Rogers stated that the real problem involved U.S. casualties and whether or not they might go up, either because of air operations in Laos or as a result of the reduction of forces available to defend the region after the ARVN corps crossed the border into Laos.[17] The president observed that the artillery positioned along the border could be vulnerable. Admiral Moorer agreed and added that there might also be some helicopter casualties.[18]

The president stated that there was little doubt the administration would get some real heat from the press and Congress, but if the operation blunted the enemy's capacity to conduct a dry-season offensive as U.S. forces drew down to less than 100,000 by 22 November 1971, the risks would be reduced. Nixon speculated, "If we fail to undertake the operation, we might be able to continue our deployments, but there was a chance we could 'get a rap' in 1972." Nixon added that the operation would be a strong deterrent to the enemy for subsequent offensive operations and might prove decisive in the overall conduct of the war. Secretary Laird agreed with the president and stated that by 1 May U.S. forces would be depleted to 45,000 first-line combat troops.[19]

The president ended the discussion with an effort to hedge against the perception of failure: "The operation cannot come out as a defeat. Therefore, we must set very limited goals such as interdicting the trail, keep our claims modest. It should be packaged as a raid on the sanctuaries. Even though this was a difficult operation, the ARVN should be able to do it. If they were not able to do it, then we must know that also."[20] While President Nixon would accept greater success, his primary aim was to conduct a preemptive strike that would prevent a 1971 dry-season offensive that would endanger his plans for troop withdrawals. There is evidence that the North Vietnamese planned an offensive during the 1971 dry season. Northern leaders found many reasons to justify such an offensive: The strategy of protracted warfare, if it continued, risked manpower shortages and economic stagnation. Le Duan, the First Secretary of North Vietnam's Communist Party, believed that the Vietnamization program and the continued withdrawal of American troops increased Nixon's chances for reelection, and reelection would give Nixon greater freedom of action in Vietnam. A successful invasion by the North Vietnamese while some American troops remained would discredit Vietnamization and help defeat the United States.[21]

Admiral Moorer's comment that there "may be some helicopter casualties" obviously concerned President Nixon. However, this concern was not a compassionate concern for the welfare of American helicopter crews; rather, he was concerned that involvement of U.S. helicopters would lead to greater public and congressional criticism. When Nixon asked Moorer why the South Vietnamese Air Force could not perform the mission, Moorer replied that he had discussed the matter twice with General Abrams, who advised him that the South Vietnamese did not have sufficient helicopters. Kissinger asked if the airmobile plan could be eliminated in favor of a ground attack. Moorer stated that the planners in Saigon considered the shock effect of an airmobile assault as an important ingredient to the overall plan. On 26 January, four days prior to the launch of Phase 1, the president asked Admiral Moorer to study the operation again to see if it could be accomplished using less U.S. airlift, so that he would not be open to the charge of lifting South Vietnamese troops into Laos.[22]

After his meeting with the president, Admiral Moorer immediately queried Admiral McCain and General Abrams on several topics. He asked them if the operation could be conducted without U.S. helicopter support, what the latest date was that Phase 2 could be canceled, whether an operation could be conducted in northern Cambodia if the attack on Tchepone were canceled, and whether a northern Cambodia operation or no operation at all was preferable. Abrams and McCain agreed, recommending that the operation be canceled. They opposed substituting operations elsewhere because they would have no more than nuisance value. Moorer quickly replied that the obstacle was "primarily political" and that Abrams and McCain should resubmit their answers. This time Abrams gave his "unqualified support" to Lam Son 719, and McCain called it an "exceptional opportunity to inflict maximum damage against enemy personnel, materiel and psychological pressure."[23]

The following day at the WSAG meeting, Kissinger again asked Admiral Moorer if the enemy would know that the ARVN was coming. Moorer deflected the question by referring back to the deception plan, stating that operations around Khe Sanh and Route 9 in South Vietnam should not stir too much concern. The voice of reason came from the State Department's Alexis Johnson, who stated that an attack on Tchepone was precisely what he had recommended in 1965, but his recommendation had been rejected because it was estimated that six U.S. divisions were required for the operation. He was astounded that people believed it could be done with two ARVN divisions, "even considering that the enemy had become much weaker in the interim."[24]

A prevailing assumption that the enemy had grown weaker, combined with unwarranted expectations of ARVN capabilities, was the foundation for failure. The Communists had suffered debilitating manpower losses during the 1968 Tet Offensive and relied more on attacks by fire during 1969 as they replenished their forces. The 1970 Cambodian incursion reduced the threat to Saigon and the southern half of South Vietnam, but it produced a false sense of confidence. Throughout the planning phase, it was continuously assumed that the NVA was still staggering from its recent losses in Cambodia. It was also assumed that North Vietnam would make an all-out effort to defend Tchepone, but that the ARVN, with U.S. air support, would prevail even though the battles in and around the A Shau Valley and the forced evacuation of Ripcord six months earlier was convincing evidence that the NVA, when not operating at the end of a six-hundred-mile supply line, was a potent military force. The realities were that North Vietnam had rebuilt its army, that it was equipped with more sophisticated weapons supplied by the Soviets and Chinese, and that the effects of airpower applied in mountainous jungle terrain were overestimated.

The various accounts of Lam Son 719 agree that the prohibition of U.S. ground forces in Laos under the provisions of the Cooper-Church Amendment was absolute and universally accepted. However, there is a body of circumstantial evidence that indicates otherwise. Returning to the president's meeting of 18 January, Nixon asked if there were any legislative restrictions on the U.S. support planned for the operation. Both Secretary Laird and Secretary Rogers, referring to the recently passed Cooper-Church Amendment, said there were none. Rogers added that the new legislation involved only the use of ground troops but that the legislation provided the authority to prevent the rebuilding of sanctuaries. Director Helms added that even Senator Fulbright—the senior senator from Arkansas and a leading critic of the war—agreed with the need to prevent the rebuilding of sanctuaries.[25] Nine days later, on 26 January, the president, Secretaries Laird and Rogers, and Henry Kissinger met in the Oval Office to discuss Lam Son 719. During a discussion of the potential impact of failure, Secretary Rogers commented that "that the idea that the U.S. could rescue the operation was shaky and therefore it would serve as a defeat for Vietnamization as well as Thieu."[26]

It is apparent that the concept of "rescuing the ARVN force" was at least discussed. Unclear is whether Nixon was looking for a loophole in the law or was considering simply ignoring it and taking the heat. Either action would have been within the realm of possibility, considering Nixon's reputation. In his book, *Inner Circles*, Alexander Haig is much more emphatic on the issue. Haig claims that it was understood by "those who briefed the president" that despite congressional restrictions, U.S. forces would immediately reinforce the South Vietnamese if the ARVN forces got into trouble.[27]

Although admittedly less than conclusive proof of Nixon's expectations, this assertion can be supported by Nixon's propensity to say one thing and expect his military commander to do otherwise. During a 30 May 1970 discussion, Nixon gave the following guidance to Abrams:

> Northeast Cambodia could be important for the security of our own forces if the enemy builds up there but our answer should be fuzzy on this issue. U.S. air power will be used for the purpose of defending U.S. forces in South Vietnam. That is what we say publicly. But now, let's talk about what we will actually do. Within the above guidelines, we may find that the South Vietnamese in Cambodia need our help and we can deal with that. In other words, publicly we say one thing. Actually, we do another. . . . Then you have authority, but publicly it is for defense of U.S. forces. Just do it. Don't come back and ask permission each time. We can deny publicly that we are providing close air support.

The president met with his advisors again on the following day, 27 January, just three days prior to the scheduled start of Phase 1. During this meeting Admiral Moorer again reviewed the concept of the operation, then turned to CIA director Helms. Helms emphasized the strategic importance of Tchepone, stating that the bulk of NVA supplies destined for the south were still north of Tchepone, "like a rock moving through a sock." The president confirmed Abrams's authority to initiate Phase 1, but withdrew the execution authority for Phase 2, the cross-border assault.[28] Nixon was obviously pensive about the pending operation.

Henry Kissinger met with Richard Nixon on 2 February to solicit Nixon's formal approval for Phase 2 of Lam Son 719. Kissinger presented Nixon with the arguments both for and against approving the operation. As an argument in favor of the operation, he stated that, based on planned troop withdrawals, this would be the last opportunity the United States would have to support a dry-season offensive, and he reiterated that Tchepone was a vital hub. He confirmed that military commanders were confident of success and added, "If the enemy stands and fights, our firepower advantage would inflict substantial enemy losses." In arguments against approval, Kissinger stated that segments of Congress and the public would criticize the operation as an expansion of the war and violation of Laotian neutrality. In addition, helicopter losses would fuel domestic reaction, and the ARVN might not have the capability to accomplish the mission. He added that the enemy was aware of the operation, had concentrated his forces in the area, and could inflict heavy casualties. President Nixon granted approval.[29]

Admiral Moorer and Secretary Laird briefed the plan of attack to President Nixon and Henry Kissinger four times between 15 December and the end of January. The plan changed during each of these briefings. No explanation was given for the changes, and no one questioned why the changes were made. While the changes (discussed in the following paragraphs) may appear relatively insignificant, each robbed commanders of precious time required to prepare for the operation.

Admiral Moorer provided Kissinger with details of the plan of attack after General Abrams's message arrived through channels on 15 December. During Phase 1 a U.S. reinforced brigade would conduct operations along Route 9, moving west from Dong Ha to the Laotian Border, and establish a forward operating base and airfield to facilitate future operations to the west. During Phase 2 ARVN forces would conduct limited objective attacks in the vicinity of Tchepone. Saturation bombing would be conducted in the area, followed by seizure of Tchepone airfield. Phase 3 was the exploitation phase; blocking positions would be established north of Tchepone, while South Vietnamese engineers repaired the airfield at Tchepone, making it suitable for operation of

C-123 cargo aircraft. Then ARVN forces would radiate out from it on search-and-destroy missions. Details on the fourth phase stated only that units from the Royal Laotian Army, guerillas, and some ARVN elements would be inserted or remain behind in the objective area. The assumption that the primary counterattack threat would come from the North was correct. However, as the plan evolved and the operation unfolded, this assumption was apparently forgotten as the ARVN Corps split its forces and deployed its more heavily armed and experienced infantry division on the south flank, undermining the original concept of the operation.

Over the next six weeks the plan took on the characteristics of a deliberate attack. Phases 1 and 3 remained essentially unchanged, but Phases 2 and 4 underwent major revisions. The Phase 4 concept of using irregular forces as a stay-behind force was amended, providing

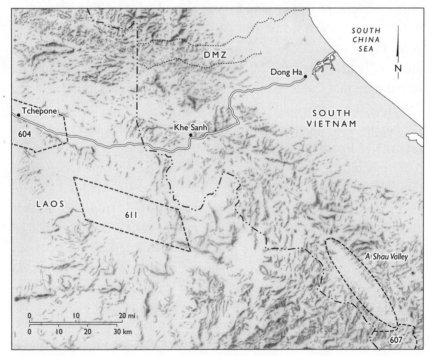

Map 2. Base Areas 604, 607, 611, and the A Shau Valley. Drawn by Bill Nelson. Copyright © 2014 by The University of Oklahoma Press.

two options for withdrawal: the ARVN force would either retrace its eastward movement west along Route 9 or, if the opportunity was there, move southwest along Route 914, reenter South Vietnam through the A Shau Valley, and move through the valley on a search-and-destroy mission. Phase 2 now called for the ARVN airborne division to execute an airmobile assault on Tchepone with the ARVN 1st Infantry Division in overall command of the ground linkup. The 1st Infantry Division's mission was to make the assault down Route 9 and establish firebases along the northern and southern rims of the Xepon River valley to secure both flanks of the penetration.[30] The plans for Phase 2 continued to change.[31]

Kissinger convened the WSAG on the following day, and the discussion of the concept of operations for Lam Son 719 continued. Admiral Moorer, who had recently returned from Saigon and meetings with General Abrams, briefed the group concerning the four phases. In his discussion of Phase 2 Moorer disclosed that while the airborne division would be responsible for the airmobile assault on Tchepone, the air assault force would consist only of a single brigade. Kissinger asked the obvious question: Would a single brigade be a large enough force to hold Tchepone? Moorer's reply was incomprehensible; he said simply that the "overall weight of preponderance in favor of the South Vietnamese would be three to one."[32]

Nixon was updated on the plan on 26 January. In Phase 2 the 1st ARVN Infantry Division would attack due west along Route 9. After reaching a point midway between the border and Tchepone— the village of Ban Dong and intersection of east-west Route 9 and north-south Route 92—the airborne division would launch its brigade airmobile assault.[33] However, this was not the plan being developed by the South Vietnamese nor the plan executed on D-Day. All briefings in Washington prior to execution stated that the 1st ARVN Division and 1st Armored Brigade would conduct ground assault down Route 9, securing the flanks with fire support bases as they moved west. However, in the plan developed by the ARVN I Corps, the ARVN airborne division—reinforced by the 1st Armored Brigade with its 11th and 17th Squadrons and the 8th Airborne Battalion—was given the mission of attacking along Route 9 and repairing the road as it advanced. An airborne battalion would conduct a helicopter-borne combat assault on Objective A Loui, the intersection of Routes 9 and 92 at the village of Ban Dong, and establish a fire support base to support continued westward movement of the ground force. At the same time, two airborne battalions and three battalions of the 1st Ranger Group would conduct air assault operations north of Route 9 to protect the northern flank.

The 1st Infantry Division's 1st and 3rd Regiments would be inserted by helicopter and establish fire support bases on the high ground south of the Xepon River to protect the south flank. The 2nd Airborne Brigade would conduct a combat assault on Tchepone as soon as Objective A Loui was secured, and the ground force would continue its westward movement to Tchepone. Two South Vietnamese Marine Division (VNMC) brigades were the corps reserves.[34] The ARVN plan was complex, far too complex for a corps commander and staff that had never conducted corps-sized operations. It also had inherent flaws. Command authority was divided between the commanding generals of the U.S. XXIV Corps and ARVN I Corps, and in an operation in which the presumption of success depended on air power, the U.S. Air Force answered to neither of the corps commanders.

The concept for Phase 2 as it was envisioned by Abrams and the U.S. Joint Chiefs of Staff and the concept that the ARVN I Corps put into motion took separate paths. After President Nixon granted his approval of the operation, Abrams and Vien turned the task of detailed planning over to Lieutenant General Sutherland, the commanding general of the U.S. XXIV Corps stationed in Military Region I, and General Lam, the ARVN I Corps commander. After their planning session, General Lam gave the responsibility for planning the assault phase, Phase 2, to General Du Quoc Dong, the brigadier general commanding the ARVN airborne division. General Lam reviewed and approved Dong's plan on the evening of 3 February, fewer than four days prior to D-Day. If Abrams was aware of the changes, he apparently failed to pass the information up the chain of command.

While the ARVN troop list containing the 1st ARVN Division, the airborne division, two VNMC brigades, the 1st Armored Brigade, and the Ranger Group may appear robust, the actual number of units originally scheduled to participate in the ARVN plan was deceptively smaller. Of the 1st ARVN Division's four regiments, only three were included in the plans for the cross-border attack. The 54th Regiment and the ARVN 2nd Infantry division were assigned missions inside South Vietnam. Only two 1st Armored Brigade squadrons were included in the plan, and the cross-border mission for the Ranger Group included only two battalions. The 37th Ranger Battalion, a battalion that had performed brilliantly during the defense of Khe Sanh during the Tet Offensive, was given the mission of occupying a blocking position in South Vietnam.

Of the two marine brigades provided by the Joint General Staff (JGS), the 258th Brigade with one artillery and three infantry battalions was already operating in an area southwest of Quang Tri. The 147th Brigade, stationed further south in III Corps, was moved by C-130 to Dong Ha on 3 February. Both brigades were initially employed as the I Corps reserves and given the temporary mission of security for ARVN forces on the South Vietnamese side of the border.

To the military professional, there is a great difference between a concept of operations and an operations plan. In its completed form, an operations plan provides the flesh and detail, all weighed against thoughtful consideration of the mission, enemy, terrain, and weather, and creating one is a process that takes time. But the approaching dry season and the large volume of enemy supplies still north of Tchepone instilled a sense of urgency for an immediate operation to prevent these supplies from reaching the North Vietnamese Army further south in Laos, Cambodia, and South Vietnam. A hasty planning process was underway, and the embryonic plan was still evolving.

In 2003, thirty-two years after participating in the decision to launch Operation Lam Son 719, Henry Kissinger reflected on the ill-founded decision and wrote:

The operation, conceived in ambivalence and assailed by skepticism, proceeded in confusion. It soon became apparent that the plans on which we had been so eloquently and frequently briefed reflected staff exercises, not military reality. The Vietnamese staff plan, approved and reviewed several times by our military commanders, had impressively predicted a rapid interruption of the trail system to be followed by a systematic destruction of the logistics structure. But from the beginning, it became clear that the South Vietnamese divisions had not been trained for the daring thrust envisaged by Lam Son 719.[35]

Given the benefit of thirty-two years of hindsight, Kissinger's assessment was correct. While some of the ARVN battalions were solid and well trained, a collection of trained battalions does not equate to a trained brigade or regiment, and a collection of trained brigades does not constitute a trained division. The South Vietnamese Army habitually fought as companies or battalions, but rarely as regiments or brigades, and with the exception of the Cambodian Incursion, never as divisions or corps. The ARVN Corps headquarters was inexperienced and poorly prepared to execute the complex tasks of coordinating fire support and synchronizing a major offensive operation.

Any operations plan is built upon assumptions. Upon the plan's implementation, the first and most crucial step is to ensure that those assumptions are valid in the current scenario. The critical assumptions of OPLAN El Paso were no longer valid. The enemy presence in the Tchepone corridor was much greater than it was in 1968, and these forces were much better equipped. Improvements to the hidden trail network provided the NVA with greater-than-anticipated mobility. More importantly, the 1970 campaigns in Cambodia and the A Shau Valley alerted the North Vietnamese to the possibility that the allied forces could, and probably would, strike southern Laos. The North Vietnamese were prepared. The South Vietnamese armed forces, supported by U.S. Army aviation, but stripped of their American advisors, would have to go it alone on the ground in Laos.

The plan was complex and underwent major changes during the last days prior to execution, robbing commanders of the time needed to prepare for their missions. The ARVN force was much smaller than the size the planners of Operations Plan EL Paso thought would be necessary, but the momentum to invade Laos was unstoppable. Phase 1 of Lam Son 719, called Operation Dewey Canyon 2, went into motion at 0000 hours, 30 January 1971.

Chapter 6

DEWEY CANYON 2

AT 0000 HOURS 30 JANUARY 1971, the U.S. XXIV Corps implemented Phase 1 of Lam Son 719. As part of the deception plan, it was code-named Operation Dewey Canyon 2, after the 1969 attack into the A Shau Valley. Its objective was to assist the ARVN forces by securing staging and assembly areas for the ARVN 1st Corps in northern Quang Tri Province; opening, repairing, and securing Route 9 from Quang Tri City to the Laotian border; reopening and repairing the abandoned combat base at Khe Sanh; and assisting the ARVN Corps with forward movement and distribution of supplies. The 101st Airborne Division, supported by artillery fires and reconnaissance patrols, staged a feint into the A Shau Valley by reopening Route 547 from Hue to the A Shau Valley.[1] The heavily reinforced U.S. 1st Brigade, 5th Mechanized Infantry Division, advanced west from Fire Support Base Vandergrift on two axes of advance. With an air cavalry troop screening in advance, the 14th Combat Engineer Battalion followed the lead elements of an armored task force, restoring or replacing destroyed and damaged bridges and culverts on Route 9, constituting the first axis. A stream of CH-54 "Sky Cranes" and CH-47s supplied replacement bridge sections and culverts. The second axis ran from a point near the Rock Pile to Khe Sanh, generally parallel to Route 9. There the U.S. 7th Engineer Battalion and the 3rd Squadron, 5th Cavalry, constructed a secondary road, the Red Devil Road, as an alternate route to Khe Sanh from the vicinity of Fire Support Base Vandergrift, which was located on Route 9 midway between Dong Ha and Khe Sanh.[2]

The brigade's three infantry battalions conducted a combat assault on the abandoned combat base at Khe Sanh at 0830 hours, encountering no enemy resistance. The battalions moved out to their assigned areas of operations while the 1st Battalion, 77th Armor, task force provided security along the central section of Route 9 in South Vietnam. In the meantime, a task force from the 1st Squadron, 1st Cavalry Regiment, conducted a reconnaissance in force along Route 9 from Khe Sanh west to the Laotian border. As soon as the infantry battalions consolidated their positions around Khe Sanh, artillery battalions arrived and prepared firing positions. At the same time, the engineers completed temporary repairs along Route 9 from Quang Tri City to Khe Sanh, making it adequate to support tracked vehicle movement as far west as Lang Vei, approximately four kilometers east of the Laotian border. The section of road between Vandergrift and Khe Sanh could only support one-way traffic, so convoys had to move day and night, shuttling supplies and troops into the Khe Sanh area.[3]

While U.S. units expanded their control of northwestern Quang Tri Province, the ARVN airborne division was airlifted from Saigon to Quang Tri; the ARVN I Corps' forward tactical operations center (TOC) was established at Dong Ha, northwest of Quang Tri City, and the ARVN 1st Infantry Division moved into positions around Khe Sanh. The ARVN I Corps and U.S. XXIV Corps completed their operations orders on 22 January but did not disseminate to the participating units until 2 February.

The weather cooperated until 4 February when rains slowed engineers' efforts to repair the roads and the derelict airfield at Khe Sanh. The old landing strip was pocked with bomb and shell craters; unexploded ordnance littered the area, and mine fields left over from the defense of Khe Sanh during the 1968 Tet offensive had to be marked and neutralized. Even without the weather delay, the scope of work required on the airfield exceeded the available time. A shorter compacted-earth runway was hurriedly constructed parallel to the old perforated steel plank (PSP) runway as a temporary facility for landing USAF C-130 aircraft. Unfortunately, this runway proved inadequate; the wheels of the first C-130 sank six inches below the surface.[4] Repairs to the PSP runway were not completed until 15 February. In the meantime, the CH-47 fleet was given the additional task of flying supplies to Khe Sanh. Helicopter refuel and rearm points were established at Vandergrift and Khe Sanh and supplemented by a forward area rearm and refuel point (FARRP) located at Lao Bao, adjacent to the Laotian border.

The rains diminished on 6 and 7 February, but low clouds and occasional drizzle persisted. Intelligence indicated that the NVA had positioned 170–200 air defense guns in the immediate area of the planned avenue of approach to Tchepone, and allied plans called for two days of preparatory tactical air strikes on 6 and 7 February. In view of the weather, General Lam, the commander of the ARVN I Corps, cancelled the air strikes, but Phase 2, the invasion of Laos, would go on as scheduled on 8 February.[5] To compensate for the cancelled airstrikes, eleven sorties of B-52 bombers pounded the area during the early morning hours of 8 February.[6] On the surface, the cancellation appears to be a serious error. But to come to this conclusion more information is needed: If there was solid intelligence information on the *exact* locations of enemy air defense weapons, and the current locations of these weapons could influence the early stages of the invasion, it could be argued that cancellation contributed to aircraft losses. But if the strikes were targeted against *suspected* locations, the strength of the argument diminishes. By this time intelligence sources had already determined that Hanoi was aware of the generalities of the impending operation, and a two-day delay would simply have provided additional time for the Communists to reinforce and prepare their defenses.

Weather claimed the first two helicopter pilots during an extraction mission in support of Operation Dewey Canyon 2. Warrant Officers James Paul and Carl Wood of D Troop, 3rd Squadron, and 5th Cavalry, encountered low ceilings and reduced visibility on 5 February 1971. As they were attempting to fly through heavy cloud cover, they crashed into the side of a mountain, and the Cobra gunship exploded on impact.[7]

The troop list for Lam Son 719 included units from all over Vietnam. The ARVN airborne division and the 147th VNMC Brigade were moved from the southern portion of South Vietnam to Quang Tri Province.[8] U.S. Army aviation units that had been selected to reinforce the U.S. 101st Airborne Division moved north. The flight of helicopters was obvious, as were the ground convoys of the aviation unit's maintenance and support equipment. These movements were apparent to the civilian populace, Communist agents, and—of equal concern—the press corps.

The press was bound to notice a change in the routine as units and supplies began moving north. It was certain that the press would publish speculative accounts, which could damage operational security. To deal with the press problem, it was decided that two separate actions would be taken: a press briefing followed by an embargo, and a deception plan; the press embargo was a catastrophic failure, but portions of the deception plan were reasonably successful. As Phase 1 began, the Defense Department and the WSAG insisted, that the press in Saigon be briefed on the military movements, but under an embargo, in order to protect security and to prevent inaccurate and misleading reports. However, the official briefings accelerated a wave of leaks. The Saigon press corps might have observed the embargo, but they were free to inform their colleagues in Washington, who were under no such restraint, of the basic facts. The Washington journalists and the TV networks not only broadcast the broadest possible hints of an imminent allied operation in Laos, they also treated the embargo as a major news story in itself, a sinister plot of deception and a cover-up. The *New York Times* published an article on 1 February reporting that unnamed officials in Washington had said that a major new allied operation involving thousands of South Vietnamese and American troops was underway in the northwest corner of South Vietnam.[9] Kissinger's concern over the press leaks was so great that he felt the president should hold execution authority for Phase 2.[10] Both Soviet premier Kosygin and TASS (the official Soviet news agency) attacked the new military action as an "outrageous invasion of southern Laos."[11]

It was impossible to conceal the fact that U.S. and South Vietnamese forces were preparing for a major military operation in northern Military Region I, as an endless stream of USAF C-130 cargo planes landed at Dong Ha and the ARVN airborne division and VNMC troops disembarked and unloaded tons of supplies. The northward movement erased any doubts.

P. J. Roths, a warrant officer aviator assigned to the 174th Combat Aviation Company, described the Operations Security (OPSEC) failure based on his personal experience.

> I arrived in Vietnam in January 1971 and [was] assigned to the 174th AHC, Duc Pho, I Corps [south of Da Nang]. It was a great unit, the Dolphins (slicks) and Sharks [UH-1C "Charley Model" gunships].[12] In early February a fellow Dolphin and I went to the steam bath one afternoon. The young women who worked here asked us, "When you go Quang Tri?" We were taken aback. "Uh . . . What?" They insisted, "Soon all GI go Quang Tri." We rushed back to our hooch and drug out a map. "Don't look south," I told the guys. Our fingers glided north over a lot of Vietnam before we found Quang Tri on the coast, not far from the DMZ. In a few days we were flying over that same ground, headed for Lam Son 719.[13]

The U.S. XXIV Corps, commanded by Gen. James Sutherland, was responsible for providing aviation, artillery, and logistical support to the ARVN I Corps. XXIV Corps placed all combat units north of the Hai Van Pass under the command of the 101st Airborne Division and gave the division the mission of supporting the ARVN Corps.[14] The reinforcing aviation units received short notice and were inadequately prepared.

In late January 1971 the 223rd Combat Support Aviation Battalion, a fixed-wing battalion headquartered in Qui Nhon in II Corps, well south of Da Nang, was preparing to stand down and redeploy to the states when the headquarters company was notified that it had a new mission. It was immediately transformed into a combat aviation battalion (CAB), given command of four helicopter companies and two air cavalry troops, and ordered to move these units north to Dong Ha. The battalion was given the highest priority for the required equipment and supplies and immediately began the trek north in air convoys and a ground convoy that stretched out over five miles in length as it made its way north on Route 1 through Da Nang and the Hai Van Pass. The subordinate units included the 48th and 173rd Combat Aviation Companies (CACs), the 238th Aerial Weapons Company (AWC) equipped with twelve UH-1C gunships, the 179th Assault Support Helicopter Company (ASHC) equipped with CH-47s, and two air cavalry troops that would later be placed under the operational control of the 101st Airborne Division's 2nd Squadron, 17th Air Cavalry.[15] With security still tight, the 223rd arrived at its destination totally unaware that it was to play an important role in a cross-border operation.[16] Lam Son 719 was still a tightly held secret to all but the enemy.

On 23 January 1971 the 14th CAB received an alert order stating that the battalion headquarters, two combat aviation companies, and one assault support helicopter company were to prepare to move from their area of operations south of Da Nang in support of an unspecified tactical operation.[17] The aviation companies did all that they could to prepare; aircraft and trucks were inspected, and repair parts and maintenance supplies were inventoried and prepared for movement. Four days later, on 27 January, the battalion was informed of its destination, Quang Tri, but received no further information. The battalion started its move on 29 January and arrived at Quang Tri on 30 January. There were no facilities available for the soldiers or their equipment. For the next week both the 223rd and 14th CABs worked around the clock digging bunkers, erecting tents and reinforcing all areas with sand bags.

THE DECEPTION PLAN

There was no way to conceal from the Communists the massive movement of South Vietnamese troops and U.S. helicopter battalions to northern Quang Tri Province. Therefore a deception plan was orchestrated in an attempt to conceal the direction of attack. The deception plan had two parts: the first was to make the Communists think the allies were massing for another attack into the A Shau Valley, and the second was an attempt to convince the Communists that the allies were preparing for an amphibious assault across the beaches of North Vietnam.

An attack into the A Shau Valley was a plausible course of action. Taking advantage of a past history of attacks into the A Shau Valley, Phase 1 was titled operation Dewey Canyon 2 after an operation of the same name that had attacked the A Shau Valley in 1969, and some of the Lam Son 719 objectives and landing zones were named after deserted villages in the A Shau Valley, A Loui and Ta Bat. These were code words that the North Vietnamese were bound to intercept. To further support this deception, the 101st Airborne reopened Route 547 leading from Hue into the A Shau Valley and launched a series of artillery raids and feints.[18] At the same time, the division had to prepared to defend against an attack from enemy forces in the valley. The presence of a powerful NVA force in the A Shau Valley could not be dismissed. Possible enemy counteractions to Lam Son 719 included the possibility of an NVA attack from the north, across the DMZ, or one eastward from the A Shau Valley into the coastal lowlands that turned north, rolling up the allied flank in the Lam Son rear area. Operation Jefferson Glen, a screening operation along the piedmont area between the mountains and the coastal lowlands, continued throughout the duration of Lam Son 719.

At the same time, marine and navy units demonstrated the possibility of an amphibious landing on the shores of North Vietnam by rehearsing amphibious operations and maneuvering ships in the adjacent waters. The South Vietnamese Navy sent its fast patrol boats north into North Vietnamese waters to attack Communist shipping and coastal installation, while South Vietnamese Marines and ground troops rehearsed river-crossing operations, selling the idea that an attack across the Cu Viet River (forming the boundary between North and South Vietnam) was imminent.[19] The most successful diversion was conducted off the coast of North Vietnam, 150 miles north of the DMZ. In a ruse developed by Admiral McCain, a marine battalion landing team went through the motions of preparing for a helicopter assault from ships in the Gulf of Tonkin directed at the North Vietnamese airfield at Vinh, an important North Vietnamese coastal port city. Day after day the helicopters, with no troops aboard, took off and flew toward the North Vietnamese coast. Just prior to reaching the twelve-mile territorial limit, they dropped down, causing the North Vietnamese radars to lose contact, then turned around and headed back to the ships. This ruse captured North Vietnamese attention and held in place enemy forces that could otherwise have reinforced the Lam Son area of operations.[20]

There is evidence that the North Vietnamese bought the idea that an invasion of North Vietnam was at hand. When President Nixon authorized the incursion into Cambodia, it constituted a major change in U.S. policies toward the war, and the North Vietnamese were uncertain of what he might do next. In a highly propagandized account of Lam Son 719 produced by the government of North Vietnam following the operation, the author wrote, "Mention should also be made of the direct participation of the 7th Fleet, which sent hundreds of its carrier-borne planes into the fray, ensured the supply by sea of the Highway 9 front, and kept North Vietnam under a constant threat of invasion by several thousand marines on board American ships cruising off the Vietnamese shore."[21] In reality, few marines were aboard.

Enemy Knowledge of the Plan

During the summer of 1970 the North Vietnamese general staff, reacting to the Cambodian incursion, anticipated a similar attack along the Route 9 corridor. The NVA 2nd Division left its heavy equipment behind and secretly moved into the Route 9 area. Once in position, it was brought up to strength in both personnel and equipment.[22] By January 1971 the NVA was ready. The North Vietnamese had over 20,000 men in the area, including 13,000 combat troops and approximately 8,000 logistics troops trained to fight as infantry. Ammunition was prestocked, defensive positions prepared, counterattack plans rehearsed, air defenses reinforced, and concealed high-speed routes into the area were improved.[23] And additional forces were en route that would more than double the enemy strength.

Then the element of surprise was lost, if it ever existed. CIA director Helms provided Kissinger with his assessment on 26 January: "The enemy probably expects an attack on their logistics complexes and has postured his troops accordingly."[24] On 27 January, twelve days before the allied forces were scheduled to cross the Laotian border, Admiral Moorer reported to the president that Binh Tram radio chatter had been intercepted confirming that Hanoi was aware of the general plan, but not the timing. When Admiral Moorer asked General Abrams if the attack should proceed, General Abrams confirmed that he favored the operation, provided that full U.S. support was assured. Admiral Moorer replied that from the North Vietnamese reaction, it was obvious they considered Tchepone a vital area. This report served to confirm a suspicion implied in one of Moorer's comments the previous day—that enemy troops in the supply system were carrying weapons, which was a departure from past practices.[25]

As the events of Lam Son 719 unfolded, it became obvious that the North Vietnamese were prepared to defend the Tchepone corridor. There was little doubt at the White House and Pentagon that this would be the fact, but many planners in Washington viewed this outcome as desirable. By their reckoning the Communists would be forced to stand, fight, and fall to superior U.S. aerial firepower.[26]

Strategically, the element of surprise never existed. But the North Vietnamese were unable to discern where the allies would attack. The A Shau Valley approach was an option open to the allies, and previous U.S. and South Vietnamese operations in the valley lent credibility to this threat. In addition, the North Vietnamese could not dismiss the possibility of an attack across the DMZ. But to their advantage, the A Shau Valley approach, the Route 9 corridor, and the avenues of approach across the DMZ, as well as potential amphibious landing sites along the southern North Vietnamese coast, were all in a relatively compact geographic area. North Vietnamese troops were positioned to provide an initial defense of all possible approaches and quickly reinforce their defense once the location of the main attack was determined.

Over the years authors have attributed the loss of surprise to a wide array of causes including press leaks, spies, increased diplomatic traffic with the government of Laos, and crash courses in English for South Vietnamese commanders and tactical air control parties. But in the final analysis, given the events of 1970 and the loss of Sihanoukville, General Giap, the North Vietnamese minister of defense, would have been derelict in his duties if he had not anticipated and prepared for an attack into the Laotian panhandle.

The MACVSOG had been operating in and around Route 9 and the Tchepone area for years and had intimate knowledge of the enemy in that area. Prior to the passage of the Cooper-Church Amendment, SOG reconnaissance teams had crossed the border to acquire last-minute intelligence.[27] While the *FRUS* documents provide no feedback or results of these patrols, author John L. Plaster does. Plaster wrote: "Three times, Chief SOG said, he gave General Abrams, the MACV J-2, and the U.S. XXIV Corps Commander [General Sutherland] a blunt recommendation, 'Stay out of there. They're in position; they know you're coming and that's a recipe for deadly results.'[28] When SOG briefed the XXIV Corps Staff, recalled Colonel Pinkerton, SOG's operation chief, General Sutherland, said his biggest worry was being able to get in there, and we told him, 'Your biggest worry ought to be how in the hell you are going to get out.'"[29]

In one week U.S. forces opened the road from Dong Ha to the Laotian border and reopened the abandoned combat base and airfield at Khe Sanh. ARVN forces moved into attack positions from as far away as Military Region III, and U.S. aviation battalions from the 1st Aviation Brigade moved from locations south of Da Nang to Dong Ha. The allied force was in position for Phase 2 of Lam Son 719, the cross-border assault. The U.S. Army lost two helicopter pilots during Phase 1, but the loss of Warrant Officers James Paul and Carl Wood was but the beginning. Helicopter warfare was about to enter a new phase.

Chapter 7

THE FIRST WEEK IN LAOS

THE ARVN AIRBORNE DIVISION, reinforced by the 1st Armored Brigade, was given the mission of conducting the main attack. The plan developed by the division after it arrived on 2 February called for air assault operations to occupy Objectives 30 and 31 (see map 3 on page 120) and secure the north flank, while the armored brigade advanced overland westward on Route 9 to link up with air assault forces at A Loui. After linkup at A Loui, the armored brigade was to continue the attack down Route 9, and a second linkup operation would be conducted as the armored force approached Tchepone. The armor-infantry thrust consisted of two 1st Armor Brigade squadrons, the 1st Airborne Brigade with its three battalions (the 1st, 8th, and 9th), the 44th Artillery Battalion, and the ARVN 101st Engineer Battalion. The task force was to advance along Route 9, repair roads as it moved, and link up with air assault units.[1]

The 3rd Airborne Brigade, consisting of the 2nd, 3rd, and 6th Airborne Battalions, was to provide security on the north flank of the penetration. The 2nd Airborne Brigade was held in reserve and given the mission to conduct the air assault on the Tchepone airfield once Objective A Loui was secured and the ground force had continued westward from A Loui to Tchepone.[2] Responsibility for security on the north flank was divided between the airborne division and the lightly armed battalions of the 1st Ranger Group, which remained under I Corps control and was tasked to conduct screening operations.

Eleven B-52 bombers made an "Arc Light" strike on suspected enemy positions during the early morning hours of 8 February, and the armored brigade task force crossed the Laotian border at 1000 hours.[3] As soon as the lead elements crossed the border, the U.S. 101st Airborne Division's 2nd Squadron, 17th Air Cavalry, crossed the border, screening the advance and searching for targets.[4]

Both Route 9 and the Xepon River are flanked by high ground on the north and south. The high ground on the south is dominated by an escarpment that rises to 1,500 feet above the valley floor and by the Co Roc Promontory, adjacent to the South Vietnamese border. The terrain north of the valley is mountainous and uneven, and elevations increase toward the north. The valley floor varies in width from approximately two kilometers at its narrowest point to approximately five kilometers near Tchepone. A significant portion of the area is covered with a thick single- to triple-canopied rain forest, and thick, nearly impenetrable, thorn-covered bamboo blankets much of the forest floor, making movements off established roads and paths nearly impossible for combat vehicles.

The terrain favored the defenders, and the NVA had controlled this terrain for years. They had intimate knowledge of the ground and its hidden footpaths. The terrain restricted South Vietnamese ground assault forces' options for avenues of approach, and once the ARVN had made its choice, predicting the landing zones (LZs) for the air assault forces became less problematic. This provided the NVA with the opportunity to concentrate its air defense weapons around likely LZs and the approaches to LZs. The NVA reinforced its defense with antiaircraft battalions from the 282nd and 591st Antiaircraft Artillery (AAA) Battalions, equipped with guns ranging from 23mm to 100mm. MACV intelligence estimated that there were 130 antiaircraft guns in the area at the beginning of the operation.[5] The additional antiaircraft battalions, combined with the scores of 12.7mm antiaircraft guns that accompanied the NVA units, posed a formidable defense against allied air operations. As a result of repeated helicopter insertions of SOG reconnaissance teams since 1965, the NVA had learned how to spot likely landing zones and developed an effective system of LZ watchers. Antiaircraft machine guns were positioned on likely air avenues of approach, and mortars were positioned to fire on likely landing zones. To preserve the element of surprise, the allies planned to use 15,000-pound "Commando Vault" bombs to blast openings in the forest canopy that could be used as helicopter landing zones. The oversized Commando Vaults were internally loaded in USAF C-130 cargo aircraft. When the C-130 approached the target area, the aft cargo ramp was lowered, and a parachute attached to the tail of the bomb was deployed to pull the bomb out and insure that the bomb would impact the ground in a near-vertical position. A fuse extender detonated the bomb six to ten feet above the ground. The blast was capable of blowing down trees within a 200-foot radius of the point of impact. The LZ would then be "fine-tuned" by tactical strike aircraft dropping 500- and 1,000-pound "daisy cutter" bombs, also equipped with fuse extenders. While effective, this tactic was not perfect. In some cases stumps up to six feet tall remained, which could prevent a helicopter from touching down, and ridges and large boulders, previously concealed by the jungle canopy, further reduced the utility of the blast area as a landing zone.

By the time Route 9 crossed the Laotian border, the road was little more than a single-lane dirt track following the meandering course of the Xepon River. It was perfect terrain for enemy ambushes, and with few opportunities for bypass, a single stalled vehicle could bring the column to a halt. The ARVN ground units advanced only nine kilometers along the road on the first day. It was a slow, arduous advance. Erosion ditches as deep as twenty feet made portions of the road impassable, and the road had been cratered by years of air strikes. The entire column would have to come to a halt while repairs were made or detours constructed.[6] As the ARVN ground force worked its way down Route 9, air assault forces secured the flanks.

While the armored brigade crossed the border, the 158th, 101st, 14th, and 223rd Aviation Battalions moved into positions at pickup zones (PZs) in and around the Khe Sanh area to launch a simultaneous, three-pronged airmobile combat assault across the South Vietnamese border into southern Laos. Eleven aircraft from the 101st Assault Helicopter Battalion (AHB), in multiple sorties, inserted the ARVN 21st Ranger Battalion into Ranger South, a position on a ridgeline west-northwest of Khe Sanh intended to screen an NVA avenue of approach into the north flank. The remainder of the 101st AHB was combined under the command and control of the 158th AHB to lift the 2nd and 7th ARVN Airborne Battalions to LZ 30, located approximately five kilometers south of Ranger South.[7]

Concurrently, the 223rd and 14th Combat Aviation Battalions (CABs) executed combat assault landings, lifting the ARVN 1st Infantry Division's 3rd Regiment command post and the regiment's 3rd and 4th Battalions to LZ Hotel to secure the southeast flank. Following this assault, the 223rd CAB inserted the 3rd ARVN Regiment's 1st and 2nd battalions at LZ Blue, located seven kilometers south of LZ Hotel. Two aircraft were shot down at LZ Blue. Capt. David Nelson Fox, the aircraft commander of UH-1H 68-16063 from B Troop, 7th Squadron, 1st Cavalry, was one of the first pilots killed in Laos during Lam Son 719.[8] His helicopter was hit by an exploding round, probably 23mm or 37mm, at an altitude of 4,000 feet. The round hit the fuel cell, setting the Huey aflame. Before he could land, the aircraft inverted and exploded. Both he and the door gunner, Sgt. Wayne Miley, were killed. Capt. Joe Bearden, the pilot, and John Seaman, the crew chief, were both rescued. The 174th AHC also lost a pilot; Warrant Officer Robert Gentry was killed by machine gun fire when an enemy gunner raked his cockpit, taking out the radios and hydraulics.[9]

On the north side of the valley, combined assets from the 101st, 158th, and the 14th CAB lifted the 3rd Airborne Battalion to LZ 31. Chief Warrant Officer Clark Stewart's aircraft was hit in the tail boom, and his tail rotor was damaged. After he was hit, he reported that he was returning to the PZ in South Vietnam, but a short time later Stewart reported that his aircraft had inverted and was going down. Stewart, his crew from the 158th, and a full load of ARVN soldiers were killed.

The 21st Ranger Battalion's combat assault to the LZ at Ranger South began at 1105 hours. The LZ was located on a position overlooking a road originating at the Ban Raven Pass on the North Vietnamese border. There the battalion was greeted with intense enemy automatic weapons fire that wounded eleven rangers. The combat assault was temporarily suspended until gunships could work the area with suppressive fires. The last lifts to Ranger South were completed at 1500 hours, at which time the Rangers immediately moved off the LZ to a ridgeline three kilometers to the east and began screening operations. Later in the afternoon gunships from 2nd Squadron, 17th Air Cavalry, engaged enemy armored vehicles near Ranger South and discovered an enemy bunker complex. When the bunker complex was attacked by fire, a series of secondary explosions ignited. Secondary explosions continued throughout the night, indicating that the bunker complex was a major ammunition cache.[10] The first day of the operation was supported by 11 B-52 sorties dropping 719 tons of bombs, 53 tactical air sorties, and 468 helicopter gunship sorties.[11] Seven U.S. Army aircrew members were killed, three aircraft were shot down and destroyed,[12] and a CH-47 helicopter was destroyed in an accident.[13] Fifteen others received combat damage.[14] The ARVN ground forces had moved nine kilometers across the border to a point midway between the border and A Loui. A total of 3,351 ARVN troops had been inserted into Laos. All flights were challenged by enemy fire, AAA fire, and enemy ground fire at all LZs with the exception of LZ Hotel.[15] Enemy opposition was light in comparison to the days that would follow.

Inclement weather shut down air operations on 9 February as rain and fog again obscured the area.[16] Route 9 became a muddy morass as the ground forces struggled to continue westward. The 8th Airborne Battalion made the only significant contact with the enemy in Laos when it encountered the NVA north of Route 9, midway between Objective A Loui and the Vietnamese border. A team of Cobra gunships from D Company, 101st Aviation Battalion, that had been released to return to its home station at Camp Eagle, departed from Khe Sanh. As the two aircraft departed in marginal weather, flying too low to the ground to avoid enemy ground fire, the second aircraft in the flight lost visual contact with the lead aircraft, and the flight separated. The trail aircraft, call sign Hawk 14, was not heard from again. It was found the following day, shot down northeast of Khe Sanh. There were no survivors.[17]

Kissinger's WSAG met daily to review the progress.[18] Admiral Moorer consistently failed to provide an accurate assessment or to answer correctly many of Kissinger's elementary but essential questions. On 7 February, the day before the ARVN crossed the border, Admiral Moorer had stated that the weather in the area of operations was "satisfactory," even though foul weather forced the cancellation of air strikes intended to take out enemy air defense positions.[19] On 8 February Kissinger had asked if U.S. losses would increase. Admiral Moorer understated the losses as "three incidents," saying that the crews on two aircraft had been rescued and one crew was missing. He added that it was possible that losses would increase, but would not exceed past levels. Moorer also reported that the NVA 2nd Division was moving west from its position in North Vietnam toward the Laotian border and one enemy regiment in South Vietnam was moving into Base Area 611 on the southern flank of the penetration.[20]

There is little doubt that Admiral Moorer was reporting the truth as he knew it. Even with the international date line separating Washington, D.C., and Saigon, the time delay between the events and the passage of reports from the field through the chain of command to MACV headquarters, and from there to Washington, made it impossible for Moorer provide timely updates. Comparing events listed in the 101st Aviation Group's duty log with the dates those events were briefed to General Abrams indicates that the time delay could have been as long as seven days.

The WSAG met again the following day. During the meeting Kissinger, concerned by the wire service reports of inclement weather, again questioned Moorer about the weather in the area of operations. Moorer's reply was, "It never rains in the operational area this time of year. . . . The troops are already in the area, where there is no rain."[21] In general terms, the weather in Laos was fair for most of the operation from mid-morning until late afternoon. But from Khe Sanh eastward to the coastal plains on the east side of the mountain range, it was still the wet season, and monsoon rains or early morning ground fog regularly shut down air operations. The helicopter units supporting Lam Son 719 were based along the coastal plain at Quang Tri, Dong Ha, Camp Evans, Phu Bai, and Camp Eagle. If the aviation units could not make it to Khe Sanh and into Laos, the ARVN ground forces were stalled and could not continue the attack. Moorer further stated that if the weather were bad, it would not affect tactical air support (TACAIR) by USAF, U.S. Navy, and USMC jet aircraft, because TACAIR was "radar controlled." He should have realized that Kissinger's concerns were probably directed toward close air support (CAS), and close air support is not "radar controlled." CAS requires a forward air controller (or an artillery forward observer, advisor, or other knowledgeable person) on the scene that has intimate knowledge of friendly troops' locations, eyes on the target, and communication with the strike aircraft. At this point in the operation, as in critical periods to come, weather was an inhibiting factor that negated the firepower superiority that the planners assumed would enable the ARVN to prevail.

For Operation Plan El Paso, General Westmoreland had selected October as the proposed start date for the operation based on available metrological history. In October the average rainfall, as recorded by the French during their occupation of Indochina, was four inches at Tchepone and two inches at Khe Sanh.[22] The records for February indicated that the average rainfall in Tchepone was slightly more than eighteen inches, while the average rainfall at Khe Sanh was thirteen inches. The document trail leading up to Lam Son 719 contains no discussion of the potential impact of the monsoons. It was the beginning of the dry season in the southern Laotian panhandle, but "dry" is a relative term. It is impossible to determine if this aspect of planning was ignored or simply wished away as both the U.S. and South Vietnamese governments pressed forward in an attempt to wage a decisive campaign before the window of opportunity to intercept the mass of NVA supplies still north of Tchepone closed.

The operation took place during the transition period of the southwest and northeast monsoons. The weather pattern in the Lam Son area of operations, east of the Annam ridgeline, was characterized by ground fog that reduced visibility to zero-zero during the early morning hours. The fog and reduced visibility typically persisted until late morning, and by noon the fog lifted. During the afternoon clouds built up and visibility deteriorated by 1800 hours.[23] This weather pattern restricted air operations and provided the NVA with opportunities to move troops and weapon systems and to conduct attacks free from the threat of air attack.

The weather cleared sufficiently to resume air operations and combat assault operations on 10 February. The 223rd CAB inserted the 4th Battalion, 1st Regiment, into LZ Delta, while USMC CH-53s from Da Nang brought in the accompanying artillery.[24] Enemy gunners opposed the landing at Delta, and the 2nd Squadron, 17th Cavalry, reported two aircraft shot down one hundred meters south of LZ Delta. An OH-6 observation helicopter was hit in the cockpit by a rocket-propelled grenade (RPG), killing the pilot. A Cobra was also hit in the tail boom by an RPG and went down. Another Cobra extracted the crashed Cobra's crew.[25] There are only two seats in a Cobra gunship, so the downed crew had two options: open the ammo bay doors, sit down, and hang on, or drape themselves over the stub wings, straddle the rocket pods, and hang on. Either way, the extraction was bound to be a memorable experience for the downed crewmen.

The 158th AHB inserted 608 ARVN soldiers from the 9th Airborne Battalion into A Loui. The LZ was located near the intersection of Route 9 and Route 92, a major intersection on the trail network. As they could have expected, the intersection was defended, causing allied losses. The enemy defensive fires at A Loui were so intense that the insertion was delayed while USAF tactical air strikes and helicopter gunships silenced the enemy gunners. Resupply missions, including heavy lift of field artillery howitzers and artillery ammunition, continued throughout the day. CH-47s from the 159th ASHB flew thirty-six sorties into LZ Ranger South and twenty-three sorties into the fire support base located at LZ Hotel.[26] An attempt was made to start heavy-lift supply missions to A

Loui, but the huge CH-47s, which had to hover over the landing zone to set down their sling loads, were easy targets for enemy gunners, and these missions were suspended until enemy fire could be suppressed. By day's end CH-47 and CH-54 helicopters delivered one six-gun battery of 155mm howitzers, a six-gun battery of 105mm howitzers, and an adequate supply of ammunition for both to FSB A Loui. Aircraft losses continued. The aerial rocket artillery (ARA) lost two Cobra gunships near A Loui; one was shot down, and the second crashed when it appeared to have lost a rotor blade resulting from suspected combat damage. In addition, the 2nd Squadron, 17th Cavalry, lost an OH-6 and its pilot in Thau Thien Province near the eastern rim of the A Shau Valley.[27] Three of the aircraft that had been downed in Laos during the first day of the operation were successfully rigged for extraction and lifted out by CH-47s.[28]

Three days into the operation, allied intentions were clear to the enemy, and NVA counteractions intensified. Perhaps the greatest disaster of the day was when four unescorted South Vietnamese Air Force UH-1 helicopters flew into the area of operations bound for LZ Ranger South. A witness from the air cavalry stated that the aircraft were northwest of LZ Ranger North, near grid coordinates XD 565552, a location that would have placed the aircraft four to five kilometers northwest of Ranger South and beyond the ARVN advance in that area. The flight was obviously disoriented, as it overflew its destination by more than five kilometers. The lead aircraft was "blown from the sky," and when the flight reversed its course, the second aircraft was "blown from the sky."[29] The ARVN I Corps' principal staff officers for operations and logistics, the G-3 and G-4, were on board; I Corps lost its primary operations and logistics staff officers. Of equal concern to the U.S. forces was the fact that they were believed to be carrying a complete set of operations plans and a copy of Communications and Electronics Operating Instructions (CEOI)—the radio codebook for the operation.[30] If they were carrying these documents, it is reasonable to assume that the documents could have fallen into North Vietnamese hands, compromising what little secrecy remained.

The ARVN 1st Armored Brigade task force completed the linkup with the ARVN airborne troops at A Loui late on the evening of 10 February. By 11 February enemy resistance was becoming more organized, and Communist gunners increasingly challenged air operations. The 39th Ranger Battalion was inserted into LZ Ranger North and the 3rd Airborne Brigade command post, accompanied by an airborne battalion, landed at LZ 31.[31] Both battalions were in contact with the enemy as they moved out of the LZs to patrol the area.[32] Unexpected encounters with enemy armor increased.

The 223rd CAB and the 158th AHB inserted 829 troops from the ARVN 1st Infantry Regiment's 1st and 3rd Battalions into LZ Don, located approximately ten kilometers west of LZ Blue. As soon as the lift to Blue was completed, the regiment's field artillery and headquarters were inserted into LZ Delta and the regiment's 2nd Battalion into LZ Delta 1. While the 1st Infantry Division expanded its area of operations south of the Xepon River, field artillery batteries of the airborne division were inserted into LZs 30 and 31. At the same time, the 14th CAB continued to fly in support of the U.S. 1st Brigade, 5th Infantry Division, securing Route 9 from Dong Ha to the Laotian border. During these missions, three 14th CAB helicopters were hit by enemy fire and two crewmembers were wounded.

Two captured NVA soldiers from the NVA 304th Division's 64th Regiment were captured near FSB A Loui on 11 February, providing indisputable evidence that a second NVA division was in the area. During interrogation the prisoners indicated that the regiment arrived in the area of operations on 4 February. This information was corroborated by a third prisoner of war (POW) captured on 14 February. On the south side of the penetration the 1st Infantry Regiment captured documents disclosing that Binh Tram 41 was located two kilometers south of LZ Blue, and that the Binh Tram was reinforced by the NVA 4th Air Defense Battalion, the 75th Engineer Battalion, and an unidentified infantry regiment suspected to be the 141st Regiment of the 2nd NVA Division.[33] The presence of this regiment provided evidence that the enemy strength in the area of operations was greater than anticipated. It was reasonable to assume that the division's remaining regiments either were in the area of operations but still undiscovered, or would soon follow. The number of helicopters lost or damaged continued to mount, and enemy activity in Laos, Quang Tri, and Thau Thien Provinces in Vietnam increased. Five 14th CAB UH-1s were hit at LZ Scotch while supporting 1st Brigade, 5th Infantry Division, operations.[34] Several aircraft from the 223rd CAB received combat damage during the insertion of the 3rd Battalion, 1st Infantry Regiment, at LZ Don. A USAF fighter-bomber, call sign Cobra 04, was shot down near Mai Loc, twenty kilometers northeast of Khe Sanh, and two UH-1Hs were shot down northeast of Khe Sanh. At the same time, the ARVN commander at LZ 30 declared a tactical resupply emergency. CH-47s, escorted by gunships, attempted to deliver supplies to both LZ 30 and LZ 31. The enemy fire at LZ 31 became so intense, however, that the mission had to be aborted. A total of twelve aircraft from the Aviation 101st Group and its reinforcing units from the 1st Aviation Brigade were damaged, and three crewmembers were wounded.[35]

The ARVN was halfway to its objective, Tchepone.[36] But having reached the intermediate objective, all westward movement by ground forces on Route 9 ceased, and the advance to Tchepone came to a halt. In his monograph General Hinh states that from the 11 to 16 February the corps commander, General Lam, met with his division commanders in the corps' rear tactical operations center (TOC) to decide what to do next.[37] In the meantime, the two regiments of the 1st ARVN Division positioned on the southern flank of the penetration moved out of their landing zones, searching for enemy supply caches. The success they enjoyed was relatively insignificant considering the fact that the mission, as understood by U.S. political and military leadership—to seize Tchepone and cut the main arteries of the Ho Chi Minh Trail—lay further west. At this point, the only segment of the trail that was severed was the Route 92 junction with Route 9. While this was significant, the NVA could bypass this intersection by rerouting their supply convoys further west. General Hinh noted, "By the end of the first week of the invasion of Laos, the I Corps armored-airborne advance along Route 9 had become much slower and more cautious."[38] This is a classic understatement.

The WSAG met at 1100 hours on 10 February. With the time zone changes it was now 2200 hours in Vietnam, and air operations in Laos were concluded for the day. Kissinger was still looking for an accurate weather report, but this time Admiral Moorer's answer was correct. Moorer also informed him that General Abrams believed the ARVN was performing well and that the North Vietnamese had brought another regiment into the area. The enemy now outnumbered the ARVN. CIA director Helms estimated that there was now an NVA division (the NVA 320th Division) in the area north of Route 9, but he quickly followed that up by saying, "That's what we want—to give them a pasting."[39] The ARVN severed a major link in the Ho Chi Minh Trail when it reached the intersection of Route 9 and Route 92 at A Loui. But this link was not indispensable; the NVA simply rerouted its traffic to an alternate route, as it had done for years, and continued to move supplies south.

From 11 to 14 February both ARVN ranger battalions were in near-continuous contact with the enemy as the NVA applied pressure

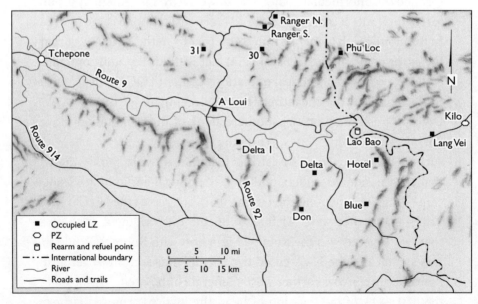

Map 3. ARVN positions at the end of 12 February 1971. Drawn by Bill Nelson. Copyright © 2014 by The University of Oklahoma Press.

to the northern blocking positions. Gunships from the air cavalry and ARA responded to multiple requests for fire support. At 1100 hours on 12 February the 37th Ranger Battalion, supported by gunships, made contact with the enemy three kilometers north-northeast of Phu Loc. An AH-1G from 2nd Squadron, 17th Cavalry, was shot down.

A second air cavalry Cobra was shot down while operating near Ranger North. Capt. Clyde Wilkinson and Chief Warrant Officer Arthur McLeod from C Troop were conducting an armed reconnaissance mission in a Cobra, tail number 68-17089. While they were attacking a target, their aircraft was hit by airburst AAA fire. The crew's next radio transmission reported that their engine oil bypass light had come on and they were going to try to make it back to Khe Sanh. A short time later, when the aircraft began to smoke and burn, the crew immediately made an attempt to land. The aircraft exploded prior to landing, and the wreckage was almost completely consumed by fire.[40] The bodies of Wilkinson and McLeod were not recovered until 1997.[41]

The battle was not confined to Laos. Enemy activity in South Vietnam, the rear area for operation Lam Son 719, continued to increase. Communist forces reacted to the invasion with an ever-increasing volume of artillery and rocket attacks against the allied fire support bases from Dong Ha to A Loui.[42] On 10 February Warrant Officer John Robertson and his observer Sgt. Joseph Pietrzak were shot down in an OH-6 while scouting the eastern rim of the A Shau Valley. Their bodies were not recovered. One day after the loss of Robertson and Pietrzak, a UH-1H from D Troop, 3rd Squadron, 5th Cavalry, was shot down northwest of the Rock Pile (a jagged peak extending up from a valley floor northwest of Mai Loc, South Vietnam) while trying to recover a downed scout. The pilot, Chief Warrant Officer Kenneth Barger, and the crew chief, Private First Class Raymond Carroll, were killed when the aircraft rolled and burned on impact.[43]

Westward movement on the south flank continued on 12 February when the 223rd CAB inserted the 2nd Battalion, 1st Infantry Regiment, and an engineer platoon into LZ Delta 1.[44] But after securing

Delta 1, all westward movement came to a complete halt while ARVN units fanned out from their fire bases, searching for and destroying or capturing relatively minor supply caches instead of pressing on to Tchepone to cut the major infiltration routes. Regardless of whether they continued to move west or operated around their firebases, there was little change in the supply consumption rate, and the logistical burden on the helicopter fleet increased as plans for ground resupply lines floundered.[45]

On 12 February the 159th ASHB completed 80 CH-47 sorties.[46] Each flight required a minimum of a light fire team (two gunships) to escort the Chinooks. This effort, while significant, did not meet all the heavy lift mission demands for the day. Escort gunships were in short supply and there were simply not enough to go around. At 1910 hours on 12 February the commander of a CH-47 company, call sign Lotus 65, notified the 101st Aviation Group TOC that his aircraft were en route to their home station and that the emergency resupply mission for the ARVN airborne division could not be coordinated for lack of gunship escort.[47] Every mission had to have gunship escorts, and the shortage of gunships would plague air operations for the remainder of Lam Son 719.

The availability of helicopter gunships for the escort mission was a major limiting factor in how many different airmobile operations could be conducted simultaneously. The aviation battalions reinforcing the 101st Aviation Group, the 223rd and 14th Combat Aviation Battalions, were equipped with UH-1C (Charley Model) gunships. However, this aircraft complicated the planning for armed helicopter support. Compared to the AH-1G Cobra, the Charley Model was slower, less powerful, and could not carry the amount of fuel and ammunition required for many of the missions.[48] Even with all its limitations, the armed helicopter proved to be the most important fire support weapons system during Lam Son 719. Armed helicopters provided the capability for detecting and immediately engaging battlefield targets of opportunity close to friendly troops. Armed helicopters, operating with the air cavalry and aerial rocket artillery and escorting troop-lift, heavy-lift, and support aircraft, virtually covered the battle area with their ability to respond immediately and accurately with fire on known and suspected enemy weapons and positions. Armed helicopters operated under low ceilings and weather conditions that restricted or precluded use of TACAIR in support of ground units or airmobile operations.[49]

On 13 February FSB 31 came under sporadic fire from enemy gunners located on a mountain ridge northwest of the base. In order to afford greater protection, the 158th AHB inserted 657 soldiers from the 6th Airborne Battalion into a position on the ridgeline to clear out the enemy. The first flight into the LZ received heavy mortar fire, damaging four aircraft. The subsequent lifts diverted to another LZ a short distance away, and the air assault was completed. Once on the ground, the airborne battalion continued to receive NVA artillery fire and retreated to a position near FSB 31 without accomplishing its mission. During its brief excursion, the 6th Battalion suffered seventy-eight casualties, and twenty-three soldiers were missing in action.[50] Increasingly heavy attacks by enemy artillery continued at FSB 31. Aerial resupply efforts intensified on 13 February with 147 CH-47 and CH-53 sorties completed.[51]

Considering the fact that the rains on 9 February had shut down helicopter support and complicated travel over Route 9, the ARVN made good progress during the three days in Laos. It reached its intermediate objective, A Loui, on 10 February. The next move anticipated by U.S. planners was the attack on the airfield at Tchepone. But the ARVN ground attack down Route 9 came to an unexpected and prolonged halt. The halt was a fatal mistake, although perhaps not the only fatal mistake in the operation. It soon became apparent that the concept of the operation, as the ARVN understood it, was a much more cautious approach. In *Lam Son 719* Major General Hinh described the ARVN understanding of the plan as a westward advance with each step "solidly anchored on a fire support base."[52]

Hinh describes a plodding, methodical movement. The plan, as U.S. planners understood it, was more akin to a raid: a bold, swift movement across enemy-held territory that would take full advantage of the tactical mobility afforded by airmobile operations. While Hinh suggests that the halt was part of the ARVN plan, Gen. Phillip Davidson claims that on 12 February, without informing Abrams, President Thieu instructed General Lam and his division commanders to "be cautious in moving west and cancel the operation once the ARVN force had taken 3,000 casualties."[53] Davidson surmises that Thieu's concern was prompted by the fact that the VNMC, the airborne division, and the 1st Armor Brigade were all part of Thieu's palace guard (his anti-coup defense) and "that their destruction would expose Thieu to dangers from his internal enemies."

Eleven years after the publication of Davidson's book, historian Lewis Sorley examined whether Thieu had issued a covert order to his commanders to withdraw after 3,000 casualties. During his research, Sorley interviewed a former special assistant to Thieu, Nguyen Tien Hung, who replied, "Thieu insists he never gave such an order."[54] Three years later Henry Kissinger addressed the issue of Thieu's covert order in *Ending the War in Vietnam*. Kissinger states that on 18 March, when the operation was all but over, "Washington" learned during a meeting with his division commanders on 12 February, that President Thieu had ordered the operation to be terminated once the ARVN force had sustained 3,000 casualties. Kissinger confirmed Davidson's allegation and stated that Nixon "would have never approved the operation had such a restriction been communicated to the White House."[55] The same allegation is buried in the footnotes to a backchannel message from Kissinger to Bunker dated 18 March 1971.[56]

As the first week of operations in Laos drew to a close, a combined team of UH-1H aircraft and gunships lifted engineers, artillery, and the 3rd Infantry Regimental command post to LZ Hotel 2 (approximately ten miles south of LZ Hotel) in an attempt to block possible enemy approaches to Route 9 from the south. The air move was contested by continuous enemy ground fire. One gunship was damaged and a UH-1H was destroyed. ARVN 1st Division units moved south, discovering and destroying NVA supply caches and reporting bomb damage assessments from previous B-52 strikes. Concurrently the ARVN 1st Armored Brigade task force conducted search-and-destroy operations along the unmapped trails north of Route 9 and east of A Loui, but made no attempt to continue westward movement.

Helicopter gunships flew 500–800 sorties every day in addition to approximately 100 daily sorties of TACAIR and B-52 bombers sorties. Losses inflicted on the enemy by these air strikes were significant. Despite U.S. tactical air and artillery support, enemy antiaircraft gunners took a heavy toll on helicopters, and the number of gunships, vital to airmobile operations, was shrinking.

By halting the westward movement, the ARVN corps surrendered one of its greatest advantages—the tactical mobility afforded by airmobile operations. This allowed the NVA time to bring reinforcements into the area to isolate and ultimately destroy, one by one, the fire support bases on the north flank in much the same manner as they isolated and destroyed the outlying French defensive positions at Dienbienphu seventeen years earlier. Once this was accomplished, Route 9 could no longer be used as an overland supply route.

While the ARVN advance stagnated, the NVA gathered forces to isolate and destroy the blocking positions on the north flank. The NVA seized the initiative as they rushed reinforcements into the battle area. There is a disparity between U.S. intelligence reports and NVA claims of enemy strength in the battle area during this period. Without specifying a specific date, the North Vietnamese stated that by early February their strength along the Route 9–Southern Laos front had grown to 60,000 troops, consisting of five divisions, two separate infantry regiments, eight artillery regiments, three tank battalions, six antiaircraft regiments, three engineer regiments, and eight sapper battalions.[57] Conversely, Admiral Moorer reported that there were 14,000 enemy combat troops in the area on 4 February, and increased the estimate to 19,000 on 8 February.[58] While there is a huge difference between 60,000 and 19,000, part of the difference in the conflicting numbers is the fact that the figures pertain to two separate areas. Moorer was referring to Lam Son 719's immediate area of operations, whereas the North Vietnamese were referring to a much larger area, one that included all of southern Laos and a portion of North Vietnam along the western DMZ. The actual number of NVA defenders in the area of operations during the first week of the operation is probably somewhere between these two figures. The issues then became the amount of time it would take the NVA to move reinforcements into the battle area and the capability of U.S. air power to seal off the area. The NVA won on both fronts. While the ARVN advance stagnated, the NVA gathered forces to isolate and destroy the blocking positions on the northern flank of the penetration.

Chapter 8

THE SECOND WEEK IN LAOS
The Attack Stalls

IT WAS APPARENT TO KISSINGER THAT THE ATTACK was not going as expected. Bypassing Defense Secretary Laird, he asked Abrams for an assessment. Abrams was in a delicate position as he replied to Kissinger's inquiry; it was a Vietnamese operation, and the Vietnamese head of state was personally involved. In his reply the general appeared to defend the ARVN failure to continue westward toward Tchepone, citing the poor weather and the worse-than-expected condition of Route 9. He opined that the ARVN performance had been good and that aircraft losses had been less than anticipated, given the circumstances and the number of sorties flown. He supported General Lam's decision to bolster his flank security, reporting that five NVA regiments were in the area and another could arrive within forty-eight hours. Westward movement, Abrams continued, would resume at the earliest possible time. In this same message Abrams acknowledged that the primary objective remained: cutting and disrupting the trail system; exploiting enemy caches was secondary.[1]

General Abrams flew to Dong Ha on 16 February to attempt to get the operation back on track and moving west to cut the major supply lines around Tchepone. During a two-and-a-half-hour meeting with Generals Vein, Sutherland, and Lam, an alternate plan emerged. In the original plan the air assault of Tchepone was to take place immediately after Objective A Loui was secured, and the armored forces would continue to drive westward to link up with the air assault force.[2] Without a functioning ground supply route, and with enemy armor present in greater-than-anticipated strength, continuation of an armored thrust down Route 9 to Tchepone was no longer an attractive option. The generals compromised; their solution was to support the assault on Tchepone by establishing a series of firebases along the escarpment overlooking Tchepone. The revised plan called for the 1st Infantry Division to conduct airmobile assaults on the higher mountaintops south of the Xepon River and to establish fire support bases to support the airborne division's push toward Tchepone.[3] They estimated that this would take three to five days. The new landing zones were named Lolo, Liz, and Sophia.

Abrams reported the outcome of his conference with Lam, Vien, and Sutherland to Washington, where it was discussed during a WSAG meeting.[4] However, the tactical situation continued to deteriorate. Operations Silver Buckle and Desert Rat—supporting attacks by Laotian special guerilla units on the western edge of the Ho Chi Minh

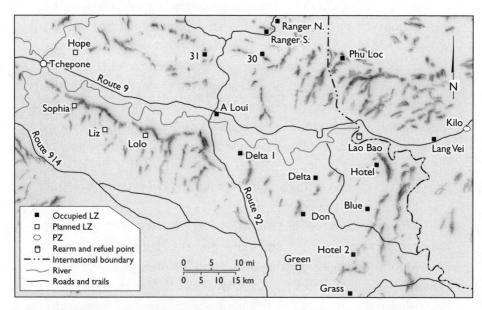

Map 4. Concept of operations as revised on 16 February 1971. Drawn by Bill Nelson. Copyright © 2014 by The University of Oklahoma Press.

Trail—had been repulsed by the NVA.[5] So had MACVSOG efforts to send teams into the A Shau Valley to reconnoiter routes for the planned ARVN withdrawal during Phase 4 and to tie down NVA forces, preventing them from reinforcing the defense of the Route 9 corridor.[6] Evidence of a larger-than-expected NVA force in the Lam Son 719 area of operations continued to mount. The 1st Airborne Battalion conducted bomb-damage assessment north of LZ Bravo on the morning of 18 February. As soldiers searched the location, they discovered a recently abandoned enemy command post—that of the NVA 308th Division, according to captured documents.

While Abrams was in his meeting with Lam, Sutherland, and Vein, the 1st ARVN Division's 3rd Regiment continued to make progress to the south. LZ Green was the preferred landing zone for this movement, but when the 223rd CAB arrived at the landing zone, it was greeted by enemy fire. The combat assault diverted to LZ Grass, approximately three kilometers east of LZ Green. After landing at LZ Grass, the 2nd Battalion, 3rd Regiment, was in a position to move out and interdict Route 914, the branch of the Ho Chi Minh Trail that ran southeast from Tchepone to Base Area 611. From this position the 2nd Battalion could block the flow of traffic on Route 914. And with Route 92 being blocked by the airborne division at A Loui, the NVA's logistical flow would be forced westward to Route 23. But still, this plan would not accomplish the mission of seizing the key transportation hub at Tchepone, thus preventing the North Vietnamese from moving their supplies south to support a major dry-season offensive in 1971 or 1972.

Abrams's 16 February efforts to regain westward momentum were soon overturned by President Thieu, who flew to I Corps on 19 February. General Lam described to Thieu the deteriorating situation and the increasing enemy resistance and questioned the advisability of continuing the attack on Tchepone. President Thieu, while not totally discarding the plan, advised Lam to "take his time and, under the present circumstances, perhaps it would be better to expand search activities toward the southwest" to cut off Route 914 which led into Base Area 611.[7] Whatever progress Abrams made in speeding up the pace of the operation during his meeting with Lam and Vien on 16 February was lost as the ARVN, under the direction of President Thieu, continued to vacillate.

ARVN forces on the south flank soon encountered stiff resistance when they attempted to move westward from LZ Grass along Route 914. The artillery batteries' attempts to move west out of FSB Hotel 2 to support the infantry battalions failed as NVA gunners successfully prevented USMC CH-53s from extracting the artillery. The ARVN was forced to destroy the guns, and Hotel 2 was abandoned. Meanwhile, two 3rd Infantry Regiment battalions were locked in close combat with the NVA. A B-52 Arc Light strike was called in to assist, and during the hours of darkness, just prior to the strike, the ARVN managed to pull back far enough to avoid damage. The NVA took the brunt of the strike, and the ARVN was able to break contact and move back north.

As the ARVN corps dallied, NVA reinforcements arrived in strength on the north flank. The isolated ARVN fire bases could not be resupplied except by air, but the NVA had encircled the fire bases with antiaircraft weapons and set up mortars to fire on the landing zones if helicopters penetrated their surface-to-air fires. Resupply and evacuation of the wounded became a complex and dangerous proposition.

Combat operations in the Lam Son rear area continued at a brisk pace. The 1st Brigade, 5th Infantry Division, capitalized on air mobility and massive firepower. Small patrols were airlifted from one terrain feature to another as they searched for the enemy. Once an enemy force was located, the troops on the ground requested artillery, gunship, and tactical air support to fix the enemy while larger ground forces were assembled and brought in to finish the enemy. It was an effective economy of force operation that allowed the brigade to maintain security over its large area of operations. The ARVN would have done well to emulate this tactic in Laos. On 15 February, during an engagement near FSB Vandergrift, the 1st Brigade killed 115 NVA soldiers.[8] Action around Vandergrift and the Rock Pile continued because, in addition to housing artillery batteries, Vandergrift was a major waypoint for the ground convoys shuttling supplies to Khe Sanh. It was also a collection point for damaged aircraft and had helicopter refueling and rearming facilities that were critical to air operations. If the Communists could destroy Vandergrift and control the surrounding area, at least temporarily, they would cut off the only overland line of supply to Khe Sanh. Realizing this, the Communists made Vandergrift one of their priority targets.

While the U.S. brigade used air mobility to its advantage, the ARVN airborne division stagnated in relatively fixed positions, patrolling only relatively short distances from its fixed fire support bases.[9] The 39th Ranger Battalion at Ranger North and the 21st Ranger Battalion at Ranger South were in near-continuous contact with the enemy. The rangers were positioned along a major infiltration route extending from the Ban Raven Pass on the border between North Vietnam and Laos. Patrols discovered and captured 37mm AAA guns, food stores, and ammunition caches, all of which indicated the presence of a major enemy force.[10] Contacts with the enemy were light at first but grew in intensity, forcing the ranger battalions to recall their patrols.

On 18 February Chief Warrant Officer Joseph Brown of the 237th Medical Detachment was at the controls of a UH-1H medevac ship, attempting to extract wounded soldiers from Ranger North. Brown launched from Khe Sanh with two Cobra escorts. While they were inbound to the LZ, they started taking heavy antiaircraft fire. The gunship team immediately responded with suppressive fire, but was unable to silence the Communist gunners. Brown's aircraft took several hits, and it was apparent to Spc. 5th Class Dennis Fuji, the crew chief, that the whistling noise coming from the main rotor meant the rotor blades had also been damaged. Brown notified the gunship team leader that he was taking too much damage and turned back. The team leader acknowledged Brown's decision and stated that the gun team would return to Khe Sanh, refuel, and wait there to try again. But while en route back to Khe Sanh, Brown reversed his course, without notifying the gun team, and headed back to Ranger North. Brown landed at Ranger North in a hail of enemy fire, and the crew began loading the wounded. When Brown attempted to take off, the aircraft was shot down. It crashed on the LZ, injuring both Fuji and the co-pilot. After impact Brown attempted to retrieve a radio from the aircraft and was mortally wounded. Supported by gunships and tactical air, a UH-1H rescue ship from the 2nd Squadron, 17th Cavalry, came in to pick up the crew. Fuji and two other crew members had been separated from the other survivors and managed to crawl into a bunker. When the rescue ship arrived, the other two survivors made a dash for safety. But Fuji, the last to leave the bunker, was just beginning his run to the ship when a mortar round exploded in front of him, knocking him back into the bunker and temporarily blinding him when a shell fragment struck him near his right eye. He quickly recovered but knew that he could not get to the rescue ship in time. Rather than see the ship destroyed by fire, he waved it off and returned to the bunker. Fuji managed to get hold of a radio and advised all aircraft to remain clear of Ranger North; it was too hot for more rescue attempts. Specialist Fuji remained on the ground at Ranger North from 18 to 20 February.[11] Rescue was impossible; the Communists had totally surrounded the 39th Ranger Battalion and had the landing zone zeroed in with mortars and field artillery, ringed with machine guns and antiaircraft weapons.

Both ranger battalions came under heavy attack by fire. The 102nd NVA Regiment, reinforced by an additional infantry battalion and five batteries of field artillery, attacked Ranger North shortly after midnight on the 18th.[12] During the hours of darkness, some of the 39th Ranger Battalion defensive outposts were overrun, even though LZ Ranger North was supported by the ARVN artillery from the ranger group's batteries located at FSBs Phu Loc and 30, as well as flare ships and AC-130 gunships.[13] By the morning of 19 February, while Thieu was in conference with Lam and his division commanders, enemy pressure on Ranger South had diminished, but the NVA attack on Ranger North had intensified.[14] ARVN artillery fired continuously in support of Ranger North throughout the day, but the enemy managed to breach the perimeter and occupy the outer trenches. Working with the ranger battalion commander, Specialist Fuji directed supporting fire from seven USAF AC-130 gunships supported by flare ships during that night. The NVA broke through the defenses and swarmed over the position. On order, the rangers took cover in their bunkers and trenches, leaving the enemy exposed, as the gunships saturated the position with mini-gun fire. Enemy losses were heavy, and the NVA was forced to pull back.

Close air support sorties continued the following morning at 0730 hours.[15] At 1430 hours the 158th AHB—under the cover of air strikes, helicopter gunships and artillery—attempted to bring in emergency supplies and extract the critically wounded. The first UH-1H was hit by enemy fire and forced to make an emergency landing at Ranger South. The second UH-1H was also hit by enemy fire, but managed to make it as far as FSB 30 before it made a crash landing and was destroyed. The resupply effort was then terminated.[16] By late afternoon the defenses at Ranger North were faltering; it had been three days since the rangers had received ammunition, food, and water. They were running out of ammunition, and some were fighting with captured weapons. Fuji radioed for help. He was told that it was on the way and that he should board the first aircraft that landed. As the chopper landed, he made a dash and was quickly followed by an ARVN captain who had been assisting the battalion commander. The perimeter defenses failed, and the NVA was inside the perimeter shooting at the aircraft's crew as they landed, loaded the wounded, and tried to take off. Maj. Jim Lloyd and Capt. David Nelson of C Company, 158th AHB, flew the first aircraft into the landing zone, which Fuji boarded. As Nelson attempted to take off, his aircraft was hit several times and caught fire, but Nelson was able to gain enough altitude to autorotate into Ranger South, a short distance away.[17] It was a hard landing. Fuji was thrown against the pilot's armored seat and stunned by the impact. When he regained his senses, he discovered that the crew of his rescue ship had been picked up, leaving Fuji on the ground again.

The ranger battalions were organized as light infantry and were not equipped to defend a fixed position. The mission assigned to the rangers was to screen the north flank. By definition, a screening force is not expected to defend a fixed position, but to detect and report the approaching enemy and fight a retrograde delaying action until heavier forces can engage the enemy. Colonel Hiep, the 1st Ranger

Group commander, requested permission for his battalion to pull back to Ranger South and join the 21st Ranger Battalion. I Corps, perhaps distracted by President Thieu's presence at the corps headquarters, never responded to his request.[18] During the afternoon of 20 February, reconnaissance aircraft reported seeing a large NVA force encircling Ranger North. Radio contact with the 39th Ranger Battalion was lost at 1710 hours. At 1856 hours the I Corps command post was notified that the able-bodied soldiers of the 39th fought their way out of Ranger North and linked up with the 21st Ranger Battalion at Ranger South. The North Vietnamese claim to have "completely annihilated" the 39th Ranger Battalion. This claim is close to correct; however, the North Vietnamese make no mention of their own losses.[19] It was a killing field, and NVA losses were heavy.[20]

Fuji's third opportunity for rescue came on 21 February. When the ship touched down in the LZ, Fuji ran out to board the aircraft. Unfortunately, he was accompanied by a large group of panicked ARVN soldiers intent on escape. Fuji managed to board the aircraft, but as the mob tried to board, the pilot, perhaps mistaking Fuji (a Japanese American) for an ARVN soldier, and fearful of being swamped and unable to get off the ground, screamed at Fuji to get off. Fuji yelled back that he was the American soldier they had been sent to rescue. The panicked pilot continued to scream at Fuji to get off, and Fuji complied with the order. Shortly after that incident, Fuji received a radio call informing him that if he could not restore order at the landing zone, there would be no further extraction attempts.[21] He relayed this information to the commander of the 21st Ranger Battalion who detailed a pair of noncommissioned officers (NCOs) to control the LZ. The next rescue attempt came the following day. After intensive air and artillery strikes, lift ships landed at Ranger South without receiving fire. In all, 122 wounded rangers were extracted with Specialist Fuji.

General Lam, believing Ranger South untenable, ordered the position evacuated.[22] The 158th AHB began the extraction on the morning of 21 February. After being delayed by weather, the first ships arrived at approximately 1050 hours. At 1100 hours Lt. Col. William Peachey, the commanding officer, notified the 101st Aviation Group TOC that ten or twelve ships had managed to get into the landing zone, drop off emergency supplies, and get out loaded with wounded rangers before the landing zone came under heavy mortar fire and the extraction effort was suspended. One aircraft was hit and forced to land at FSB 30, and a second UH-1H was hit but was going to attempt to make it back to Khe Sanh.[23]

On the same day, a combined effort by the 158th AHB and the 223rd CAB extracted 400 6th Airborne Battalion troops, in sixty sorties, from FSB 31 to a landing zone on the Vietnam side of the border near Route 9.[24] The 6th Airborne, a battalion that failed in its mission to clear a ridgeline northwest of Fire Support Base 31 on 13 February, was the first battalion-sized force to be extracted from Laos. It is unclear why a fresh battalion was not inserted, because enemy pressure was building on the northern flank of the penetration. Mission accomplishment dictated holding the flanks of the penetration, and the situation called for reinforcements—not extractions. The following day, General Sutherland described the circumstances surrounding the extraction to General Abrams, reporting that the battalion was "put in the wrong place and never able to get it together" and that General Dong, the airborne division commander, decided to pull it out. And Sutherland, assuming that another battalion would be inserted, supported Dong's decision.[25] Sutherland's assumption, while logical, was wrong.

In the meantime, the troops remaining at FSB 31 were resupplied by twenty-eight CH-47 sorties, while FSB A Loui received thirty-seven CH-47 sorties, and the 37th Ranger Battalion at Phu Loc received twenty sorties. The 1st ARVN Division's fire support bases on the south side of the penetration received twenty-six CH-53 ammunition resupply sorties. Units of the 1st Infantry Division moved further south, striking along Route 92 and finding a number of enemy installations, but also making numerous contacts with the enemy and receiving attacks by fire. The 8th Airborne Battalion and armored elements engaged the enemy two kilometers north of Ban Dong, destroying one T-34 tank and a 23mm antiaircraft gun position.

As the duty logs for this period indicate, 18 to 21 February was a period of intense combat throughout the area of operations. Although many of the U.S. Army air activities were resupply and medevac missions, every mission required gunship escorts, and the escorting gunships were piling up flying hours, combat damage, and maintenance requirements. The fleet was getting ragged, aircrews were becoming exhausted, operational UH-1C and AH-1G gunships were in short supply, and aircraft and crew losses continued.[26]

Helicopters are a mass of rotating parts, and this inevitably leads to vibration and wear. The ratio of maintenance to flying hours is high. This high maintenance requirement, combined with combat damage, accidents, and losses, was consuming aircraft faster than the maintenance crews could perform the required inspections and make repairs. The operational ready (OR) rate plummeted for all types of helicopters.[27] There were periodic shortages of critical repair parts, and few, if any, aviation units had a full complement of crew chiefs, mechanics, maintenance supervisors, and technical inspectors. And despite periodic rain and

Figure 5. Using the ammo bay door as a bed and his body armor as a pillow, a Cobra pilot gets some crew rest at Khe Sanh. Photograph provided by Wayne Twiehaus.

fog that shut down air operations out of Khe Sanh, dust was a problem. With hundreds of landings and takeoffs each day, the rotor wash dried the ground and sent up huge clouds of dust. It was one of those unique environments where a soldier could stand in mud and have to shield his eyes from dust. The turbine engines ingested dust, increasing wear and reducing power. On a clear, dry day, Khe Sanh's location was marked by a red dust cloud that was visible for miles.

The 101st Group duty log for 14 February noted that Maj. John Klose, the 223rd CAB S-3 (operations officer), reported that his battalion had only twelve of thirty-six gunships available for operations. The situation became worse on 24 February, when the 223rd CAB advised the group headquarters that there was only one operational Charley Model remaining in the battalion.[28] Both the 223rd and the 14th CABs were equipped with UH-1C gunships, and the Charley Model OR rate continued to be a problem. During a 2001 address to the aviation battalion commander precommand course at Fort Rucker, Alabama, Klose, now a retired colonel, described the Charley Model as "totally ineffective at the weight, density altitude, and fuel load required. . . . It was beyond its capabilities." From 14 February until the operation was concluded, the 101st Aviation Group duty log has multiple recurring entries of the 223rd requesting aerial rocket artillery or gunship support. The Charley Model fleet had been crippled by combat damage and by the maintenance problems that resulted from operating the aircraft in an environment beyond the aircraft's capabilities.

There was a second, but intangible, factor that contributed to the plummeting Charley Model OR rate—pilot experience. That is not to say that the Charley Model pilots were not experienced; rather, they were inexperienced in an environment so different from those where they had previously flown. By 1971 the highest threat area in South Vietnam was northern I Corps and the A Shau Valley—and the Charley Model–equipped units all came from areas farther south. The 101st Airborne Division aviation units had a distinct advantage. It had been just over six months since the conclusion of Operation Texas Star in the A Shau Valley and the crucible of the hot extraction at FSB Ripcord. Lt. Col. Bill

Peachey, the 158th AHB commanding officer, was a veteran of Ripcord, and while many aviators who had flown Ripcord missions had departed, they had passed on a legacy of experience and knowledge. Of equal, if not greater, importance was that 101st Airborne Division aviators supported SOG cross-border operations and were familiar with the enemy threat as well as the terrain and flying conditions. The hurried manner in which the southern aviation units were moved north and assembled for Lam Son 719, combined with the fact that participants in the SOG cross-border operations were sworn to secrecy, made it impossible to brief or train them for what they were about to encounter; it was a "come as you are" operation. And, all of this was aggravated by what can be described as blissful ignorance on the part of senior U.S. planners. There was no time and no effort was made to train the aviation units coming in from other areas of Vietnam.

In 1971 Rick Freeman was a chief warrant officer aircraft commander assigned to C Battery, 4th Battalion, 77th Aerial Rocket Artillery (ARA). Rick had been in C Battery since 1969 and had voluntarily extended his tour in Vietnam. At the onset of Lam Son 719 he was one of the most, if not the most, experienced Cobra pilots in the 101st Airborne Division. Rick described pilot training and familiarity with the area of operations:

I was there the whole time and flew a lot of reconnaissance with MACVSOG from April 69 until Nixon told us we weren't there. Because I flew that AO [Area of Operations] for quite a while I have different opinions about the whole fracas. . . . I wasn't that concerned about flying in my back yard. I knew what the threat was and how to avoid it. I knew how to navigate because I had been flying there for some time. We didn't have the major losses that everyone talks about. We didn't lose anybody during the whole war, a helicopter now and then, but not very many. I saw whole [Charley Model] gun platoons get shot down and all of them within a hundred meters of each other on the ground, in about a five-minute time frame. Really sad.[29]

Annex D of the 101st Airborne Division's after action review is a tabular listing of U.S. helicopters destroyed or damaged during Lam Son 719. Each incident is identified by unit, type of damage, and aircraft altitude, airspeed, and the phase of the mission it was in when hit. An analysis of annex D illustrates Freeman's observations.[30] Except for their mission of aerial fire support, the two helicopter gunships of Lam Son 719—the AH-1G Cobra and the UH-1C Charley Model—have little in common; comparing a Cobra to a Charley Model is akin to comparing a ballerina to a bullfrog. Charley Model tactics were not totally discretionary, but forced on them by aircraft limitations.

Setting aside the air cavalry Cobras, which had an entirely different mission, the mission of the Charley Models in the 14th and 223rd CABs was identical to that of the Cobra gun company of the 158th AHB. Both were escort gunships. On average, the 158th's Cobras were hit at an altitude of 1,310 feet, whereas the mean altitude for Charley Model hits was 736 feet. The median altitude for Charley Model hits is even more telling—400 feet. The 223rd CAB's 48th Aviation Company Charley Models provide an even more stark comparison. The 48th's gun platoon, call sign Joker, sustained more hits than any other Charley Model unit by a margin of almost two to one. The average altitude of a Joker hit was 320 feet. The statistical analysis of the Joker's hits shows the statistical median and mode to be even more descriptive: both values are 100 feet above the terrain. The Charley Models were slower, flew lower, and were less lethal. The UH-1C simply could not match the Cobra's performance in power, airspeed, agility, or weapons systems. It was clearly inferior to the Cobra, and that difference was bound to have an impact on the UH-1H lift ships escorted and protected by the two different types of gunships.

The lack of familiarity of the terrain and threat not only handicapped the Charley Model pilots, it handicapped all of 223rd and 14th CAB pilots who moved north on short notice to reinforce the 101st Airborne Division. Consider the facts revealed by a statistical comparison of the 223rd CAB, supporting the ARVN 1st Infantry Division on the south flank of the attack, and the 101st's 158th AHB, supporting the ARVN advance down Route 9 and the forces on the north flank of the attack. Both faced formidable air defense and ground fires. In the first eleven days of the operation, the 223rd CAB had thirty-six aircraft damaged or destroyed by enemy fire, twenty-three of which were assigned to the 48th Aviation Company. The 158th AHB had a total of seven aircraft hit during the same period.

The events of the second week in Laos were a harbinger for the events that followed. It was a time of wasted opportunities, procrastination, and indecision. When the ARVN attack came to a self-imposed halt on 11 February, the Communists used the opportunity to reinforce, concentrate their air defense weapons around the stationary ARVN forces and air avenues leading to these positions, and mass their field artillery fires. On 16 February Abrams, in a meeting with Lam and Sutherland, thought he had the movement to Tchepone back on track, only to have this plan upset by Thieu's meeting with Lam on 19 February, when Thieu advised to Lam to wait and see what developed. The ARVN was never able to benefit from the use of Route 9 as a resupply route, and the burden of logistical support fell entirely on the U.S. Army's helicopter fleet—a resource being rapidly consumed as the ARVN dallied. The northern blocking positions began to crumble, and the South Vietnamese chose not to reinforce.

Chapter 9

COLLAPSE ON THE NORTHERN FLANK

BY THE BEGINNING OF THE THIRD WEEK IN LAOS, ARVN refusal to continue westward movement provided the North Vietnamese the time needed to concentrate their forces and isolate ARVN positions on the north flank. By week's end the NVA would own the north flank.

After overrunning Ranger North, the Communists turned their attention to Ranger South. Throughout the night of 21 February NVA artillery pounded the rangers with unrelenting fire. At approximately 1200 hours on 22 February, USAF helicopter gunships and tactical air and field artillery hit the NVA forces around Ranger South with a masterfully coordinated two-hour barrage of preparatory fire. As soon as the preparation was completed, thirteen UH-1H lift ships and medical evacuation (Dust Off) aircraft, protected by the suppressive fire of escorting Cobras, landed in the LZ and evacuated 122 wounded 39th Ranger Battalion survivors. All thirteen aircraft were able to get into and out of the LZ, and the extraction was completed in less than an hour.[1] The force remaining at Ranger South numbered approximately 400 men, including 107 from the 39th Ranger Battalion.[2]

Approximately twelve hours after the fall of Ranger North, President Nixon called Admiral Moorer for an assessment of Lam Son 719. Some of the answers Moorer gave the president were overly optimistic, and some were just wrong. Moorer explained the rationale for the delay in the movement to Tchepone as it had been described to him: ARVN forces needed to establish fire support bases to support the movement.

He added that the special guerilla units had arrived at Route 23, south-west of Tchepone, and that Routes 92 and 914 had been cut. Then, referring to the battle at Ranger North, he stated: "We feel that at least two battalions of the 102nd NVN [North Vietnam] regiment were rendered ineffective as a result of this action over the weekend. . . . [A]s you noted on the map, that particular one [Ranger North] was the most exposed because it was right up there in the path of all the reinforcements coming down from NVN and it was a helluva fight and they laid on a lot of fire power and I think they got the results they wanted. . . . As you know the 39th Battalion joined the 21st just slightly to the southwest."

When the president asked if the South Vietnamese were capable of "putting one or two more corps in there," Moorer's reply was, "Yes."[3] While, on paper, the ARVN may have had the capability of committing another corps to this operation, in reality it could not. South Vietnam had a total of fourteen divisions. The majority of three of these divisions was committed to Lam Son. Portions of two other divisions were committed to operations in Cambodia. That left nine divisions, all of which, with the exception of the ARVN 2nd Infantry Division, were stationed in the southern three military regions. Many of these divisions were lightly committed, if not idle. The problem was that, historically, the ARVN divisions were not mobile; they did not deploy outside of their home areas and away from their families. Their soldiers were recruited or conscripted from the local area and often spoke a regional dialect. Previous attempts to move these divisions to areas where there was a greater military need had met with disaster. In the best of times, the accession rate for new conscripts and recruits barely kept pace with the desertion rate. And when divisions were relocated, the problem got completely out of hand as soldiers deserted to rejoin their families.[4] If Moorer had consulted with General Westmoreland, he would not have made this mistake.

Although Moorer was incorrect when he replied that the ARVN could introduce a second corps into the battles, he was correct in his statement that the ARVN I Corps had reserves available. The problem was that the reserves were not committed. General Lam had approximately 30,000 soldiers under his command, but the maximum number committed in Laos was less than 18,000.[5] Moorer, like Sutherland, *assumed* that that Lam would use his reserve forces. And, like Abrams, Moorer *assumed* that the ARVN airborne division's assault on Tchepone was imminent.[6]

Moorer's description of the action at Ranger North as a "helluva fight" in which the loss of ranger lives, as compared to the enemy, had been "highly satisfactory," and that the 39th Ranger Battalion "joined the 21st just slightly to the southwest," was grossly understated. Moorer received his information from Abrams, and Abrams received his information from his staff. During a weekly update, the briefing officer described the action at Ranger North: "On 20 February the 39th Ranger Battalion evacuated its position due to enemy pressure and joined the 21st Ranger Battalion."[7] A more accurate description would have been that Ranger North, an important blocking position on the north flank, was overrun, and that the 39th Battalion had suffered a 70 percent casualty rate and was no longer an effective fighting force.[8]

As the operation progressed into its third week, enemy resistance steadily increased. Having overrun the 39th Ranger Battalion at LZ Ranger North, the NVA now directed its attacks on the remaining fire support bases on the northern flank—Ranger South and the airborne division troops at Fire Support Bases 30 and 31. The 158th Aviation Battalion spent most of the week operating under intense fire as its aircraft approached the landing zones.

All resupply and medevac missions required gunship escorts, and after the first two weeks in Laos, aviation commanders realized that missions that would have required a single light fire team of two gunships in South Vietnam required a minimum of two fire teams in Laos. But gunships were in short supply. The duty logs for the 101st Aviation Group provide precise detail on the shortages. On 22 February the 2nd Squadron, 17th Cavalry, reported that only six of its twenty-seven Cobras were flyable. On 23 February the squadron's A Troop had only one operational Cobra, C Troop had none, and 1st

Brigade, 5th Infantry Division, was forced to call off a combat assault because the 14th CAB could not provide Charley Model gunships. In the air over Laos, gunship missions began to resemble a pick-up game of basketball as gunships completed one mission and immediately transitioned to another without the benefit of prior planning or the opportunity to rearm and refuel. The orders often contained no more information than the call signs and radio frequency for the supported aircraft on the next mission.[9]

While the airborne division faltered on the north flank, the ARVN 1st Infantry Division made progress on the south flank. By 23 February the 1st and 3rd Infantry Regiments had continued their southerly movement and had reached Route 914. From there they continued northwest along Route 914, destroying enemy stockpiles and logistics facilities. They came upon the pipeline segment destroyed earlier by the 2nd Squadron, 17th Cavalry, and continued its destruction for another five kilometers. On 23 February the ARVN 3rd Regiment received orders to move back north and west, to LZs at Delta 1, Brown, and Brick in order to facilitate the continued westward movement of the operation. But by this time the regiment's 2nd Battalion was heavily engaged by the enemy and could not break contact. The 3rd Battalion was brought in to reinforce, but still, the NVA refused to disengage and continued to "hug" the ARVN force, staying as close as possible to prevent artillery or airstrikes.[10] In a daring use of air power, the regiment called for a B-52 strike on the NVA, with the time on target scheduled for early the next morning. The grid coordinates for the target were so close to the friendly positions that, given the probable error of such strikes, the ARVN force was at risk. In the darkness one hour prior to the strike, the ARVN quickly pulled back to a safe distance. After the strike, the force reentered the area to conduct bomb-damage assessment. The NVA had suffered heavy casualties, and contact was broken. Instead of exploiting this success, the battalions were moved back to LZs along the edge of the escarpment. The 4th Battalion, 3rd Infantry Regiment, and the regimental command post conducted a combat assault into LZ Brown, and the

2nd Battalion was lifted to LZ Delta 1. The 1st Battalion moved north to a position approximately four kilometers north of the intersection of Routes 92 and 914. It did not take the NVA long to fill the void as it moved north, applying pressure to the fire support base at Hotel 2, making closure of the fire support base a prolonged and costly affair.

On 24 February General Lam came to the conclusion that the position held by the 21st Ranger Battalion and the survivors of the 39th Ranger Battalion from Ranger North was untenable. The extraction of the 39th Rangers' wounded from Ranger South had required a maximum effort of artillery and air support, as did all resupply missions to what was now the northernmost outpost. Lam ordered the rangers to move overland to FSB 30 to be extracted and redeployed to FSB Phu Loc in South Vietnam.[11] Again, the ARVN commander withdrew his forces when the logical action would have been to reinforce them, especially since the extraction of both ranger battalions and the 6th Airborne Battalion during the previous week had reduced ARVN strength on the northern flank by three battalions.

On 24 February General Abrams was receiving a staff update briefing when the meeting was interrupted and he was handed a note. The note described the condition of the Lam Son helicopter fleet. The operationally ready (OR) rates were so low that the entire operation was at risk. All types of helicopters were involved, but the Charley Model OR rate was under 25 percent. Abrams was taken by surprise by this turn of events. Gen. Fredrick Weyand, Abrams's deputy, and Maj. Gen. John Carley, the deputy chief of staff for operations (or J-3), had just returned from Da Nang where they had discussed two specific issues with the XXIV Corps commander, General Sutherland. Sutherland, who had previously been granted priority of effort by Abrams, requested an additional CH-47 company to supply aviation fuel to Khe Sanh and an AWC (Aerial Weapons Company). He needed more gunships—but not Charley Models.

Brigadier General Smith, Sutherland's aviation expert, stated that the UH-1C gunships were inadequate. Carley suggested that XXIV Corps solve its gunship problem by transferring Cobras from the U.S.

23rd Infantry Division and replacing them with Charley Model gunships. Smith quickly rejected the proposal. He needed Cobras.

During his briefing, General Carley told Abrams, "the problem, I honestly believe, is one of maintenance."[12] The cross-border attack had been underway for over two weeks, aviation units had been subjected to punishing antiaircraft fire, and Carley characterized the situation as a maintenance problem! Abrams exploded: "The way this thing is supposed to work is that, once I said *what* the priorities were and *what* was going to be done around here, *goddamn it* . . . USARV's [United States Army Vietnam's] responsible to have maintenance people up there, keeping track of this, *goddamn it*! And they should know what is happening! That's their job!" Abrams turned to his deputy, General Weyand, for his thoughts. Weyand responded:

> Well, I guess I'm not too forgiving on Jock [Sutherland]. I recognize the truth in what you're saying but goddamn it, you've got a corps commander up there who is supposed to be keeping track of every fucking bird in the place every hour of the day. . . . You've got an organizational problem of some kind. He just doesn't know what the hell is going on. A battalion on [Route] 914 for two days before he knew about it—we knew about it—tells me that the coordination and tie-in between his headquarters and Lam's is not fully effective. I think we have an organizational problem. . . . and [in] reference [to] the UH-1C problem[,] it sounds to me like General Smith has gone completely ape. Those aircraft can't be totally ineffective.[13]

This exchange between Abrams and his staff reveals more than just the fact that the Lam Son helicopter fleet was in trouble. The MACV staff was not keeping up with the battle. It was apparently depending on routine reports to keep its commander informed, and Lam Son 719 was far from being a routine operation. It also reveals the pervasive ignorance about aviation matters that permeated much of the army's senior officer corps. America's involvement in the Vietnam War had been going on for the past ten years, and helicopters came of age during this period. But that was not to say that there was anyone in that conference room that had firsthand experience in helicopter warfare. These were officers that, for the most part, were veterans of World War II. Attempts to rectify the gap in senior officer knowledge of aviation operations included sending senior officers to a VIP version of flight school. This effort produced marginal results. While the senior officers may have mastered the elementary skills of flying, the VIP flight school could not replace experience.

It is difficult to understand why Abrams allowed himself to be surprised by the report. Lam Son 719 was an operation of great personal interest to President Nixon, and common sense dictated that he should have had a greater knowledge of day-to-day events. Apparently his staff took the same hands-off approach.

The second disturbing aspect of this exchange is the reaction of the J-3. While Southerland and his staff were guilty of failing to raise the issue before the situation was nearly in a state of collapse, it is obvious that Southerland—or more specifically Brigadier General Smith—brought the matter to the J-3's attention and that the J-3 gave Southerland and Smith the classic "staff shuffle." Instead of taking a proactive approach and solving the problem, the J-3 said, "put the request in command channels, we will look at it and give the boss our recommendation"— staff language for "hell no." This reaction, followed by the J-3's off-the-cuff remark that attributed the situation to a "maintenance problem," could have been avoided had the J-3 flown one mission into Laos.

When questioned by Abrams, General Weyand placed a portion of the blame on Lt. Gen. Sutherland. Abrams ordered the acting commander of the 1st Aviation Brigade, Colonel Cockerham, to meet him at Sutherland's office in Da Nang. When Cockerham arrived, at approximately 1300 hours on Monday, Abrams's tirade at Sutherland was still in progress. Abrams asked Cockerham how long it would take to bring the Lam Son fleet back up to an OR rate of 80 percent, and Cockerham replied that the job would be done by Wednesday evening. This was an impossible task; the entire aviation maintenance chain was already working at full capacity, and aviation maintenance officers were near the point of physical exhaustion. But the situation was about to improve.

Knowing that he had Abrams's full authority backing him, Cockerham partially restored the fleet through a mass infusion of replacement aircraft, transferred from other units throughout Vietnam, and additional aviation units. At 2230 hours on 24 February, the same day that Abrams had learned of the problem, Colonel Davis, the commander of the 101st Aviation Group, was asked if he would accept an aerial weapons company (AWC) instead of the two ARA batteries he had requested; he accepted.[14] An Aerial Weapons Company had the same number of Cobras as two ARA batteries. In addition to the 235th AWC, the MACV also ordered one ARA battery (B Battery, 2nd Battalion, 20th ARA) to move north to support Lam Son 719. B Battery arrived and was infused into the 4th Battalion, 77th ARA, providing each of its batteries with an additional platoon. Charley Model gunships were rounded up from all over Vietnam and sent to the 14th and 223rd CABs. This action filled the shortages of these two battalions, but the success was temporary. The replacement Charley Models fared no better than the original fleet. In addition to transferring aircraft from other units in Vietnam and sending additional aviation companies as temporary reinforcements, USARV sent an immediate message to the Department of the Army requesting emergency shipment of additional AH-1G Cobras from the United States. Twenty-four AH-1Gs and eleven UH-1Cs were released from depots and immediately shipped, and another fifteen AH-1Gs followed, shipped on a priority basis. Eight more were shipped in March.[15]

THE FALL OF FSB 31

After the NVA overran Ranger North and General Lam ordered the withdrawal from Ranger South to FSB 30, the NVA's 64th Regiment, reinforced by the 9th Tank Company, intensified its attack on Fire Support Base 31 with a coordinated tank-infantry attack, supported by artillery and rocket fire.[16] FSB 31 had been under intense pressure since the second week in Laos, and General Dong, the commander of the airborne division, made two unsuccessful attempts to reinforce it. The first attempt was the insertion of the 6th Airborne Battalion, the battalion that had faltered and was extracted on 19 February and had not been replaced. His second effort was an attempt to reinforce FSB 31 with a combined armored and infantry task force from the 1st Armored Brigade, operating along Route 9 in the vicinity of Objective A Loui.[17] Accounts of the battle at FSB 31 tell conflicting stories.[18]

At the onset of operations in Laos, the 3rd Airborne Battalion (with its 31st, 32nd, 33rd, and 34th Infantry Companies) and the 3rd Brigade Headquarters landed at FSB 31 and were quickly followed by a 105mm artillery battery. Two infantry companies went out to patrol the surrounding area, and two remained behind to defend the base. By 25 February two of the infantry companies, the 31st and the 32nd, were still patrolling north of FSB 31. The 34th Infantry Company—under-strength as the result of casualties sustained earlier—and the 33rd Infantry Company were at FSB 31.[19] As NVA pressure on the northern flank and FSB 31 intensified, a reinforcing column was ordered to move north from FSB A Loui to FSB 31. According to Maj. Gen. Nguyen Duy Hinh's account, in *Lam Son 719*, the 31st and 32nd companies received orders from the airborne division commander to move south and link up with a reinforcing column, composed of the 17th Armored Cavalry Squadron and two companies of the 8th Airborne Battalion.[20] The first major conflict in the accounts of the battle concerns the orders given to the relief column. Fulghum and Maitland's account of the battle, in *South Vietnam on Trial*, is based, in part, on an interview with Col. Arthur Pence, the senior advisor to the ARVN's airborne division, and makes no mention of the 8th Airborne Battalion. According to this account, Col. Nguyen Trong Luat, the ARVN 1st Armored Brigade's commander, refused to follow Major General Dong's order, even after General Lam, the I Corps's Commander, repeated it.

Gen. Donn Starry, in *Mounted Combat in Vietnam*, disagrees. Starry, who also makes no mention of the 8th Airborne Battalion, states that the 17th Armored Task Force received conflicting orders from I Corps and the airborne division. According to Starry, I Corps ordered the 17th Armored Cavalry to move north from A Loui to reinforce Landing Zone 31, and the airborne division ordered it to stop south of the landing zone and wait to see if the site was overrun. As a result of the confusion, the 17th Armored Cavalry, reinforced with tanks from the 11th Armored Cavalry, arrived at Landing Zone 31 on 19 February, after some airborne elements had been pushed back. By Starry's account, the 17th Armored Squadron and one airborne battalion continued to hold FSB 31 for six days, until they were pushed back by intense NVA direct and indirect fire.[21] General Hinh states that the armored task force was "on its way" to FSB 31 when it fought a major battle with the NVA on 25 February.[22]

The next controversy concerning the fall of FSB 31 involves the United States Air Force. According to General Hinh, the 31st Infantry Company, operating south of FSB 31, reported enemy armor moving in the area at 1100 hours on 25 February. The artillery battery at FSB 31 began firing on the tanks and called for artillery support from FSB 30 and FSB A Loui. There was no FAC present due to an error in grid coordinates, and by the time the FAC arrived at 1400 hours, FSB 31 was surrounded, and NVA tanks had reached the south side of the defensive perimeter. The first sorties of tactical air support aircraft destroyed a number of tanks on the southern perimeter and managed to force the remaining tanks to withdraw. Then, at 1520 hours, twenty NVA tanks, supported by infantry, attacked from the northwest and east. At same time, an F-4 fighter-bomber was shot down, and both the pilot and weapons system officer ejected. According to Hinh, the FAC departed the area to direct a search-and-rescue effort for the downed aircrew. With the FAC gone, close air support ended, and FSB 31 was overrun. Hinh speculates that FSB 31 could have held if the FAC had remained on station and air strikes had continued.[23]

The USAF account of this incident in *Project CHECO* [*Contemporary Historical Examination of Current Operations*] Report gives a different version. According to that report, air support was terminated at 1540 hours due to a thunderstorm that made air support impossible until 1735.[24] In the narrative description of the action at FSB 31, contained on pages 57 and 58 of the *CHECO Report*, there is no mention of an F-4 being shot down or a USAF search and rescue operation. However, sixty-five pages later in the *CHECO Report*, Figure 17, located between pages 122 and 123, lists an F-4 shot down at coordinates near FSB 31 and indicates that a search-and-rescue operation was mounted.

The 101st Aviation Group duty log for 25 February supports Hinh's version. An entry at 1625 hours states that the air cavalry observed an F-4 being shot down and two pilots ejecting and parachuting to the ground at grid coordinates southeast of FSB 31.[25] The report also states that the air cavalry's attempts to rescue the pilots were turned back by intense ground fire.[26] The duty log contains further evidence supporting Hinh's account: at 1630 hours Lt. Col. Kirklighter, commanding officer of the 223rd CAB, terminated his battalion's effort to complete the extraction at Hotel 2 and the insertions at LZs Don and Delta 1 due to a "lack of TACAIR," but reported that his battalion would continue resupply sorties elsewhere in the area of operations. Army aviation continued to fly until 1855 hours, when the weather shut down air operations.[27]

There is little doubt that the USAF abandoned support of FSB 31 and diverted all air assets in the immediate vicinity to attempt to rescue the downed aircrew. After a contentious meeting in the tactical operations center, Col. Arthur Pence, the senior U.S. advisor to the ARVN airborne division, subsequently leaked the matter to the press and was immediately relieved of his duties by General Sutherland, and Gen. Benjamin Harrison, the senior advisor to the ARVN 1st Infantry Division, was assigned the dual responsibility as advisor to the airborne division.[28]

Enemy fire continued to pound the airborne troops. The Communists overran FSB 31 on 25 February and captured the commanding officer and executive officer of the 3rd Airborne Brigade. Within a few hours of his capture, the brigade commander was on the radio calling for ARVN soldiers to lay down their weapons and surrender.[29]

The USAF's search-and-rescue operation failed to recover the downed aircrew before nightfall on 25 February, and the operation continued on the following day. Seventy-five fighter-bomber sorties were expended, but the crew was eventually rescued.[30]

After Landing Zone 31 was lost, the 17th Armored Cavalry and the surviving 8th Airborne Battalion troops were isolated southeast of the fire support base. Enemy pressure on the armored cavalry remained heavy, and this battle continued into the following week. On 27 February the ARVN force, supported by tactical air and air cavalry helicopter gunships, reported destroying fifteen tanks while losing three armored cavalry assault vehicles. Later, on 1 March, still southeast of Landing Zone 31, the ARVN armored cavalry was attacked again. In this battle, which lasted throughout the night, the cavalry was supported by South Vietnamese artillery, U.S. tactical air strikes, and air cavalry gunships. Fifteen enemy tanks were destroyed, and the 17th Armored Task Force lost six armored cavalry assault vehicles.[31] On 3 March the 17th Cavalry moved south to more defensible ground and fought a delaying action until it rejoined the 1st Brigade at A Loui.

After the fall of FSB 31, the ARVN force concluded that it was not equipped to deal with an NVA armored threat. It was a role reversal of sorts. Throughout the war the NVA had been forced to deal with allied armor, but the allied forces had not been exposed to an armor threat except for a brief exchange at Ben Het in 1969 (when U.S. forces were equipped with M-48 tanks and the NVA was equipped with the light amphibious PT-76) and during the siege of Khe Sanh in 1968 (when the NVA had used PT-76s at the Lang Vei Special Forces camp). Although the ARVN was equipped with the M-72 LAW (light antitank weapon), heretofore it had been used mainly as a "bunker buster"; the ARVN was not experienced in using this weapon to engage enemy armor. After its early engagements with tanks, the ARVN declared that the LAW was ineffective. In order to meet the threat, 90mm recoilless rifles and 3.5-inch rocket launchers (the obsolete predecessor to the 90mm) were gathered up from depots and rushed to the area of operations.[32] Subsequent tests of the M-72 LAW confirmed that it was an effective weapon—when properly employed.

From 26 to 28 February the 101st Aviation Group struggled to relocate the 3rd Infantry Regiment back to rim of the escarpment and complete the extraction of the remaining rangers, who were now located at FSB 30, back to Phu Loc. NVA pressure on FSB 30—the last remaining fire support base north of Route 9—continued to mount. In an effort to maintain security of Route 9, which was required for the eventual withdrawal of the 1st Armored Brigade, General Lam ordered the airborne division to establish two new fire support bases, Alpha and Bravo, along Route 9 between A Loui and the border of South Vietnam. The encirclement of ARVN forces was tightening and the NVA strength was growing. In the aftermath of Abrams's heated meeting with his staff and General Sutherland concerning the status of helicopter OR rates and poor coordination between the ARVN and U.S. Corps, XXIV Corps collocated a portion of its staff with ARVN TOC to create a joint coordination center.

Most of the action during the third week in Laos was on the north flank, in the airborne division's area of operation, with the 158th AHB heavily engaged in support. By the morning of the 26 February, D Company (the gun company) had only one set of flyable Cobras. Fortunately, the 227th AWC arrived at 2235 hours on the following day with nineteen Cobras.[33] On 28 February the last ARVN rangers were extracted from FSB 30, but the airborne battalion and field artillery continued to defend FSB 30.

The Communists were prepared to clean up this last FSB on the north flank. Prior to the fall of FSB 31, the ARVN 2nd Airborne Battalion at FSB 30 had come under attack by enemy artillery. The Communists stepped up their artillery and mortar attacks every time a resupply or medevac ship had attempted to land. Every resupply mission was necessarily a coordinated operation with air strikes, gunship, artillery, and air-delivered smoke screens to mask enemy observation. Even then, some helicopters had been shot down, others damaged, and some of the supply missions had been aborted.[34] Now supplies were running low, and the numbers of dead and wounded awaiting evacuation continued to increase.

THE DESTRUCTION OF FSB 30

FSB 30 was established on 8 February, the first day of operations in Laos, and was, at least by strength of numbers, the strongest ARVN position on the north flank. The 2nd Airborne Battalion and two batteries of field artillery occupied it. Two infantry companies defended the fire support base, and the two remaining companies conducted local patrols and search operations. By 11 February supplies of artillery ammunition were running low, and a tactical emergency was declared. An emergency resupply was completed by CH-47s escorted by Cobras, while tactical air strikes and artillery fire suppressed enemy gunners. Resupply became increasingly difficult as enemy strength grew and air defense weapons choked the air avenues of approach to the fixed ARVN positions. By 26 February it became clear that FSB 30 was under siege. Over the next four days the 158th Aviation Battalion continued efforts to extract the ARVN rangers while resupplying the artillery batteries and the 2nd Airborne Battalion and evacuating the dead and wounded. In the meantime, the volume of enemy artillery fire on FSB 30 steadily increased. As the end of the third week in Laos approached, elements of the NVA's 308th Division attacked FSB 30.

At 0100 hours on 1 March the NVA launched a ground attack on FSB 30. Intense artillery fires preceded the attack, and as daylight broke, a combined force of NVA infantry supported by armor made its way to the outer defenses. FSB 30 was located on a high mountain with steep slopes. The enemy armor did not attempt to negotiate the side of the mountain, but instead took up positions well out of antitank weapons range and engaged the defenders with direct fire.[35] AC-130 gunships and two B-52 Arc Light sorties were diverted to support the ARVN defenders. With the defenders at FSB 30 decisively engaged and the 17th Armored Squadron in heavy contact, NVA armor began to appear on Route 9. Eight NVA tanks were spotted by AC-130 gunships near Route 9, approximately eight kilometers west of A Loui. The gunships attacked, destroying an undetermined number of tanks. Later, USAF strike aircraft spotted and attacked two T-54 tanks south of Route 9, between A Loui and the Vietnamese border.[36] The ARVN force had enemy tanks in its rear.

The effort to resupply FSB 30 continued on 2 March. UH-1H aircraft delivered supplies and evacuated the killed and wounded. At 1105 hours Lt. Col. William Peachey, the 158th battalion commander, reported that the evacuation effort was continuing in the face of light mortar fire, but they were having difficulty getting the troops to leave their bunkers and assist in loading the dead and wounded.[37] By 1200 hours Peachey was having a different problem: the only soldiers that were supposed to be extracted were the killed and wounded, but now the healthy, including the 2nd Airborne Battalion commander, were leaving their bunkers and boarding the UH-1Hs. Peachey immediately suspended the mission and met with the U.S. senior advisor to the airborne division. The 101st Aviation Group commander, Colonel Davis, raised the issue to the G-3 of XXIV Corps, who in turn contacted the ARVN I Corps. At 1340 hours XXIV Corps notified the 101st Aviation Group that the ARVN Corps had no knowledge of a planned extraction of FSB 30.[38] General Lam's orders to the airborne forces were to break out of the encirclement at FSB 30 and conduct mobile operations.[39] It appears that the 2nd Airborne Battalion, led by its commander, was attempting to "bug out." But circumstances and orders soon changed.

Five minutes later an FAC reported that ten NVA tanks were in the vicinity of FSB 30. Less than an hour later, the 101st Group received a report that "most of the ammunition hauled to A Loui today is burning and rounds are cooking off [exploding]." At 1504 hours a liaison officer reported that General Lam had now approved the extraction. But the extraction was still on hold; Brig. Gen. Sidney Berry, the assistant division commander of the 101st Airborne Division, held up execution until confirmation was received from General Sutherland. That confirmation came half an hour later at 1538 hours.

One minute later the 2nd Squadron, 17th Cavalry, reported that LZ 30 was taking incoming and was on fire. All thoughts of attempting to extract the artillery batteries were quickly discarded. There was no way the big CH-47s and -54s could survive incoming artillery as well as the detonations of burning ARVN artillery ammunition. General Berry sent instructions to attempt the extraction of the killed and wounded. At 1616 hours the air cavalry reported that FSB 30 had taken another hit and the smoke from the fire was over a mile high. This report was quickly followed by a report that A Loui was being hit with the same type of heavy artillery that was hitting FSB 30. The explosions were two to three hundred feet high.

General Berry launched his command and control aircraft and arrived at the scene. At 1643 he informed the 101st Group that the entire landing zone was now just a series of explosions. Extraction of the killed and wounded was left to the discretion of Lt. Col. Peachey, the commander of the 158th AHB. While Peachey prepared the 158th for the extraction, Colonel Davis flew to FSB 30. Davis reported that the ammunition on the ground was continuing to explode. The commander on the ground cancelled the extraction stating that there was no way his people could get out of their holes, even if the helicopters managed to land. Already airborne, the 158th diverted and continued its efforts to evacuate the dead and wounded from the 1st Armored Brigade Task Force that was still in contact with the enemy following the fall of FSB 31. The 158th continued efforts to extract the killed and wounded of the 17th Armored Task Force, the 8th Airborne Battalion, and the survivors of FSB 31 and FSB 30 for the next three days.[40]

By the conclusion of the third week in Laos, the ARVN forces were preparing to continue their offensive. But the delays of the past two weeks had provided the NVA time to concentrate its forces around the fire support bases on the northern flank of the penetration. FSB 30, the last remaining ARVN bastion on the north flank, was surrounded and under heavy NVA mortar and artillery attack. The 17th Armored Squadron and elements of the 8th Airborne

Battalion were in contact with the enemy southeast of FSB 31. The crisis in helicopter availability was far from over, but MACV was scrambling replacement aircraft and reinforcing aviation units to the Lam Son 719 area of operations.

Chapter 10

ONWARD TO TCHEPONE

ARVN FORCES CONTINUED THEIR EFFORT to reach Tchepone during the fourth week in Laos, but at the cost of a staggering number of helicopters destroyed or damaged. Security on the north flank totally collapsed. NVA reinforcements continued to arrive while some ARVN forces left Laos and returned to South Vietnam. By early March the enemy strength in the area of operations had swelled to approximately 36,000, and additional troops were still on the way. Intelligence sources verified that the NVA 324th Division, the defenders of the A Shau Valley, arrived on the battlefield intent on turning back the ARVN incursion into Base Area 611. The ARVN force was outnumbered by a margin of more than two to one.

Enemy activity in the Lam Son rear area surged through the night of 28 February, involving units from the U.S. 1st Brigade, 5th Infantry Division, in the rear area. At 0730 hours on 1 March the 14th CAB reported that Vandergrift was taking mortar fire, and at 0750 hours D Company, 158th AHB, reported that the refueling point at Vandergrift was on fire. Forty thousand gallons of fuel were destroyed. Aircraft damage continued to mount; at one point, the airstrip at Khe Sanh was shut down until the Cobras and Charley Models that had come in on emergency landings could be cleared from the runway.[1]

In preparation for the renewed offensive, the 101st Airborne Division alerted its 3rd Brigade to be prepared to move up to the DMZ to relieve the ARVN 2nd Division and remain available as a corps reserve.[2]

To strengthen the defenses within South Vietnam against the rising tempo of NVA attacks, the U.S. 11th Brigade, 23rd Infantry Division, moved from its area of operations south of Da Nang to reinforce the 101st Airborne Division.[3] Brigadier General Berry, the assistant division commander of the 101st Airborne Division, was designated as the aviation officer for the operation and given the task of coordinating aviation support.[4]

On 1 March the 223rd CAB extracted the 2nd Battalion, 3rd Infantry Regiment, and returned the battalion to South Vietnam. The remainder of the regiment was extracted from the area around Hotel 2. The regiment's command post and 1st Battalion were inserted at Delta 1, and the 3rd Battalion was inserted at LZ Brown, on the high ground on the northern edge of the escarpment, south of Route 9.

President Thieu, who met with General Lam at the ARVN I Corps headquarters on 19 February, had decided that Tchepone was less important than the roads and trails leading out of the village and that elements of the ARVN 1st Infantry Division would move south along Route 92, cut Route 914, and continue movement northeast along Route 914 toward Tchepone.[5] This plan was apparently discarded sometime prior to 27 February, and by 28 February General Lam was in Saigon discussing another new plan with President Thieu. General Abrams apparently was not brought into this discussion until his meeting with President Thieu on 1 March.

President Nixon was growing impatient with the lack of progress and the number of changes in the plan for the assault on Tchepone. On 1 March 1971 Henry Kissinger asked Ambassador Bunker to meet privately with General Abrams and discuss Kissinger's concerns about how the operation was evolving. When Kissinger requested this meeting, he had no idea that the plan was being changed by Thieu and Lam yet again. Kissinger reminded Bunker that the president had approved Lam Son 719 on the premise that the operation would disrupt the trail network and undermine the enemy's capability to launch an offensive during the 1971 and 1972 dry seasons. The president had originally been told that the ARVN force would seize Tchepone four to five days after D-Day. When that time period had come and gone, the president had been told that weather and the condition of Route 9 had delayed progress, but that Tchepone would be seized eight to ten days after D-Day. Now the plan had been changed again; the president was being told that Tchepone was less important than cutting the trails southeast of Tchepone. Kissinger worried about the level of ARVN commitment. More specifically, he wondered why ARVN reserves had not been brought into the battle "at a time when the enemy has obviously committed his full resources."[6]

Bunker replied to Kissinger on 3 March, acknowledging that weather and enemy tactics had forced changes in the concept of the operation, but insisted that the overall goals were being met. Bunker said enemy traffic on Routes 9 and 92 had been eliminated and that the traffic on Route 914 had been greatly reduced.[7] Bunker's message temporarily alleviated concerns at the White House, but it was not entirely accurate. Traffic on Route 92 had been eliminated, and would continue to be eliminated as long as the ARVN airborne division and 1st Armored Brigade held the intersection of Routes 9 and 92 at Objective A Loui. But the NVA still held all of Route 9 west of A Loui, past Tchepone, to its intersection with southbound Route 23, another major branch of the Ho Chi Minh Trail. And, the 1st ARVN Division's presence on Route 914 was terminated when the 3rd Regiment encountered heavy NVA resistance, broke contact, and moved north. By the time Kissinger had received Bunker's message on 3 March, the revised plan for the assault on Tchepone was under way.

Westward movement toward Tchepone finally continued with a combat assault on LZ Lolo on 3 March. It was a defining day for the aviators flying the mission and the first test of "new management" since Abrams's outburst on 23 February and the resulting XXIV Corps efforts to field a functional tactical operations center. The results were horrific.

The 223rd CAB, the battalion that had been organized around a headquarters company that had been a fixed-wing airplane battalion until the last week in January, was assigned the mission of direct support of the 1st ARVN Division.[8] By 3 March the battalion and its commander were still an untested and unproven organization, and the battalion's helicopter fleet was reduced to the point that they could provide only a small fraction of the forty lift ships needed for operation. Instead, a fleet of forty UH-1Hs was assembled from the 223rd, 14th, and 101st Aviation Battalions. Plans called for the 561 members of the 1st Battalion, 1st Regiment, to be lifted to Lolo in three separate, forty-ship lifts. After the infantry was on the ground, heavy-lift helicopters would bring in bulldozers for construction of bunkers, artillery, and supplies. Two light fire teams of Charley Model gunships were assigned as escorts.[9]

The 14th CAB duty log for 2 March provides a glimpse of the preparations for the assault. The duty log states that the pickup zone would be at Kilo, located a few kilometers southwest of Khe Sanh near Route 9 and that the LZ would be "in the vicinity of Violet," at grid coordinates XD 3937. The combat assault was scheduled for 1000 hours, with the commander of the 223rd to lead as air mission commander. Four hours later a duty log entry amended the PZ to be FSB Delta and the LZ to be grid coordinates XD 431372, a location approximately five kilometers east of Violet, which would forever after be known as LZ Lolo.[10] Aircraft commanders and gunship team leaders attended a mission briefing at Khe Sanh at 0830 hours the following morning.

Dan Grigsby, a platoon leader and aircraft commander from the 71st AHC, attended the mission briefing. Both Grigsby and Gary Arne, another pilot who attended the mission briefing, recall questions by pilots concerning LZ preparation and gun cover for the insertion, questions that were seemingly dismissed by the briefing officer because the landing was supposed to be a "piece of cake."[11] The LZ was scheduled to be hit with a B-52 Arc Light the night before the CA, and enemy opposition was expected to be light.

While the mission briefing was in progress, the air force attempted to prepare the LZ. According to the *CHECO Report*, at "approximately 0800 hours" the FAC contacted the air mission commander, who informed the FAC where to put the ordnance around the LZ. Six sorties dropped a combination of 500-, 1,000-, and 2,000-pound bombs, all equipped with fuse extenders, to aid in LZ construction. These were followed by three more sorties that dropped a combination of 500- and 1,000-pound bombs in the tree lines north and south of the LZ, and CBUs (cluster bomb units) along the avenue of approach east of the LZ.[12]

The flight departed Khe Sanh as scheduled, en route to the PZ at Delta, and the air cavalry reconnoitered the landing zone. The combat assault on LZ Lolo was far from a prototypical event in which the troops boarded at a secure pickup zone, then were flown to what may be a hot landing zone. Rather, aircraft were taking fire en route to the pickup zone, in the pickup zone, and at the landing zone. The lead company, the 71st AHC, managed to pick up their passengers and depart the PZ without incident. But by the time A Company, 101st AHB, arrived at Delta, the PZ was taking mortar fire, and the Charley Model guns assigned to escort the lift apparently became involved in attempts to suppress fires around the PZ.[13]

Jesse Dize, an aircraft commander of a UH-1H from the 48th Aviation Company, was shot down west of the PZ, near LZ Brown, well short of LZ Lolo. He described the situation as "sort of like being thrown out of the game before entering the stadium."[14] When the call went out over the radio that Dize had been shot down, Doug Womack, Chalk 3 in the flight and somewhere ahead of Dize, grasped the seriousness of the situation: aircraft were being shot down, and they weren't even at the LZ yet.[15] NVA mortars, machine guns, and infantry were dug in at and around Lolo, and the air cavalry had failed to detect the enemy trenches and field fortifications during their LZ reconnaissance. When the lead lift ships arrived, the NVA opened up with a withering barrage.

Understandably, veteran accounts of the action at Lolo contain conflicting details. Every crew was totally focused on its task at hand, and the fog of war was thickened by the fast pace of events. Some veterans report that no gunship support was present. One of the Charley Model's deficits was airspeed, and presumably, the gun teams were delayed by their efforts to suppress the enemy at the PZ. But Charley Model gunships were there and made one, possibly two, gun runs before being shot down. Three Charley Models were hit in the vicinity of Lolo between 1000 and 1015 hours.[16] The limited number of gunships on station simply did not have enough firepower to suppress a determined, and numerically superior, enemy force, let alone survive, and the Charley Model gunships were out of their depth. The air mission commander (AMC), Lieutenant Colonel Kirklighter, the commanding officer of the 233rd Aviation Battalion, immediately requested all available gunships.[17] None were close at hand, but he did not suspend the assault until nearly an hour later. Multiple entries in the 101st Aviation Group's duty log indicate that this was a mistake, one that Lt. Col. Bill Peachey, the commanding officer of the 158th Aviation Battalion and a veteran of the extraction at FSB Ripcord, would have been unlikely to make.

Dan Grigsby was the flight lead. When he arrived at the LZ, he quickly determined that the conditions were far removed from what had been briefed and called for the assault to be suspended until either additional prep of the LZ was completed or more gunship support arrived. The air mission commander refused, and Grigby's was the first ship in. His passengers were all killed, either as he decelerated or as they left the ship. Gary Arne was in Chalk 2. Just prior to touching down in the landing zone, his tail rotor and hydraulics were shot out. The loss of the tail rotor caused the Huey to go into a violent spin; his ARVN passengers were flung out and, in all probability, killed on impact. Arne was able to maneuver his crippled ship over the escarpment before he crashed. He and his crew were able to make their way back to the LZ and take cover in one of the trenches that had been dug by the NVA prior to the air assault until they could be extracted.

Womack went in third. He made a 360-degree turn, waiting for the reply as to whether or not the lift was going to be suspended. When it became clear that the lift was still on, Womack made a straight-in approach. His load of ARVN was probably the first to survive the insertion, at least temporarily. While he was hovering and his ARVN disembarked, his ship was hit by AK-47 fire and fragments from an RPG that hit a stump rather than his aircraft. Womack's ship was seriously damaged, but he managed to nurse it back to Khe Sanh.[18] Kerry McMahon, Chalk 4, was shot down, and his aircraft burned in the LZ. Chalk 5 extracted the crew from McMahon's aircraft. In all, nineteen ships went into the LZ. The ten aircraft from the 71st were all hit; five of them were shot down, and two of those five were destroyed. A Company, 101st AHB, had six ships hit, and two were destroyed. The 48th had one lift ship destroyed en route to the LZ, and three of its Charley Models were hit and unable to continue the mission.[19]

At 1057 hours Lieutenant Colonel Kirklighter finally notified the group headquarters that he was suspending the lift. At this point, twenty loads of ARVN soldiers were still aboard aircraft, which left those on the ground—the portion of the ARVN landing force that had survived the initial attempt, as well as the downed aircrews—in a precarious situation.

When the flight arrived back at Khe Sanh, Womack cannibalized parts from Ed Albrick's ship to repair his own, while the other crews inspected their aircraft and, in some cases, swapped damaged ships for aircraft with less damage.[20] Womack also combined the two ships' crews. The pilots gathered to talk about the situation. They were determined to go back, deliver another load of ARVN soldiers, and pick up the downed aircrews on Lolo.[21] In the meantime, the group TOC advised XXIV Corps that they needed all the aircraft that had been supporting the 1st Brigade, 5th Mechanized, as well as the aircraft on corps general support missions, and notified the group rear TOC at Camp Eagle to send ten more aircraft and crews to Khe Sanh by 1300 hours.[22]

Major Bob Clewell, the commanding officer of A Company, 101st AHB, led the second effort. After refueling and returning to PZ Delta for another load, Clewell's group of determined pilots was on its way back to Lolo. The first slick got in and out of the LZ at 1304 hours, but the second slick went in and was immediately shot down, and no more than four aircraft made it in to the LZ before the second effort was suspended at 1320 hours. The TACAIR sorties that continued efforts to silence enemy guns around Lolo failed. More air strikes were called in, and an Arc Light strike was scheduled for 1500 hours.[23]

Forty lift ships cranked for the third lift at 1518 hours, and all available gunships supported the flight. The first ship went into the LZ at approximately 1545 hours. The helicopters were still under fire and taking hits, but the ARVN on the ground had eliminated many of the enemy on and immediately around the LZ. At 1600 hours Colonel Davis reported that all forty sorties had been in and out.

※※※※

The combat assault at LZ Lolo is one of the most controversial events of Lam Son 719. The shock waves continued to reverberate in the concentric hallways of the Pentagon long after Lam Son's conclusion. Nine helicopters had been destroyed and forty-four had been damaged at, or en route to, the LZ.[24] It was a poorly planned, uncoordinated blunder. The absence of adequate gunship escorts had proved disastrous. The escorts available had been too few and of the wrong type.

The Charley Models were beyond their depth, but still, one additional team could have been available except for the interference of the XXIV Corps staff. It is safe to assume that after General Abrams had first heard the facts of helicopter availability rates on February 23, he had lit a fire under XXIV Corps. While the renewed interest of the corps commander and his staff was probably beneficial, it had come at a price. Early in the operation XXIV Corps directed the 101st Aviation Group to supply one, and sometimes two, UH-1H helicopters to transport reporters to areas of interest in Vietnam. It was not unusual for reporters to catch a ride on helicopters on a space-available basis, but dedicating aircraft to the press was extraordinary. However, the MACV imposed rules prohibiting transporting members of the press into Laos on U.S. helicopters—a rule that chaffed members of the press who were constantly underfoot and complaining. On or about 26 February the MACV relaxed the prohibition, and the XXIV Corps public information officer generated a requirement for the Aviation Group to provide dedicated helicopters to transport reporters into Laos as well as escort gunships and a chase ship to follow the flight in case it was needed.[25] This order defied logic: operational helicopters, and gunships in particular, were in short supply, and on 3 March a team of Charley Model gunships that should have been supporting the combat assault at Lolo was instead escorting members of the press to LZ Delta 1.[26]

In addition, President Thieu intervened and demanded last-minute changes to the planned assault on Lolo, delaying execution and compromising the element of surprise. On the afternoon of 28 February General Lam flew to Saigon to confer with President Thieu concerning a change of plans. Thieu wanted the VNMC to relieve the airborne division. Lam convinced Thieu that the VNMC should relieve the 1st ARVN Division's 2nd Regiment and that the 2nd Regiment should make the assault on Lolo. The 2nd ARVN Regiment was already committed, operating on the south flank of the penetration, and in contact with the enemy.[27] Relieving the 2nd ARVN Regiment while simultaneously replacing it with the VNMC and preparing the 2nd Regiment for the air assault on Tchepone would take time, and Lam had already set in motion the preparations for the assault on Lolo when he had given the grid coordinates for the Commando Vault bomb that would clear the LZ. General Abrams was not notified of the change until the following day.

Thieu's motivation to relieve the airborne division is not completely clear, but by 28 February it was becoming apparent that the 3rd Airborne Brigade was failing in its mission to hold the north flank. The 3rd Brigade Commander had been captured three days earlier, when the NVA overran FSB 31. While Thieu's move to relieve the airborne division may have been justified, the timing was terrible. Lam's alternative was even worse. The VNMC brigades were still uncommitted, in reserve, and the air assault on Lolo could have been launched in less time giving the NVA less time to prepare their defenses and the operation could have been launched from a relatively secure PZ in South Vietnam alleviating the need for the escorting gunships to suppress enemy fires at the PZ and allowing more of the gunships to support the landing.

The delay resulting from shifting the assault mission first from the 2nd Airborne Brigade to the VNMC, and then again shifting the mission to the 2nd ARVN Regiment, disrupted the timing of an operation that was underway after the air force dropped the Commando Vault bomb. It took two days to prepare the 2nd Regiment for Lam's new plan. Given the delay, the Commando Vault bomb that blasted away the trees on Lolo was dropped far too early and compromised the location of the LZ. But apparently no one gave any thought to selecting a new location for Lolo.

The expectation that the LZ would be prepped with a B-52 strike led to an assumption that minimal gunship support would be needed. The experience of the past three weeks, however, should have led to the conclusion that two teams of Charley Model gunships were insufficient; XXIV Corps had already argued that these gunships were handicapped in the Lam Son environment. Eight B-52 Arc Light sorties went in at 0455 hours on 3 March, on grid coordinates provided by General Lam. The closest point of impact was one kilometer south of Lolo.[28]

Because of the problems posed by eleventh-hour changes in plans, greater than expected enemy resistance, and insufficient gunship support, the heavy lift and logistical missions scheduled for Lolo on 3 March were not completed. The senior advisor to the ARVN division informed the TOC that the ARVN division planned to continue with the next step to Tchepone, the assault on LZ Liz on 4 March, as previously scheduled, then later return to complete the Lolo sorties.[29]

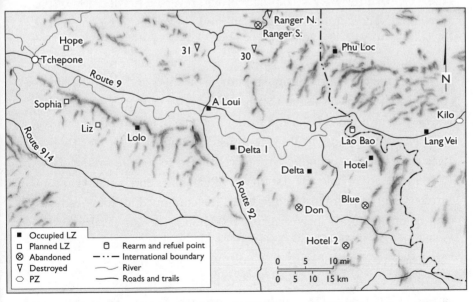

Map 5. ARVN positions at the end of 3 March 1971. Drawn by Bill Nelson. Copyright ©
2014 by The University of Oklahoma Press.

※※※※

Landing Zone Liz was located approximately seven kilometers west of Lolo on the escarpment. At 2330 hours on 3 March General Berry announced the air preparation plans for LZ Liz. The west side of Liz would be hit with eight B-52 Arc Light sorties before daylight, eight tactical air sorties at 0710 hours, twelve CBU sorties at 0940 hours, and two air-delivered smoke sorties; meanwhile, the ARVN 155mm artillery at A Loui would work over the east side of the LZ. In addition to the normal escort gunships, four sets of guns would be on standby and two sets of guns would cap the mission.[30]

The Commando Vault bomb that cleared the LZ had been deployed on 1 March, giving the enemy forewarning, just as the early bombing of Lolo had done. Fourteen B-52 sorties hit Liz and the surrounding area during the early morning hours of 4 March, the last hitting at 0635 hours, and by 0720 hours USAF strike aircraft were beginning the air preparation. Thirteen sorties were completed by 0945 hours. Unfortunately this assault was doomed when the senior advisor informed the TOC that the ARVN commander had reversed his decision of the previous evening: now he wanted all the Lolo sorties to be completed before starting the assault on Liz.

The air assault on Lolo had not been completed on 3 March as planned, and the effort continued into the morning and early afternoon of 4 March. After an initial weather delay, the 1st Battalion, 1st Regiment, was inserted at Lolo, and sorties bringing in bulldozers to prepare ARVN positions and artillery continued throughout the day. The LZ was cold, but the incoming aircraft continued to receive fire from the ridgeline south of Lolo. The 1st Infantry Regiment's 2nd Battalion and an artillery battery were inserted at Lolo. The continued lift into Lolo was not completed until approximately 1500 hours. The air cavalry reconnoitered Liz and drew heavy automatic weapons fire. General Berry held up the air assault until additional airstrikes could be brought in.[31]

It was the dry season in Laos, and a continuous arc of fire burned around LZ Liz, reducing visibility to less than one quarter mile at times.

The first ship into the LZ landed at 1717 hours, and by 1731 hours the thirty-first and final ship of the first lift cleared the LZ. The second lift of thirty-one ships started at 1745 hours and was completed at 1805 hours. Eighteen aircraft had been hit and one destroyed, but the 4th Battalion, 1st Regiment, was on the ground—one step closer to Tchepone.

At the same time, the VNMC brigades were lifted into LZs Hotel and Delta to secure the southeast shoulder of the penetration and intercept the NVA regiments that were moving north from Base Area 611 in an attempt to cut off the ARVN route of withdrawal. With the combat damage from the past two days of operations, the Lam Son helicopter fleet was below 50 percent operational, even with the replacement aircraft that had been pumped in after the meeting between Abrams, Sutherland, and Cockerham on February 24.

The 1st ARVN Division took another step closer to Tchepone on 5 March when the 4th and 5th Infantry Battalions of the 2nd Regiment, and an artillery battery, were lifted to LZ Sophia. Unlike the movement of the 1st Regiment to LZs Lolo and Liz, this combat assault had the advantage of starting from a relatively secure pickup zone at Khe Sanh. But after loading the troops, the flight received antiaircraft fire all the way from the Vietnamese border to LZ Sophia. Improved planning and execution bolstered success at Sophia. Unlike LZs Lolo and Liz, the Commando Vault bombs had not been dropped early, and the location of the LZ was not compromised. Rather five Arc Light strikes were completed by 0610 hours, and a sixth Arc Light strike hit at 0740 hours, followed by tactical air strikes. The tactical air strikes and LZ construction with Commando Vaults and Daisy Cutters began at 0745 hours and took three hours. At the end of the construction phase, the air force raked the area with thirty-six tactical airstrikes. In the meantime, howitzers, artillery ammunition, bulldozers, and bunker construction materials were rigged for delivery by heavy lift helicopters. LZ reconnaissance began at 0820 hours, and preparation started at 0830 hours.[32] At 1240 the slicks cranked and arrived at the Kilo PZ at 1250. At 1315 hours the first slick arrived at Sophia, and by 1328 the LZ was obscured with a smoke preparation.[33]

At 1333 hours Captain David Nelson, the same Captain Nelson shot down while attempting to rescue Specialist Fuji on 20 February, reported that his aircraft was hit in the LZ. According to the 223rd CAB duty log, Nelson reported that the crew chief was wounded in the head and several of the ARVN on board were wounded. He departed the LZ on a heading of 100 degrees. After the other aircraft had disembarked their troops and were on their way back to the fire support base, some of the other crewmen said they saw a chopper, which they believed to be Nelson's, burst into flames, crash, and explode. As soon as the ball of flame was observed, attempts were made to establish radio contact. There was no response. Enemy antiaircraft fire and ground activity made a search-and-rescue effort impossible. All aboard the aircraft were declared killed in action, but their bodies were not recovered until September 17, 1990.[34] By the time troop insertion was completed at 1646 hours, six more aircraft had been shot down.[35] Heavy lift of artillery and supplies was underway. While the lift into Sophia drew little enemy fire compared to the insertion at Lolo, the NVA air defense gunners were active all along the routes east of Sophia. Eighteen aircraft were damaged and two were shot down.[36]

While the combat assault into Sophia was underway, a maintenance UH-1H from the 174th AHC, with a crew of four and three additional men on board to assist in field repairs or rigging aircraft for recovery, went down approximately one kilometer west of A Loui. The alternate command-and-control aircraft immediately diverted to attempt to assist the downed aircrew. But as the pilot approached the location, his engine failed and he announced that he would attempt to autorotate to A Loui. A Dust Off aircraft went in to rescue the crew and managed to get one pilot on board before being driven off by enemy fire. The air cavalry immediately launched the Hac Bao, an elite ARVN reconnaissance company, to attempt the rescue but did not have enough gunships to cover the insertion.[37] The crew managed to find a hiding place after skirmishes with the enemy.

On the following day an air force search-and-rescue team attempted to rescue of the downed crew. During the four hours of continuous airstrikes that supported the operation, one A-1E "Sky Raider" was shot down, and a CH-53 "Jolly Green Giant" received extensive damage. The USAF search-and-rescue attempt failed, and the crew remained on the ground, running low on ammunition, water, and hope. Later that afternoon General Berry, call sign Big Ben, called the stranded crew members and told them that one more attempt would be made to rescue them. At 1815 hours the air cavalry, supported by air strikes, gunships, and artillery, successfully inserted the Hac Bao approximately one kilometer from the stranded aircrew. The reconnaissance company immediately moved off the landing zone and encountered the enemy in close combat. Throughout the night the Communists engaged the Hac Bao with small arms, and the Hac Bao responded with hand grenades. The following morning the Hac Bao started a series of grass fires to flush out the enemy and provide smoke to cover its movements. The company linked up with the downed aircrew, moved to a landing zone, and both groups were extracted by late afternoon. While ten Hac Bao soldiers were wounded during the two-day operation, the company killed approximately sixty Communists.[38]

The NVA could probably have killed or captured the downed crew at will. But this crew was more valuable to the NVA alive than dead, because it served as bait for the search-and-rescue effort the NVA knew would follow, which would cause air assets to be diverted to the rescue attempt. During its later debriefing, the crew reported hearing the sounds of vehicles making repeated trips to and from the downed aircraft. The NVA was dismantling and carrying away the aircraft, piece by piece. While the crew did not see the vehicles, it reported that the vehicles sounded like electric golf carts, which, if correct, was a clever use of technology; electric motors produce less heat, making the vehicles less susceptible to detection by infrared surveillance devices.[39]

The assault on Tchepone continued on 6 March. The two remaining battalions, the regimental reconnaissance company, and the command post of the 2nd Infantry Regiment landed at LZ Hope, overlooking the village of Tchepone. As 120 UH-1H aircraft assembled at Khe Sanh to execute the combat assault, B-52s and TACAIR hammered the landing zone, while the 2nd Squadron, 17th Cavalry, conducted reconnaissance in and beyond Tchepone. But NVA gunners pelted the assembly area at Khe Sanh with 122mm rockets, forcing the assault to launch ahead of schedule.

The reinvigorated involvement of the XXIV Corps and 101st Airborne Division TOCs played a role in the tardy, but successful, raid on Tchepone. The XXIV Corps positioned its forward operations center adjacent to the ARVN 1st Corps' operations center, expediting the coordination of support. General Berry's actions as the aviation officer pulled together the dwindling air assets for the huge airmobile assaults on Lolo, Liz, Sophia, and Hope. An air assault of this magnitude, deep into heavily contested territory, bristling with enemy air defense batteries, was unprecedented. The allied forces learned from the mistakes at LZ Lolo and massed superior, coordinated aerial firepower to pave the way to Liz, Sophia, and Hope.

The NVA began to react to the ARVN's presence in the Tchepone area on 7 March. NVA artillery and mortars hit Fire Support Base Lolo, an attack by fire that persisted throughout the day, hit the last remaining fire support base that could influence the action on the north flank, Fire Support Base A Loui, delaying and complicating resupply and evacuation missions. But the ARVN had reached Tchepone. Unfortunately, this successful move to Tchepone was counterbalanced by more NVA successes and ARVN failures: blocking positions on the north flank collapsed, enemy pressure increased on the Lam Son rear area in Quang Tri Province, and NVA gunners continued to score kills on helicopters. Enemy fire hit 145 helicopters during the fourth week in Laos, destroying twenty.[40]

After landing at LZ Hope, reconnaissance patrols from the 2nd ARVN Regiment swept through the rubble east of Tchepone unopposed. They found a few supply caches, but most of these caches had already been hit with airstrikes. Operating at altitudes under 100 feet, the air cavalry located enemy installations and supply caches and passed the targets to the air force ten to twelve days prior to the arrival of ARVN ground forces.[41]

The 2nd Regiment reached Tchepone during the late afternoon of 8 March and crossed to the south side of the Xepon River later that night. On 9 March the regiment began the climb up the escarpment en route to FSB Sophia. Far from completing its search of the hills east of Tchepone, the ARVN force made no attempt to cross the Xe Bang Hiang River to exploit the western side of Tchepone, the area believed to contain the largest supply caches. The original plan had been to deal the enemy a decisive blow by occupying and destroying its logistical network in southern Laos. But this was replaced by a meaningless public relations ploy to make good Thieu's announcement from the onset of the operation, that the ARVN force was going to Tchepone.[42] With that, the invasion of Tchepone was complete. Meanwhile General Lam flew to Saigon to meet with President Thieu to explain his plans for withdrawal.

The 2nd Infantry Regiment abandoned FSB Sophia on 11 March. The regiment left its field artillery howitzers in place to be destroyed by U.S. airstrikes and established three new fire support bases—FSBs Brick, Brown, and Sophia East—near Route 92, approximately nine kilometers south of FSB A Loui. Replacement artillery pieces were airlifted into FSB Brick and infantry battalions were inserted south and west of the FSB to interdict Route 914 and search for and destroy cache sites.[43] According to the plan, the 1st Regiment would withdraw from the vicinity of FSB Lolo after nine to ten days, then the 2nd Regiment from Brick and the 3rd Regiment in the area of LZ Brown and FSB Delta 1 would follow. The VNMC brigades and the remaining elements of the airborne division would withdraw after the 1st ARVN Division. General Lam expected to complete these movements by 31 March. After resting and reorganizing the 1st ARVN Division, two marine brigades and an airborne brigade would stage an attack into the eastern portion of Base Area 611 and the A Shau Valley. Lam projected the operation to be concluded by 15 April.[44] But even these plans were forced to change. The eastward movement of the 2nd Regiment thinned ARVN forces on the western end of the penetration, leaving the 1st Regiment vulnerable to a growing enemy presence.

Chapter 11

THE RETREAT FROM LAOS

ON 15 MARCH HENRY KISSINGER forwarded to President Nixon a summary of General Abrams's status report of Operation Lam Son 719.[1] Abrams's report, based on his meeting with President Thieu three days earlier, was detached from reality. Because Abrams's headquarters was located five hundred miles from the action, the reporting system was not keeping pace with action on the ground. Abrams provided his estimation of enemy losses, stating that six of the ten NVA regiments committed to the battle had suffered significant casualties. Abrams endorsed Thieu's plans to abandon Tchepone and sweep southward into Base Area 611. The decision not to exploit Base Area 604 concerned the White House, and Kissinger immediately dispatched his assistant, Brig. Gen. Alexander Haig, to Vietnam to assess the situation and report directly back to him.

As the sixth week in Laos opened, the poor weather and occasional rains continued to restrict the hours available for air operations. Enemy gunners made aerial resupply dicey, as incoming artillery and mortar intensified every time resupply ships attempted to approach landing zones. However, the Lam Son heavy lifters, escorted by gunships, delivered seventeen loads to A Loui, six to LZ Bravo, four to A Loui, and nineteen to the VNMC brigade at Hotel. But only two CH-47 loads, for the 147th VNMC Brigade, were able to get into FSB Delta, and all attempts to resupply the 1st ARVN Regiment at FSB Lolo failed.

When it became apparent that there was no way the CH-47s could get into Lolo, the 223rd CAB attempted to bring in supplies with

174

UH-1Hs. This effort also failed as the enemy raked the incoming aircraft with intense ground fire, hitting six UH-1Hs, two Charley Models, and one Cobra. The 223rd CAB commander attempted to organize a night mission to resupply Lolo, hoping that under the cover of darkness a UH-1H with a sling load of the most critical supplies could get through. But this attempt also failed when fog and low clouds obscured the area.[2]

EXTRACTING THE 1ST REGIMENT, 1ST ARVN DIVISION

NVA pressure on the 1st Infantry Regiment was unrelenting. The 1st ARVN Infantry Division's positions on the south flank were spread too far apart for the ARVN to conduct a mutually supported defense. The NVA recognized this weakness and concentrated its forces on the isolated ARVN battalions.[3] By 13 March the 1st Regiment at Lolo was under unrelenting NVA artillery and rocket fire as NVA ground forces moved to encircle the defenders. On 14 March, with casualties mounting and ammunition running low, the regiment made hasty plans for retreat: the regimental headquarters and the battalions outside of FSB Lolo would withdraw to the east, and the 4th Battalion would remain at Lolo as a rear guard, then break contact with the NVA and rejoin the regiment.[4] Press reports stated that the 1st Regiment "fled," but in reality, it was a well-executed retrograde movement, followed by a heroic rearguard defense by the 4th Battalion. Although Admiral Moorer was probably unaware of the dire circumstances that had forced the regiment to withdraw, he reported to Nixon that the regiment had "just moved to higher ground at the same point."[5] The 4th Battalion fought a continuous four-day battle as it moved eastward, occupying successive defensive positions.

At 2350 hours on 17 March the ARVN 1st Corps declared a tactical emergency. The 4th Battalion was surrounded, under attack, and in need of an emergency resupply of small-arms ammunition and hand grenades. The mission was immediately passed to the 223rd CAB. Weather posed a challenge: at Khe Sanh there was a broken layer of clouds at 300 feet and 500 feet, the sky was overcast at 1,000 feet, and visibility was reported as one and a half miles in the fog. The FAC, call sign Hammer 264, was orbiting the battalion and reported the weather as having scattered ceilings and five miles of visibility. The weather pattern in the area of operations indicated that conditions would continue to deteriorate through the night making visual flight impossible. No landing zone was available; the supplies would have to be delivered by sling load. The combination of night and weather called for the best-qualified aircrews available for the sling-load operation. The crews selected went by call signs Traps 86 and Spasm 10. These two UH-1H crews (plus a team of Charley Model gunships) launched from Dong Ha, flew to Khe Sanh to refuel and pick up sling loads of supplies, then headed to Laos. When the 223rd requested flare ship support, the mission was passed to the 14th CAB. Khe Sanh tower was notified to have the ground controlled approach (GCA) radar on standby.[6]

At 0030 hours the 101st Aviation Group was notified that the 4th Battalion's commanding officer and executive officer had been either killed or captured and that the call sign for the new acting commander was "Quebec Whiskey."[7] In the meantime, Hammer 91 replaced Hammer 264 as FAC controlling USAF gunship fire 250 meters south of Whiskey's location. Pathfinders were alerted to set up flares to assist in guiding the inbound helicopters to the refueling point, and the division support command was alerted to have fuel handlers ready to refuel the aircraft. UH-1H crews Traps 86 and Spasm 10 and their gunship support were inbound to Khe Sanh at 0145 hours and reached the refueling point five minutes later. After refueling their aircraft, the aircrews were briefed on the mission and were on their way to pick up their sling loads at 0315 hours. The 108th Artillery lit up the route between Khe Sanh and the Laotian border with flares, and the mission was under way.

At 0340 hours Hammer 267, who had relieved Hammer 91 as FAC, reported that he was uncertain of the survivors' location and requested that the helicopters hold east of the area until the location could be confirmed. By 0345 the Charley Model gunships were running low on fuel, and the resupply team had to return to Khe Sanh to refuel. In the meantime, Hammer 80, who took over on station for Hammer 267, located the 4th Battalion, and the helicopter flight launched again. By the time the flight reached the vicinity of FSB Hotel, the weather had deteriorated to zero ceiling and zero visibility, forcing the helicopters to turn back to Khe Sanh.[8] Khe Sanh was shrouded by fog, and by 0645 hours was receiving incoming mortar fire.[9]

As daylight broke, a commander identified by the call sign "Fixer Alpha" called to cancel the resupply effort and order that the extraction of the 1st Regiment continue.[10] The 4th Battalion was surrounded by the enemy and fighting their way through to a new location. He also requested an aerial rocket artillery section to relieve the USAF gunship on station, because the ceiling was so low that the AC-130 was vulnerable to ground fire every time it descended below the clouds to fire.[11] An ARA section was dispatched, and General Berry ordered the air cavalry to support the extraction.

The 4th Battalion fought its way through the enemy encirclement while air cavalry, 68 sorties of TACAIR, and Cobra gunships from D Company, 101st AHB, provided covering fire in an effort to keep the NVA at bay. The battalion split into two groups: one group tried to escape and evade, and the other group (eighty-eight soldiers led by Quebec Whiskey) moved to the new PZ, a bomb crater near the bottom of the escarpment. The remnants of the battalion were out of ammunition, exhausted, and for all practical purposes defenseless. At 1150 hours General Berry declared a tactical emergency, and the 223rd CAB immediately launched aircraft to extract the survivors.[12] The NVA had surrounded the bomb crater and was using loudspeakers to call for the survivors to surrender. As the rescue flight approached, Capt. Keith Brant from D Company, 101st AHB, volunteered to lead the aircraft to the PZ. Brant and his copilot/gunner, Lt. Alan Boffman, had been on station all day, providing covering fire and making repeated trips back to Lao Bao to rearm and refuel their aircraft. But now he was out of ammunition again. As he went in to mark the location for the 223rd, his hydraulics were shot out and his ship caught fire before he could show the flight the location of the PZ. Instead of saving himself, he made a

360-degree turn, pointed his aircraft at the PZ, and said, "The friendlies are at twelve o'clock." Then he turned and announced that he was going to try to make it to the Xepon River. When he realized that he was not going to make it to the river, he keyed the microphone one last time and said, "Give my love to my wife and children."

The first ship into the PZ was immediately swamped with evacuating ARVN and lifted off with soldiers dangling from the skids, some of whom fell to their deaths. The second ship was shot down. Of the sixty-one ARVN soldiers that made it out of the LZ, twenty-four came out on the first ship. Reporters and photographers were present when the flight returned, and some ARVN soldiers were still clinging to the skids. Press accounts insinuated cowardice, but nothing could have been further from the truth.[13]

The 1st Infantry Regiment headquarters, and its 2nd and 3rd Battalions, moved to a position approximately two kilometers southwest of FSB A Loui, where they were picked up and flown back to Khe Sanh during the afternoon of 18 March.

In the meantime, Alexander Haig arrived in Saigon and began a stream of messages to his boss, Henry Kissinger. Haig's first report, based on a conversation with Ambassador Bunker, was optimistic. He reported that Bunker was confident in Thieu's determination to see the operation through, and that the operation would continue "largely through the month of April."[14]

THE 2ND INFANTRY REGIMENT RETREATS

The 2nd Infantry Regiment's 2nd Battalion encountered strong enemy resistance on 17 March while conducting search-and-destroy operations north of Route 914. The battalion retreated north and linked up with the regiment's remaining battalions in the area around Sophia East and LZ Brown the next day. The Communists, fully aware of the withdrawal of ARVN forces, were making an all-out effort to block the withdrawal.[15] With his losses mounting and the tempo of enemy attacks increasing, General Lam met with his division commanders on the night of 18 March at Khe Sanh. There was really not much to discuss. With the evacuation of the 1st Infantry Regiment and one battalion of the 2nd Regiment earlier that day, the remaining ARVN force in Laos faced insurmountable odds and was in danger of total annihilation. General Lam ordered the pace of withdrawal accelerated. Preparations for the immediate withdrawal of the 2nd Regiment from LZ Brown and FSB Delta 1 began immediately.[16] What had been intended as an "orderly withdrawal" of ARVN forces became a full-scale, disorganized retreat.

The decision to accelerate the withdrawal did not sit well in Washington. Kissinger received the news and sent the following message to Ambassador Bunker:

It would be hard to exaggerate the mystification and confusion caused here by the ARVN's latest scheme of maneuver which envisages a rapid pullout from Laos. For a week, we have been briefing on the assumption that we were proceeding along the lines of your latest conversation with President Thieu envisaging a slow pullout through Base Area 611. I do not want to get into details of military operations. However, it is intolerable to have the President vulnerable to constant changes of plans which are unilaterally implemented. The President will go on television on Monday night. We must have an agreed strategy by then. From here, last week's scheme looked preferable. As you know, we originally approved Lam Son to disrupt supplies during the dry season. For this reason, careful consideration should be given to operations along Route 914 and through Base Area 611. But whatever the scheme, we must be part of the planning and have adequate advance warning. I hope Thieu understands that the President's confidence is an asset he should not lightly dissipate and that this may be his last crack at massive U.S. support.[17]

Haig immediately flew north to the I Corps tactical operations center at Dong Ha to make a personal assessment and report back to Kissinger. While Haig's presence at the TOC rankled some of the military leadership that considered Haig more of a politician than a military professional, Haig's assessment was nonetheless accurate. Haig reported, "ARVN enthusiasm for continuation of Lam Son 719 is completely lacking." The greatest challenge now facing Abrams, Haig believed, was how to engineer an orderly withdrawal. Haig recommended that pressure from Washington on the ARVN to reinforce or delay the withdrawal be terminated, as the limited success of Lam Son was preferable to total defeat. Haig also reported that President Thieu had apparently called General Lam and informed him that he was moving the ARVN airborne division back to Saigon as soon as it could be extracted from Laos.[18]

The 29th and 803rd Regiments of the NVA 324th Division surrounded the 147th VNMC Brigade Headquarters, the 7th Marine Battalion, and the brigade's artillery at FSB Delta. Five of their ten howitzers had been knocked out by enemy fire. The 812th NVA Regiment had the 258th VNMC Brigade pinned down at FSB Hotel and its positions on the Co Roc promontory farther to the east.[19] The NVA 308th Division was attacking from the north, and the 64th and 24th Regiments from the NVA 320th and 304th Divisions were attempting to encircle A Loui. The NVA hit FSB Delta 1 with 120mm rockets and 75mm recoilless rifle fire, destroyed four 105mm howitzers, and detonated 1,400 rounds of artillery ammunition. This action was supported by 686 sorties of helicopter gunships and AC-130 gunships, 246 tactical air sorties, and 14 B-52 strikes, which delivered 1,158 tons of bombs.[20]

On 20 March U.S. air assets exerted a maximum effort to pummel the Communists with tactical air strikes, helicopter gunships, and B-52s in an attempt to enable the South Vietnamese forces to break contact and withdraw. At the same time, NVA antiaircraft gunners, recently reinforced by two additional air defense battalions, made their maximum effort to shut down air support. In the 2nd Infantry Regiment's area of operations, 580 soldiers from the 3rd Battalion were successfully evacuated from a pickup zone west of Sophia East in an extraction "with absolutely no casualties—a super extraction that lulled us into a false sense of security," as John Klose described it.[21]

The Regiment's 2nd and 4th Battalions were still on the ground, south of Sophia East, near LZ Brown. After refueling and rearming, a flight of forty lift aircraft launched from Khe Sanh to resume the extraction. The result was a nightmare. Forty ships went in and thirty were hit; the damage was extensive. The tattered flight returned to Khe Sanh to refuel and inspect the damage to its aircraft. Ten to twelve ships, some of which were damaged, appeared capable of making a second attempt and were soon en route back to Brown. Maj. Jack Barker, the commanding officer of B Company, 101st AHB, was near the middle of the formation as it approached the landing zone; his crew included Capt. John Dugan, Sgt. William Dillender, and PFC John Chubb. It was not Barker's first tour in Vietnam, but it was his first tour as a helicopter pilot, and both he and Private Chubb were relatively inexperienced. It was a highly decorated crew; between the four, their awards included five purple hearts, three Silver Stars, two Distinguished Flying Crosses, and a Distinguished Service Cross.[22]

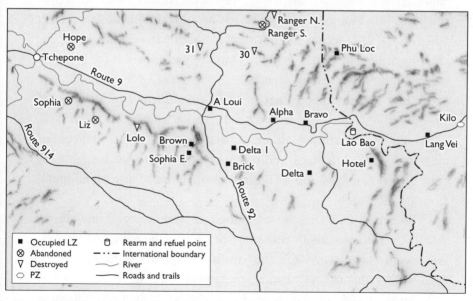

Map 6. ARVN positions on the morning of 20 March 1971. Drawn by Bill Nelson. Copyright © 2014 by The University of Oklahoma Press.

Behind Barker was Maj. Dale Spratt, commander of the 174th AHC. Spratt's aircraft was 500 to 1,000 feet from Barker's when Barker's aircraft was hit. The aircraft disintegrated as it fell to the earth, and it was obvious that there were no survivors.[23] General Berry, who was observing the action from his command-and-control ship high above the landing zone, immediately aborted the mission. If the remaining members of the ARVN 2nd Infantry Regiment were going to be extracted, they would have to break contact with the enemy and move to a more secure landing zone.

The remaining 2nd Regiment battalions were under unrelenting enemy attacks and had been without a resupply of water for so long that the men were drinking their own urine. Lt. Col. Tran Ngoc Hue, a highly decorated national hero and former commander of the Hac Bao company, commanded the 2nd Battalion. Hue called in B-52 strikes so close that the defenders were showered with bomb fragments. By the time the order to break out and move to another extraction site was received, Hue had been seriously wounded by an incoming mortar round. In order to ease the burden of his battalion as they attempted the break out, Hue requested to be left behind. He was taken prisoner when the NVA overran the position and spent the remainder of the war imprisoned in North Vietnam. Only sixty members of the battalion arrived at the new landing zone.[24]

While the combined fleet of the 14th, 223rd, and 101st Aviation Battalions worked to extract the 2nd Regiment, the 158th AHB extracted the remaining airborne battalions. Forty-five helicopters sustained combat damage, and six more were destroyed, bringing the total to 108 damaged and 11 destroyed since the beginning of operations on 19 March.[25]

The NVA's 2nd Division continued its attempt to annihilate the ARVN 2nd Infantry Regiment's survivors during the night of 20 March. As dawn broke on 21 March, the fighting subsided and the ARVN battalions were able to break contact and move toward FSB Delta, where they were picked up and flown back to Khe Sanh. Both battalions absorbed heavy casualties. Again, the action in the pickup zone was chaotic, as the battle-weary ARVN soldiers rushed the lift ships. Even after the main body of remaining 1st Infantry Division troops had been extracted, helicopters continued to search the area and pick up stragglers. Helicopters from the 101st Aviation Group evacuated over 991 ARVN soldiers before the day ended.[26] During the final days of the withdrawal, Gen. Benjamin Harrison, the senior army advisor to the ARVN divisions, was at the Khe Sanh airfield to observe every returning UH-1. Each was fully loaded with ARVN troops, with four to six more hanging onto the skids.

THE 1ST ARMORED BRIGADE RETREATS

General Lam ordered the armored brigade and the airborne units located at A Loui to abandon the fire support base and fall back to the area of FSB Alpha on 19 March; he allocated two air cavalry troops to cover the move. What followed was a classic example of poor coordination between the major ARVN commands as well as the tendency for the commanding general of the airborne division to ignore the corps commander's orders.[27] At the onset of the operation the armored brigade was under the operational control of the airborne division, and there is no record of this aspect of the task organization being changed. However, the corps commander's intent was clear—two air cavalry troops were to cover the withdrawal. But the airborne division commander intervened and directed the air cavalry to other missions in support of his division. The majority of field artillery howitzers at A Loui were rigged for sling load and picked up by heavy-lift helicopters. The three remaining 105mm howitzers were attached to M113 armored personnel carriers to be towed back to Vietnam. The convoy departed A Loui with the 11th Armored Cavalry Squadron acting as the rear guard, the 7th Armored Cavalry Squadron in the lead, and the logistical units in the middle.

The convoy was ambushed at a stream crossing between A Loui and FSB Alpha. Four M-41 tanks from the unit ahead of the 11th Squadron were abandoned in the middle of the crossing, blocking the route, the extent of their damage unknown. The portion of the convoy that had managed to negotiate the crossing before the tanks were abandoned continued eastward with the accompanying airborne infantry soldiers. After considerable delay and a three-hour fire fight with the enemy, the 11th Squadron managed to move two abandoned tanks, complete the stream crossing, and close in on FSB Alpha during early morning hours of 20 March. The survivors of the convoy reorganized at FSB Alpha and continued east on 21 March with the 11th Squadron in the lead. At 1130 hours, three kilometers east of FSB Bravo and only five kilometers from the Vietnamese border, the convoy was ambushed again. By this time it had lost nearly 60 percent of its vehicles, and some crews had abandoned their vehicles and fled to the east on foot.[28]

The squadron commander anticipated more ambushes along the remaining five kilometers of Route 9 and suspected the road would be littered with damaged vehicles. He found a crossing site on the Xepon River, crossed over to the south side, and continued east through the jungle. On 22 March he reached the point where the river turns south with the Vietnamese border just across the river. But he could not cross. The riverbanks were too steep for the vehicles. The U.S. 1st Battalion, 77th Armor was guarding the border and reported the situation to higher headquarters. Two CH-54 Sky Cranes delivered bulldozers, which immediately began to cut down the banks and prepare a crossing site.[29]

Enemy tanks were closing in on the convoy while the bulldozer operators were working frantically to cut down the steep banks. At approximately 1430 hours a forward air controller reported twenty enemy tanks eight kilometers west of the stranded convoy. A second FAC confirmed the sighting five minutes later and reported that the enemy tanks were on Route 9, moving east at approximately thirty miles per hour. The FAC requested strike aircraft, and by the time two F-100s arrived on the scene, the enemy tanks had closed to within five kilometers. In a quick-paced air-to-ground battle, the lead F-100 rolled in with 500-pound bombs and napalm. He missed. His wingman rolled in, but his aircraft was hit with antiaircraft fire and exploded before he could deliver in ordnance. The flight lead rolled back in for a second pass and scored a direct hit on the NVA T-54 tank leading the enemy column. Unable to bypass its lead tank, the column was temporarily stopped.[30] With NVA tanks in hot pursuit, the convoy crossed the river on 23 March, while U.S. airstrikes turned back the enemy armor.

By this time in the operation the NVA had captured scores of ARVN radios, and many operating frequencies were compromised. Both ARVN and U.S. radios were being jammed. It is not clear if the 11th Squadron commander failed or was unable to report his situation, but neither the brigade nor corps headquarters was aware of his situation. Some accounts state that, after the battle on March 21, the commander learned from a prisoner of war that there was another ambush site ahead of him on Route 9. The ARVN corps headquarters heard the same report a week earlier and gave the 11th Airborne Battalion the mission of clearing and securing the border crossing. But that information was never sent to the 1st Armored Brigade.[31]

In his account of Lam Son 719, Gen. Donn Starry was never able to determine the number of armored and cavalry units that were sent in with the 1st Armored Brigade. While there is an accurate record of brigade strength when the column crossed the border on 8 February, reinforcements were sent in gradually. The reinforcements were so piecemeal, and the troops came from so many units, that it was difficult to tell just who or what was committed. Many units never reached A Loui and simply became part of the withdrawal problem.[32] On 23 March a briefing officer reported to General Abrams, "They went in with sixty-two tanks and they brought out twenty-five. A U.S. advisor met them at the border and made a personal account. They went in with one hundred sixty-two APCs [M-113 armored personnel carriers] and brought out sixty-four."[33] While all that he said may have been correct, it is unlikely that all piecemeal replacements were counted.

After the 1st Armored Brigade withdrew through FSB Alpha, the next order of business was to close the fire support base. Helicopters lifted seven 105mm howitzers and four 155mm howitzers from the fire support base on 20 March. The four depleted aviation battalions were able to extract 642 ARVN airborne soldiers from the 2nd and 7th Airborne Battalions, all of which were flown to Dong Ha to await transportation back to Saigon.

Bringing out the Marines

The Marine Division's 147th and 258th Brigades were the last major South Vietnamese units to enter Laos and the last units to leave. The 147th Brigade, commanded by Col. Hoang Tich Thong was inserted at LZ Delta. Two of Thong's battalions moved off the landing zone to conduct mobile operations, while the brigade headquarters, the remaining battalion, and the brigade's artillery remained at Delta. All brigade units were soon in heavy contact with the enemy. By 20 March the defenders at Delta were surrounded. The NVA employed one of its common tactics, hugging. This tactic was particularly successful at Delta; Colonel Thong consistently refused to clear artillery and air strikes—including his own artillery—within a thousand meters of his position because he lacked confidence in the accuracy of his supporting arms. The brigade's artillery was accustomed to operating in the Mekong Delta where the terrain is flat, but artillery gunnery is much more complicated in mountainous terrain. Intervening crests between the guns and the target can dictate the use of high-angle fire, and Thong was skeptical of his artillery's proficiency.[34]

Earlier, on 12 March, the 147th VNMC Brigade had been the victim of a friendly-fire incident. A heavy team of three Charley Model gunships from the 14th CAB observed persons moving south of FSB Delta and requested clearance to fire. Clearance was granted, and the three gunships, two from the 174th Aviation Company and one from the 71st Aviation Company, rolled in. Thirty-three marines were wounded and four were killed.[35] While this scenario implies error on the part of the gunships, that is not necessarily the case. When the gunships called in their request to fire on the suspected enemy, they were advised that no friendly troops were at that location and received permission to fire.

Even after Colonel Lan overrode Thong's restriction on clearing fires, the VNMC could not break the NVA's hold on FSB Delta.[36] NVA antiaircraft guns surrounded FSB Delta, while NVA artillery and RPGs pounded the unfortunate marines. By 20 March NVA soldiers were firing small arms at inbound helicopters from positions dug under the base's perimeter wire. The enemy had a firm grasp on FSB Delta, and NVA gunners had turned back every CH-47 that had attempted to bring in a sling load after 15 March. There was no way CH-47s could hover over the fire support base long enough to deliver their loads. Instead, the resupply effort was continued by the smaller and more agile UH-1Hs of the 14th CAB. But that Huey's load capacity was much smaller, and supply reserves continued to shrink.

Every flight into the LZ was a high-risk affair. Aircraft were attacked by machine-gun, small arms, and antiaircraft fire while en route to the LZ, and the NVA would pelt the LZ with mortar fire as aircraft arrived. Although escorting gunships did their best to suppress the NVA gunners while en route, once the aircraft reached the LZ, mortars and artillery would open up. The Huey pilots did their best to conceal their intended touchdown points on the firebase in order to avoid being caught in the bursting radius of the incoming rounds. But all LZs, carved from the forested terrain, had typically no more than two or three options for landing sites. The favored technique was to land at one of these sites, wait a few seconds, then quickly hover over to another. Mortars fire with a high trajectory, and depending on the range from the mortar to the target, the time of flight required for the mortar round to impact on the LZ may be as high as fifteen to twenty seconds. Employing a technique wryly referred to as "Musical Mortars," pilots would bet their lives that they could entice the NVA to fire at their original landing site, then shift to another and deliver their loads before the enemy had time to adjust their fire. After two or three days of using this tactic at FSB Delta, the NVA adjusted its tactics. As a Huey approached, the NVA fired at all of the landing sites, and the pilots had little choice but to abort the mission. During the course of Lam Son 719, mortar fire in landing zones hit forty UH-1Hs, destroying ten.[37]

The 174th Aviation Company resorted to improvised airdrops in attempt to deliver supplies. Crews installed rollers—the same type used to load and unload cargo trucks—in the cargo compartments of the UH-1Hs. Supplies were loaded on to a pallet or in a box, and a parachute with a short static line attached to the ripcord was fixed to the load. The improvised system was completed during the late afternoon, and at 1720 hours the flight of UH-1Hs flew over the LZ at an altitude of 1,000 feet. As the pilot maneuvered to avoid enemy fire, the crew pushed the load out. The drop missed the landing zone. A second attempt was made. The pilots increased their altitude by another 1,000 feet in order get out of small arms range. The effort met with mixed results; most drops missed the landing zone, and at least one package exploded when it crashed to the earth.[38] The resupply effort continued until 1830 hours, when an aircraft from the 176th AHC was blown out of the sky at an altitude of 5,000 feet.[39]

At 0600 on 21 March two NVA regiments launched a ground attack against Delta, preceded by mortar fire and what appeared to direct fire from tank guns.[40] The fire hit the command bunker, destroying the radio antennas. The other bunkers near the TOC were destroyed, and the howitzers were damaged.[41] The VNMC requested evacuation of FSB Delta, but General Lam denied the request, stating that the artillery had to be extracted, even though helicopters had been unable to land at Delta. Lam also allocated 2,000 rounds of 8-inch artillery and 5,000 rounds of 155mm artillery to support the 147th. The senior marine advisor, Lt. Col. Alexander McMillan, later observed that by the time Lam finally allocated long-range artillery to support the brigade, the artillery had been withdrawn to positions that were out of range.[42]

The 147th Brigade was running out of ammunition, and most of its artillery had been knocked out by enemy fire early on 23 March. The NVA infantry attacked the FSB and managed to gain a foothold inside the defensive perimeter. The NVA infantry mounted a second attack, this time supported by ten flame-throwing tanks. The marines knocked out two tanks with M-72 LAWs, a third with tactical air, and a fourth was destroyed by a land mine. But the six remaining tanks continued the attack, and the brigade headquarters and the 7th Battalion were forced to move out.[43] The marines withdrew toward FSB Hotel and the 258th VNMC Brigade. The 2nd and 4th Battalions came to the aid of the retreating force, but while en route to FSB Hotel, the NVA ambushed the column. The brigade and its battalions managed to fight through the ambush, but casualties were high. All three battalion commanders were wounded, as were the majority of company commanders. But the 147th managed to link up with the 258th Brigade at Hotel. Two hundred thirty wounded were immediately picked up and flown to Khe Sanh. After the initial count, 134 marines were missing. But, as the day wore on, small groups continued to filter into FSB Hotel or cross the border back into South Vietnam. Later that day the remainder of the battalion was extracted back to Khe Sanh. The marines held the southeast corner of the shrinking penetration just long enough to prevent the NVA from closing its trap on the retreating ARVN force.

The ARVN corps was in full retreat, and the NVA continued to ratchet up the pressure on Khe Sanh. A successful Communist attack on Vandergrift destroyed 20,000 gallons of aviation fuel on 21 March. On 22 March the control tower at Khe Sanh sustained a direct hit by NVA artillery. To the west of Khe Sanh, the refueling point at Lang Vie was under sporadic, indirect fire attack, and aircraft attempting to land at the facility were increasingly being greeted with ground fire. The 159th ASHB reported air burst antiaircraft fire north of Khe Sanh, and at 1910 hours, and just as low clouds and thunderstorms began to move into the area, a pilot from D Company, 158th AHB, reported taking enemy fire just off the east end of the Khe Sanh airfield. Shortly after midnight the NVA made a coordinated indirect fire and ground attack at Khe Sanh. At 0240 hours the base was hit with mortar and artillery fire, followed by a ground attack by sappers at 0250 hours.[44] The sappers planned their attack well. One of the most vulnerable areas in a defensive perimeter is the boundary between units. It is a point where a coordinated defensive effort is least likely, and the NVA managed to locate the boundary between D Troop, 2nd Squadron, 17th Cavalry, and the 4th Battalion, 77th ARA. The sappers were cleaned out of Khe Sanh after two and a half hours of fighting, but in the meantime, the sappers, combined with enemy mortars and artillery, managed to destroy six aircraft and seriously damage six more. In addition to the aircraft, the sappers destroyed the aerial rocket rearm point. The North Vietnamese claim to have "destroyed forty helicopters, thousands of rounds of ammunition and one million liters of oil and gas, and killing one hundred enemy, mostly pilots and technical personnel" during this series of attacks.[45] Their claims about the destruction of ammunition and fuel are probably close to correct, but their claims of helicopters destroyed and pilots killed are grossly exaggerated.

On 24 March the NVA began to probe the 258th VNMC Brigade defenses at FSB Hotel. The marine division commander had no intention of entering into another battle like the one at FSB Delta and countermanded Lam's order for the brigade to remain at Hotel.[46] The first battalions of marines, followed by the field artillery, were extracted during the late afternoon of 24 March. The following morning B-52 Arc Light and tactical air sorties pounded the areas west and southwest of FSB Hotel, and the 258th Brigade, the last remaining South Vietnamese unit in Laos, was air lifted back to Khe Sanh.[47] All that remained were stragglers. Momentum propelled the NVA all the way to the border of South Vietnam. Communist tanks appeared at several locations and were immediately attacked by USAF fighters and gunships.[48]

Aircrews continued to report stragglers after the last units were extracted. But each group had to be approached with caution until the soldiers' identities could be confirmed. By this time the NVA had captured scores of ARVN radios and aviation survival radios and were actively engaged in ploys to lure helicopters into ambushes. During the night of 21 March an air force FAC monitored a survival radio beeper signal and observed a strobe light, but no downed aircrew could be confirmed as being in that location. On the following day another aircraft reported a wounded man crawling east along Route 9, and again the individual could not be confirmed as friend or foe. On 24 March another FAC reported twelve persons approximately one kilometer north of abandoned FSB Bravo. The people on the ground set up flares in the shape of a triangle in an obvious attempt to attract attention. The group was within five hundred meters of a planned Arc Light strike, and the strike was cancelled.[49]

On 26 March the 101st Aviation Group was notified that all air operations in Laos, with the exception of air cavalry and ARA support of the cavalry, were terminated. When President Thieu announced the change to Lam Son 719 on 19 March, he stated that the operation would continue into the month of April. In order to save face, the Hac Bao was ordered to conduct two meaningless raids, the first on 31 March, and the second on 6 April.[50] The Ho Chi Minh Trail was in full operation one week after the ARVN withdrawal.[51] Operation Lam Son 719 was officially terminated on 6 April 1971.

The failures of Lam Son 719 are rooted in the unintended consequences of a decision to launch a major military operation involving corps from two nations that did not share a common objective. President Nixon's objective was in the near term; he hoped to prevent the North Vietnamese from launching an offensive that could endanger, and even delay, withdrawal of American forces remaining in Vietnam. President Thieu also hoped to cripple the North Vietnamese, but his objective was to give South Vietnam more time to prepare to meet the North Vietnamese without direct U.S. military assistance and without sacrificing his best divisions.[52]

Chapter 12

AFTER LAM SON 719

THE 1ST ARVN DIVISION SUSTAINED HEAVY CASUALTIES. Like the other ARVN divisions, it was populated by soldiers recruited and conscripted from the local region, and the pain of lost family members was particularly intense among the civilian population of Quang Tri and Thau Thien Provinces. As the division's convoys made their way back to Dong Ha, they were inundated with old men and women and children, dressed in white, the traditional color of mourning.[1] Confidence and morale were shattered.

On 7 April 1971 President Nixon addressed the United States in a televised speech. The primary purpose of the speech was to announce his decision to increase the rate of troop withdrawals, a decision he justified by using Lam Son 719 as proof of the success of the Vietnamization program. He declared the operation in Laos a success and stated that, while the South Vietnamese had suffered heavy casualties, the North Vietnamese casualties were even heavier, but more important, the enemy's supply lines and their capability to conduct offensive operations in South Vietnam had been disrupted.[2] Operation Lam Son 719 was over, but the controversy and recriminations were just beginning.

There is little doubt that the South Vietnamese armed forces had improved under the Vietnamization program. But Lam Son 719 served as convincing evidence that ARVN forces were still not capable of defending their country without U.S. military support. While their

forces had improved, so had the capabilities of the North Vietnamese—a fact brutally proven one year later, during the North Vietnamese Easter Offensive, when the NVA rolled over ARVN defenses and
was stopped only by massive U.S. airpower. During the battle in Laos,
the ARVN forces were outgunned by the Soviet-equipped NVA. At
the direction of the president, the United States took immediate steps
to improve and modernize South Vietnamese forces within congres-
sionally mandated budget restraints.

But none of these efforts could address the ARVN's greatest
weakness—ineffective leadership at the top of the chain of command.[3]
During a discussion with Sir Robert Thompson on 25 March, General
Abrams described the situation with the war as being analogous to
a game of Liar's Dice: "We're betting on Vietnamization and he [the
NVA] is betting on getting that stuff [supplies coming down the Ho
Chi Minh Trail]. . . . Someday somebody's going to lift the cup—and
instead of four fives, it's gonna be garbage."[4]

While President Nixon was satisfied that the operation met the
limited objective of averting a major North Vietnamese offensive
during the 1971 dry season and was instrumental in reducing American casualties, it is safe to assume that the results of Lam Son 719 fell
short of his expectations.[5] General Abrams's inability to influence the
outcome led to a deterioration of the president's trust and confidence
in him and planted the suspicion that Abrams was reacting to conflicting orders from Secretary Laird.[6]

The concept of a westward attack along Route 9 had existed long
before Operation Lam Son 719, but the origins of the specific plan
for the operation remain unclear. Most early accounts of Lam Son
719 attribute the plan to Creighton Abrams, and the documents in
the State Department's historical files, make it appear that Abrams
spawned the plan. But this answer is too obvious, too compact, and
too much out of character for Abrams. Because Abrams was still on
active duty, and bound by a code of silence, when he died in 1974, he
was never in a position to defend himself against the allegation that
he originated the plan.

The *FRUS* documents confirm that Admiral McCain sent Abrams a draft plan on 10 November 1970 and asked Abrams to refine and develop a plan for an invasion of Laos. But we do not know if the plan that originated in McCain's office was Lam Son 719. There were competing plans at that time, such as Westmoreland's proposal to launch the attack along Route 19, further south and further away from NVA reinforcements.

Prior to the release of the seventh volume of *FRUS, 1969–1976*, which covers the time period between July of 1970 and December of 1971, Lewis Sorley theorized that Alexander Haig delivered the plan for Lam Son 719 to Abrams during his trip to Vietnam in early December. However, this theory is contradicted by document 91 of volume 7, a 17 December memorandum that describes Haig's conversations with General Abrams, Ambassador Bunker, and President Thieu during Haig' trip to Southeast Asia. During Haig's first meeting with General Abrams, Haig described stated that the president envisioned a "bold and imaginative thrust into the enemy's logistic nerve center either in Northeaster Cambodia or in Southern Laos in the Bolevens area," a concept identical to the plan favored by General Westmoreland. However, Abrams informed Haig that President Thieu and General Vien had already concluded that a two-division thrust into Tchepone would achieve even greater results.

In *Hell on a Hill Top* M. G. Harrison, who served as the senior advisor to the ARVN 1st Infantry Division and the ARVN airborne division, briefly discusses Lam Son 719. He states that planning for a Southern Laos–Route 9 campaign started in ARVN circles long before any U.S. senior officials were involved.[7] General Vien, the chairman of the Joint General Staff, offered a conceptual plan for severing the Ho Chi Minh Trail along the Route 9 corridor as early as 1965, but his plan could not advance without U.S. support. Another source indicates that the South Vietnamese began planning for an invasion of the Laotian panhandle as early as the spring of 1970: During his discussion with Sir Robert Thompson on 25 March of that year, General Abrams stated that he had been called to President Thieu's office on 1 May to discuss cross-border operations.[8]

President Thieu's actions serve as another indicator that the plan may have originated within the South Vietnamese government. Thieu took ownership of the operation by interceding and directing changes that far exceeded his competency level. His greatest error was halting the westward movement of the attack. While it is debatable as to when Thieu ordered the halt—12 February according to Davidson or 19 February according to Hinh—it is significant that when Kissinger questioned the reason for the halt, Abrams defended the logic for the delay. This is in sharp contrast to Gen. Phillip Davidson's *Vietnam at War*, which describes Abrams's reaction to the delay as "stunned and furious."[9]

In this regard Abrams is an enigma. Lam Son 719 was a high-priority operation in the eyes of President Nixon, but Abrams's demeanor during the operation did not portray the same sense of urgency. Abrams believed that he had no control over the operation. During his weekly intelligence update briefing on 6 February, Abrams remarked, "The thing they [Washington] don't seem to understand is the whole thing is in the hands of Lam and Sutherland and their subordinates and the hourly and minute to minute decisions that are being made by them. That's the way the whole—you can't change it. That's just the way it is. There isn't anything I can tell them, or anybody else."[10]

Abrams's conduct during the operation was probably best described by General Westmoreland during a discussion with Henry Kissinger on 12 April 1971: "Abe was in the most difficult position you can hear of. Thieu took it over. Americans were taken out because Thieu talked to the field commanders. On one occasion we talked Thieu into a course of action and orders sent to [Lam] who talks with Thieu and reverses it. It's awkward. You have to fully appreciate the position that Abe was in."[11] Abrams was not in a position to challenge South Vietnam's head of state. Such a challenge would have to come from the American head of state, Richard Nixon.

There are two documents in the State Department's files that refer to dates in April and May of 1970 and contain specific directives from Nixon to his subordinates to plan an operation in southern Laos. The first document refers to a 29 April 1970 meeting between Admiral

McCain and President Nixon.[12] The second document refers to Nixon's conversation with General Abrams a month later, on 30 May 1970, during which Nixon stated, "In summary then, I would like you to prepare adequate plans which provide for offensive operations in Laos."[13] Given the direct orders from their commander in chief, it is inconceivable that either Abrams or McCain would have failed to immediately follow through. And it is highly unlikely that the South Vietnamese would have been excluded from the planning process. But this does not necessarily make a good case to argue that planning for Lam Son 719 did not begin until late November or early December. It only supports an argument that the beginning of planning for an offensive in the Laotian panhandle had begun, not necessarily Lam Son 719. There were other plans.

Gen. Cao Van Vien, the former chairman of South Vietnam's Joint General Staff claims he received the proposal for an offensive in the Tchepone corridor from "MACV" (probably meaning General Abrams) in early January 1971 and that after President Thieu gave his approval for the concept, General Lam was tasked with planning the operation.[14] While it is possible, perhaps even probable, that Abrams approached Vien with a proposal for an operation in Southern Laos, Vien's timeline appears to be contradicted by *FRUS* documents. McCain sent a draft concept plan on 10 November 1970. On 8 December, presumably after Abrams responded to McCain, McCain authorized Abrams to begin planning efforts with Vien. But we don't know what plan this was; multiple plans to deal with the threat of a Communist push during the 1971 dry season were under consideration. On 15 December McCain informed Moorer about "the plan" in a CINCPAC message, noting that he had asked Abrams to develop it.[15] McCain gave his "wholehearted" support to the plan. General Haig arrived in Saigon on or around 16 December and, on 17 December, sent a message to Kissinger stating that, in his first meeting with General Abrams, he had learned that President Thieu and General Vien had already concluded that a two-division attack over Route 9 would achieve greater results than the plan proposed by General Westmoreland.[16]

Abrams was under pressure from Washington to come up with a plan. Given the Vietnamization program, the dwindling number of U.S. combat forces, and the Cooper-Church Amendment, the ground forces would have to come from the South Vietnamese troops, and Thieu was in a position to veto any plan that did not meet with his personal approval. It is entirely possible that Abrams agreed simply because he had no alternative. It is equally possible that the plan to attack down the Route 9 corridor originated with Abrams. But regardless, Abrams became involved in the plan and rejected the Route 19 plan that General Westmoreland favored.

Gen. William Westmoreland, the army chief of staff and the general who had commanded all U.S. forces in Vietnam for five years, was a forgotten man during the planning of Lam Son 719. Perhaps stained by his association with Lyndon Johnson and the "surprise" of the 1968 Tet Offensive, Westmoreland was ignored by policy makers. On 23 February 1971, after it became apparent that ARVN progress was falling short of expectations, Henry Kissinger called Westmoreland to his White House office to discuss the operation. Westmoreland stated that he had not been consulted concerning the plan and gave his view that targeting Tchepone with less than two divisions was too ambitious. In an indirect reference to Operation Plans El Paso and Full Cry, he stated that when he commanded the MACV he had concluded that four divisions would be required to cut the trail.[17]

Admiral Moorer was piqued by Westmoreland's statement and retorted that Westmoreland had been present when the concept was briefed to the Joint Chiefs of Staff on 18 January and had not objected.[18] While Westmoreland may have remained silent at this briefing, he had stated his position earlier. The first occasion was when he sat in for the Chairman of the Joint Chiefs of Staff during the 11 December meeting of the WSAG and stated that if operations were conducted in the Tchepone area, the balance of forces would be heavily in favor of the enemy.[19] His position was also apparent when he recommended that the thrust be along the Route 19 approach in northern Cambodia. Westmoreland stated his position, but nobody was listening. Admiral

Moorer's insistence that Westmoreland was consulted appears somewhat disingenuous. In a 15 December diary entry Moorer stated that he was inclined to "go for what Abrams wants us to do it and in no other way."[20]

In the years following the war, Henry Kissinger distanced himself from responsibility for the policy decisions that culminated in Operation Lam Son 719. He argued that he was never informed of the projected force requirement of two U.S. corps contained in Operation Plan El Paso until his 23 February meeting with General Westmoreland.[21] However, that assertion is not entirely accurate. On 19 January, during a meeting of the WSAG that Kissinger chaired, Undersecretary of State Alexis Johnson stated that he had previously recommended an attack on Tchepone but had been overruled by estimates that "six U.S. divisions were required for such an operation."[22] Kissinger was apparently not listening, or he simply chose to ignore Johnson's comment. The record of the meeting includes no further discussion of this topic. Henry Kissinger provided additional insight into his opinion of State Department input in *The White House Years*:

> What happened in 1971 was that the governmental consensus of the December 23 and January 18 meetings began to evaporate as soon as Rogers was exposed to the passionate opposition of his experts. By January 21 it became apparent that State was dragging its feet. At WSAG meetings Under Secretary Alex Johnson began to surface objections that did not challenge the decision but would have delayed its implementation indefinitely—a bureaucratic maneuver in which Johnson was superbly skilled.[23]

This statement is misleading. In anticipation of Secretary Rogers's objections, Kissinger personally devised a plan to exclude the Secretary of State from the discussions until 18 January. Therefore "governmental consensus" did not exist during the 23 December meeting and Rogers was not prepared for the 18 January meeting and his comments during the 18 January did not reflect clearly indicate consensus.[24]

Lam Son 719 was a bold, audacious plan that would have required a commander blessed with the same attributes. Gen. Bruce Palmer, who served as the 2nd Field Force Commander from 1965 to 1966 and the Deputy Commanding General of United States Army Vietnam from 1967 to 1968, stated, "Only a Patton or a MacArthur would have made such a daring move; an Eisenhower or a Bradley would not have attempted it."[25] The commanding general of the ARVN I Corps was certainly not a Patton or a MacArthur. The most complimentary description of General Lam that can be found is that he was a "competent administrator," or perhaps an able military governor of Military Region I, but he was definitely not the right choice for maneuvering an ARVN corps on the battlefield. Lam's shortcomings were readily apparent, and plans were made to replace Lam with General Tri, the capable corps commander who commanded ARVN troops during the Cambodian incursion. Unfortunately, Tri was killed in a helicopter crash before he could arrive to assume command of the operation.[26]

Lam Son 719 was clearly a failed operation, but it is difficult to determine if the failure is rooted in the plan, the execution, or both. Both were deeply flawed. Reflecting back on Lam Son 719 Lt. Gen. Sidney Berry stated, "By any objective standard, planning and coordination for Lam Son 719 were, at the Corps Commanders' level, of unacceptably low quality."[27]

The ARVN force in Laos was too small to accomplish the mission. But General Lam never committed all of the forces that were available to the corps. This could have been incompetence on Lam's part. It is also possible that the failure to commit a significant portion of the reserve was tied to Thieu's personal control of the operation. The troop list for the operation included his airborne and marine divisions; these two divisions were his strategic reserve, and given the fact that his remaining divisions were tied to their home areas, the loss of these divisions could have had drastic consequences.

When the North Vietnamese determined that the objective of the operation was to sever their strategic supply line, they committed all available forces to the battle, knowing that, if the effort succeeded, it could validate the Vietnamization program and compel the North Vietnamese to concede at the Paris Peace Talks.[28] While the NVA threw all available reserves into the battle, the South Vietnamese hesitated. When reserves were committed, they were committed piecemeal, in such small portions that they had little impact on the tactical situation.

The slow, plodding ARVN advance, with "each step solidly anchored on a fire support base," allowed the NVA to concentrate its forces and eliminate the fire support bases one at a time.[29] The voluntary halt of westward movement after 12 February surrendered the initiative to the enemy. The tactic of semi-fixed fire support bases was a tactic that the ARVN had learned from U.S. forces during operations in South Vietnam and the same tactic that had failed at Ripcord. This was a profound failure to adapt to a changing situation.

The cost of deploying the ARVN field artillery batteries may have outweighed the benefits. Every field artillery insertion required multiple sorties of heavy-lift helicopters and a continuous stream of sorties to bring in ammunition. And every sortie of CH-47, CH-54, or CH-53 required a gunship escort, tying up gunships that could have otherwise been used to provide fire support. Once the artillery ammunition was delivered, the ARVN forces frequently failed to secure it in protective bunkers, and NVA gunners were successful in hitting it with mortars or artillery. The resulting detonations were far more destructive than the incoming rounds.[30] The artillery tethered the ARVN to the semi-fixed bases, and once the enemy isolated the bases, extraction was nearly impossible. Most of the guns were lost. The ARVN would probably have been better off if it had not inserted its artillery, placed greater reliance on mortars, and preserved its ground mobility.

If you measure the outcome of the operation against the avowed objective, it was a failure. However, failure, like success, cannot be measured in absolute terms. One of Nixon's objectives was to preempt a major North Vietnamese offensive and provide time for U.S. troops to withdraw. This objective was partially achieved. Although the NVA was unable to launch a major offensive in 1971, heavy combat continued in

Military Region I, and from the American perspective it continued to be a helicopter war. American ground troops continued to disengage and pull back to the populated areas along the coastal plains while the ARVN, supported by U.S. Army aviation, moved into the front-line positions.

Lam Son 719 rekindled a contentious debate between the air force and the army, regarding both service's claims on aviation. The real issues behind the debate centered on the differing philosophies of each service and the slice of the defense budget each service would claim for aviation. The USAF promoted a doctrine that air assets should be centrally controlled by the air force, but the army favored greater decentralization with some air assets immediately responsive to the ground commander. This was a continuation of the debate between the two services that had occurred during the early 1960s when the findings of the Howze Board were debated in Congress.[31] The greatest congressional concern was overlapping budgets: McNamara supported the army's requirement for airmobility because he believed that in the past the air force had failed to meet the army's requirements. Senator Barry Goldwater, an air force reserve major general, opposed the board's recommendation. The Howze Board recommendations were accepted, and the result was the creation of the first airmobile division.[32]

The chief of staff of the air force, Gen. John Ryan, claimed that General Sutherland and other army generals had sought to use Lam Son 719 to demonstrate helicopter capabilities and failed to properly use USAF tactical air power until the loss of FSB Lolo proved that helicopters could not operate by themselves. John Klose's briefing to the precommand students at Fort Rucker in 2001 circumstantially supports this allegation. Klose stated that after the mission briefing for the assault on Lolo was concluded, General Sutherland told him and Lieutenant Colonel Kirklighter, "take them to Tchepone at all costs. The credibility of Army Aviation depends on it."[33]

Ryan's next point was probably closer to the main issue. He maintained that the air component commander should have control over airmobile operations until such time as the assault force was established on the ground.[34] This argument probably caused concern among the army's ranks that the air force was attempting gain control over army aviation.

In *Vietnam at War* General Davidson supports the allegation that General Sutherland failed to take full advantage of USAF tactical air support. Davidson states that during the planning phase, the 7th Air Force contended that the only way helicopters could survive the assault would be for the air force to use large quantities of fighter strikes to soften the area up before the helicopters went in, and that XXIV Corps thought that the air force had exaggerated the threat.[35] Davidson also refers to the interservice dispute between the army and the air force over which service should be the proponent for airmobile operations. The dispute was supposedly settled in 1966 by an agreement that the respective service chiefs signed. The army agreed to turn over all fixed-wing Caribou aircraft to the air force, and the air force agreed to army control of its helicopters.[36]

Ryan's complaints continued. He made the point that there was little coordination between the ARVN 1st Infantry Division, airborne division, and marine division and that as a result, the air force did not know where emergencies were occurring and continued to split its sorties equally between the South Vietnamese divisions. Ryan also stated, "it took a long time for us to realize that the ARVN had never before operated two divisions side-by-side."[37] While it is possible, perhaps even probable, that the chief of staff of the air force had little knowledge of the tactical situation or the evolving concept of the operation, it is not logical to assume that the commanding general of the air component in Vietnam was uninformed. Air force liaison officers were part of the staff at every army senior command.

The dispute could be related to the number of sorties allocated to Lam Son 719 by the 7th Air Force. For budgetary purposes, Secretary Laird limited the number of sorties that could be flown during the fiscal year, and the 7th Air Force was responsible for allocating sorties for all operations throughout the theater of operations. On any given day the requirement, based on the unpredictable needs of combat, could have easily exceeded the daily allocation. Admiral Moorer authorized an increase in the monthly allocation of tactical air sorties but stated that the funding level for the fiscal year of 1971 could not be exceeded.[38] In *The White House Years* Henry Kissinger refers to this problem: on 6 May 1972, during the Easter Offensive, Kissinger states, he did his best to avoid the mistake of the Laos operation (Lam Son 719) by attempting a major blow with insufficient forces. He instructed Ambassador Bunker that if either he or Abrams concluded that more air was required, it should be promptly requested and "we will get it to you."[39]

The second possible clue to the origin of the dispute is recorded in Colonel John Klose's briefing. Klose stated that the night before the combat assault, the battalion was assured that a B-52 Arc Light strike would be included in LZ preparation. As we know, there was a B-52 strike, but the closest point of impact was one kilometer south of Lolo. Tactical air support was planned and used at Lolo, but there was an obvious need for more sorties when the first lift landed on the LZ.

The issue of insufficient air support could also have come from the Vietnamese. In a 1985 monograph, General Vien stated that the operation "suffered from insufficient air support, including helicopters."[40] He is correct. Once the ARVN discovered that they could not use Route 9 as a resupply route, the logistical mission passed, by default, to the army's helicopter fleet. At that point enemy air defenses shut down many of the resupply efforts, and gunships were constantly overtaxed. It is also safe to assume that, from the ARVN perspective, USAF air support was inadequate. One prominent example was the loss of FSB 31. There was never enough fire support available when air support was redirected from support of the ARVN defense to efforts to rescue a downed USAF aircrew. There should be little doubt that Colonel Pence's comments to the press; the same comments that led to his relief, concerning the incident at FSB 31, were incendiary.

Search-and-rescue (SAR) operations were always high-priority events. The morale of aircrews was sustained by the knowledge that their band of brothers was committed to the creed that no man would be left behind. No command directive could have changed this. SAR missions took on even greater importance in the later days of the Vietnam War. U.S. prisoners of war became an emotional issue with the American public and a bargaining chip for the Communists. While there is no evidence that diversion of air support for SAR operations was an established policy during operation Lam Son 719, the practice was entrenched by April of 1972. During the opening hours of the 1972 Easter Offensive, a USAF EB-66 was shot down over the North Vietnamese Army's attacking troops, just south of the DMZ. Lt. Col. Iceal Hambleton, the only survivor, had ejected from the stricken aircraft and landed in the midst of the invading army. Not only were hundreds of sorties diverted to support the rescue effort, a no-fire area 27 kilometers in radius was established around him. This fire control measure, which encompassed the entirety of the immediate battle area, meant that no air strikes, naval gunfire, or artillery missions could be performed within this area without the express permission of the SAR commander.[41] When the ARVN brigade commander learned of the restriction, and that it was put in place for the benefit of a single American airman, he held up his finger and asked, "Just one?"[42]

Ryan's comment during the hearing at the Pentagon that "it took a long time for us to realize that the ARVN had never before operated two divisions side-by-side" also deserves consideration. The original concept for Lam Son 719 stated that the ARVN infantry division, reinforced by the ARVN armored brigade, would make the thrust down Route 9, and that once they had reached the intermediate objective, A Loui, a brigade of the airborne division would be launched on a helicopter-borne assault on Tchepone. This description of the concept of operations remained consistent in every Washington briefing until the operation was launched. At that point there is a change. The 1st ARVN Division was given responsibility for the south flank, and elements of the airborne division, armored brigade, and ranger group were on Route 9 and the north flank. This change put two divisions on line, and the corps headquarters retained control of the ranger group. This scheme of maneuver complicated battlefield coordination. In what now appears to be an obvious attempt at placating the air force, the XXIV Corps after action review characterizes tactical air support as "highly responsive to requirements . . . a primary factor for success against enemy armor and holding key terrain around major fire support bases."[43]

There is no argument that Lam Son 719 was a poorly executed, uncoordinated operation, beset by fundamental flaws. The ARVN I Corps command post was located at Dong Ha, and the XXIV Corps command post was at Quang Tri City, eight miles away, making close and continuous coordination all but impossible. Although both of the corps established forward command posts at Khe Sanh, these forward command posts were understaffed and ineffective.[44] The XXIV Corps had no representative in the forward area with authority to coordinate the activities of all U.S. units supporting the ARVN Corps, and the ARVN corps staff at Khe Sanh did not have senior staff officers with sufficient competence and authority to react to battlefield emergencies during the absence of General Lam.[45] Three weeks after the first ARVN troops crossed the border, and one week following Abrams's explosive reaction to the tardy report concerning helicopter availability, XXIV Corps finally established a viable joint coordination center. But it was too late.

Unity of command is one of the fundamental principles of military operations drilled into an aspiring officer's education, and Lam Son 719 is a classic object lesson of the consequences of failing to adhere to this basic requirement. General Lam never exercised absolute command authority over the ARVN airborne division or the VNMC division. In reality, the only force that he really commanded was his own 1st ARVN Division and the ranger group.[46]

There is an allegation that General Lam's effectiveness was impaired by insubordination on the part of the politically connected VNMC and ARVN airborne division commanders, and that President Thieu failed to give Lam the authority to ensure that his orders to these two units were carried out.[47] The airborne division and two brigades of the VNMC were included in the original troop list for Lam Son 719. The 258th Brigade was already stationed in I Corps, and the 147th Brigade was redeployed from the Mekong Delta and arrived at D-Day+1. The VNMC division headquarters and the 369th Brigade did not arrive until D-Day+32 (approximately 12 March), after Thieu nixed plans for the 2nd Airborne Regiment to conduct the air assault on Tchepone.[48] Only the 147th and the 258th were deployed to Laos. The 369th Brigade remained in South Vietnam with the division headquarters as part of the I Corps reserve. The USMC advisors to the VNMC generated two documents that provide a parochial view of the conflict between the VNMC and General Lam: *The U.S. Marines in Vietnam, 1970-1971* published in 1986 by the USMC Museums and History office, and *The Co-Vans: U.S. Marine Advisors in Vietnam* written by retired colonel John Miller, the advisor to the VNMC Division operations section during Lam Son 719 and a contributor to the USMC Museums and History publication.

The commanding general of the VNMC Division was Lt. Gen. Le Nguyen Khang. While Lam was also a lieutenant general, Khang was senior to Lam. Perhaps as a matter of pride, Khang never took an active role in the commander's conferences at the I Corps Headquarters, but instead turned matters over to his deputy, Colonel Lan. According to Miller, there was a history of distrust between Lam and Khang and a suspicion that Lam would take out his frustrations on the marines. The marines' fears of Lam's motivations increased when Lam briefed his plan for withdrawal and the 147th Brigade—to move southeast, away from Khe Sanh, and to reenter South Vietnam in the vicinity of the A Shau Valley—and no mention was made of air or logistic support for the brigade.[49] Apparently Miller and his VNMC counterpart failed to detect that this same plan also applied to the 1st ARVN Division and the 147th was not expected to go it alone.

After the 147th Brigade was decisively engaged at FSB Delta, both USMC sources claim that during the evening briefing on 22 March Lam allocated 2,000 rounds of 8-inch artillery and 5,000 rounds of 155mm artillery to the marines, but purposely positioned the artillery batteries out of range for FSB Delta.[50] If, as the marines allege, the 155mm and 8-inch artillery was out of range of FSB Delta, there is no evidence of malice on the part of General Lam. However, there is abundant circum- stantial evidence to indicate that it was more likely another case of poor

AFTER LAM SON 719

planning and coordination.[51] The 155mm and 8-inch artillery may have been out of range, but the marines were never out of the range of the 175mm batteries. With a maximum range of approximately thirty-four kilometers, the 175mm gun had over twice the range of the 155mm and 8-inch howitzers. But take note of the description of the artillery weapons. The 155mm and 8-inch artillery systems were howitzers, and the 175mm was a gun. Guns fire at a higher muzzle velocity and lower trajectory than howitzers, are less suited for engaging targets located on reverse slopes in mountainous terrain, and have a significantly larger range probable error (meaning that the impact of artillery projectiles fired at lower trajectories and higher velocities will be more likely to impact at greater distances both short of and over the target—even when fired with identical propelling charges and tube elevations), particularly when engaging targets at the upper end of their range capability. The 175mm gun was not well suited to provide close fire support for the marines. This controversy may be the source of a comment by Alexander Haig that the U.S. artillery had been positioned too far away from the battleground to provide optimum support.[52]

While it may have been no more than a misunderstanding generated by a misleading briefing by General Lam, these controversies aggravated the atmosphere of distrust between the VNMC and General Lam. Both accounts are probably in error. Hinh's error may be that of omission. No record or document places him in a position to have first-hand knowledge of events at the I Corps headquarters during Lam Son 719. On the other hand, Colonel McMillan and Major Miller were present. But there is no record of either of these officers raising this issue with General Sutherland or anyone on the XXIV Corps staff.

It is impossible to resolve the conflicts between the accounts of the USMC and General Hinh. The marines interpreted Lam's actions as a sinister plot designed to ensure that the VNMC was subjected to the same punishing losses that the ARVN experienced.[53] I have found only one acknowledged instance of the VNMC failing to follow orders, and that involves the extraction of the 258th Brigade. But considering the circumstances at hand, the actions of the VNMC division were reasonable and saved lives. The 147th Brigade had little choice but to withdraw; otherwise they would have been annihilated. Although there are incidents of airborne battalions failing to adhere to orders, acts of insubordination personally attributable to the airborne division commander are difficult to document. The South Vietnamese force and its commander were simply beyond their depth.

Many must share the blame for the failure of Lam Son 719, an operation that could have been the decisive battle of the Vietnam War. Abrams's assessment of the progress of Vietnamization was overly optimistic. Nixon pressed for an attack that approached the outer limits of the possible, and Thieu's interference muddled the operation. One of the greatest failures was the failure to recognize when it was time to withdraw. The final move to Tchepone that started on 3 March with the insertion at Lolo was a move approved by both Abrams and Thieu. But their motivations were at odds. Abrams saw the continuation of the attack as a means of accomplishing the mission, and he probably assumed that the ARVN force would commit reinforcements if required. For Thieu it was an exercise in saving face, and he had no intention of placing additional units at risk.

On 30 March 1971 the *New York Times* published an article written by Max Frankel with a headline reading "Nixon Aides Insist Drive in Laos Was Worth Price." Frankel alleged that there was an intelligence failure: the intelligence community, led by the CIA, failed to correctly assess the enemy's reinforcement, antiaircraft, and armor capabilities, as well as the enemy's determination to defend his infiltration route.[54]

Kissinger's memorandum addressed each alleged set of failures by attaching copies of intelligence assessments and memorandums that had been sent to the White House during the lead-up to Lam Son 719. A memorandum dated 14 December stated that there was a higher concentration of antiaircraft weapons due the presence of the 559th Group and the large numbers of antiaircraft gunners assigned to protect the Group's routes and way stations. The response to the allegation of failure to predict the armor threat was contained in a 3 February memorandum that stated that the NVA 198th Armor Battalion was "possibly" located near Muong Phine, the intersection of Routes 9 and 23. The postmortem analysis documented previous CIA estimates of Communist troop strength and predictions of Hanoi's intentions and concluded that the CIA "came about as close to calling the shots as one is ever likely to come in the real world."[55]

While the CIA's assessment of its intelligence effort can be fairly criticized, a greater error was the overestimation of American airpower. Planners overestimated the ability of air power to dominate the battlefield and underestimated the North Vietnamese Army's resolve to defend its strategic supply routes in Southern Laos. During a 10 February meeting of the WSAG, following a brief discussion of the successful use of B-52s in the defense of Khe Sanh in 1968, Admiral Moorer reported that the North Vietnamese were moving reinforcements from the north across Route 9. CIA Director Richard Helms added that there was now the equivalent of a North Vietnamese division north of Route 9 and added, "That's what we want—to give them a good pasting."[56] The evidence of NVA resolve was there, but ignored. The A Shau Valley, located close enough to North Vietnam for the Communists to be able to quickly reinforce, was an integral part of the NVA's supply and infiltration route, and no allied force had been able hold a position in the Valley. The lessons learned during Ripcord and Hamburger Hill had been overlooked.

However, there is no fault to be laid at the feet of the army aviators. Although many were inadequately prepared and some were poorly equipped, they met the challenge with unwavering courage and devotion to duty. Without their performance the outcome would have been much worse. True, there were exceptions. There were occasions when some pilots refused to fly, and some may have aborted their mission with insufficient justification. Television anchor Harry Reasoner said it best: "This is a war we could not have considered without helicopters. The pilots are beginning to feel like Mark Twain's man who was tarred and feathered. If it weren't for the honor of the thing, they'd just as soon have missed it."[57]

From a purely military perspective, the war in Vietnam was lost in Laos. Bui Tin, a former colonel on the North Vietnamese general staff, stated the case succinctly in *From Enemy to Friend*: "It defies imagination to think that the American side was willing in May 1970 to send U.S. troops into Cambodia, yet at no time did they dare to touch this strategic link to the southern theater."[58] An attack on the Ho Chi Minh Trail between 1965 and 1969 would have crippled the North Vietnamese war effort. But after 1969 withdrawal from Vietnam and the Vietnamization program became the primary policy considerations, and President Nixon authorized Operation Lam Son 719 as a preemptive strike that would allow withdrawals to continue during 1971. Traffic on the Ho Chi Minh Trail may have been reduced, and even delayed, but 3 April intelligence sources reported that traffic was higher than it had been in April of 1970.[59]

Nixon's announcement of the conclusion of Lam Son 719 did not end the battle. With momentum on their side, the Communists continued to carry the fight into northern Military Region I and moved long-range field artillery to positions on the north side of the DMZ, causing Kissinger to speculate that perhaps U.S. forces had been withdrawn too soon.[60] The NVA 304th Division infiltrated across the DMZ and pushed the remaining U.S. and ARVN forces out of western Quang Tri province.[61] By late May Hickory Hill (also referred to by some as Telstar) was under attack. Hickory was an electronic intelligence collection station, defended by U.S. and ARVN rangers, located on a mountaintop just north of Khe Sanh. On 1 June NVA troops overran the small force of defenders, and an AH-1G with tail number 68-15002, affectionately referred to as "Balls Deuce" by the Redskins of D Company, 158th AHB, was shot down, killing Chief Warrant Officer Don Wann and Lt. Paul Magers. Ironically, D Company had made it through Lam Son 719 without losing a single pilot, and Balls Deuce had made it through the operation unscathed by enemy fire. (See figure 8 on page 218 for a photograph of Balls Deuce.)

Three weeks later the NVA launched a massive ground attack on Fire Support Base Fuller, located northeast of Hickory, overlooking the DMZ. The attack was preceded by a month of heavy bombardment by NVA artillery from north of the DMZ. The NVA launched its attack during the afternoon of 23 June. The area around Fuller was a "target rich environment." Using rearm points at Quang Tri and the refueling facilities at Mai Loc, both located just a few minutes' flying time from Fuller, the Cobras could expend two or three loads of ammunition for every load of fuel. But the North Vietnamese just kept coming. During the night the ARVN defenders, shell-shocked and demoralized by a month of incessant shelling, slipped out of the fire support base, leaving an Australian advisor, call sign Delta X-Ray, and his team alone on the smoldering mountaintop. Delta X-Ray and his team huddled in their bunkers and called for the Cobra gunships to turn their fires directly on the base. Everyone above ground was an enemy. The advisor and his team managed to slip out of Fuller just before dawn. With the coming of the new day, the weather cleared enough for tactical airstrikes, and the fighters laid down a blanket of napalm and iron bombs. Heavy enemy contact continued around Fuller for two more days. On 25 June the Redskins lost another pilot, Captain Albert "Pat" Carden. Carden was hit by a single round in the chest while Cobra 68-15042 was breaking out of a gun run.[62] Northern I Corps was a dangerous place. Thirty U.S. Army air crewmen, twenty of them pilots, were killed in sixteen separate actions between 31 March and 3 July 1971.[63] One year later aviators faced an even more sophisticated array of enemy air defense weapons, as the helicopter war moved from Tchepone to An Loc.

Following Lam Son 719, the Soviet Union and China provided military aid programs for North Vietnam, replaced and upgraded lost equipment, and provided the NVA with state-of-the-art air defense weapons. At the same time the U.S. continued fiscally restrained efforts to modernize and train the South Vietnamese armed forces. The NVA launched a cross-border invasion in the spring of 1972. The South Vietnamese were able to blunt the offensive, but only with massive U.S. air and naval support. President Nixon's rage with General Abrams continued to grow, and Abrams, like his predecessor General Westmoreland, was "kicked upstairs" and appointed as the army Chief of Staff.[64] The search for a negotiated settlement eluded Nixon until December 1972, when he authorized Operation Linebacker 2. U.S. air and naval forces mined North Vietnam's harbors, blockaded the ports, and sealed the overland supply routes coming in from China with a destructive bombing campaign.

The peace accords were signed in January 1973. In the wake of the Watergate scandal, Nixon left office, and Congress voted to shut off all military and financial aid to South Vietnam; meanwhile the Communist bloc continued to provide assistance to North Vietnam. The outcome of the war was inevitable.

Appendix A

THE HELICOPTERS OF LAM SON 719

AS THE 16 MARCH 1971 EDITION of *Newsweek Magazine* described it, the Vietnam War, at least from an American perspective, was about to become "The Helicopter War." The helicopters of Lam Son 719 were among the most advanced in the world at the time. But they were far from the technological marvels of today's army. No sophisticated GPS or navigation systems existed. Rather, navigation was done by map and compass, time, distance, and heading. There were no radar altimeters or terrain-avoidance devices; it was seat-of-your-pants flying in visual flight rules (VFR) conditions. If the pilot was forced into instrument weather flight (IFR), most aircraft were poorly equipped. A single automatic direction finder (ADF) receiver was the common configuration in most utility, attack, and observation helicopters. By 1970 the majority of the pilots graduating from flight school departed with a "tactical" instrument ticket, meaning that their qualifications were substantially less than those required to fly in IFR conditions under FAA regulations. Prudent pilots practiced IFR approach procedures at every opportunity—and prayed that the ground controlled approach (GCA) radar crew would be on the air when it was needed.

A variety of helicopters was involved in Lam Son 719, and a basic understanding of the various models and their functions aids in understanding the role of army aviation in that operation. The designations for various aircraft were preceded by the letters UH (utility helicopter), CH (cargo helicopter), OH (observation helicopter), or AH (attack helicopter), depending on their functions.

Figure 6. A UH-1H Iroquois "Slick" at Camp Evans, Vietnam, February 1971. Photograph from author's collection.

The UH-1, or "Huey," became the icon of the Vietnam War. The Huey was used for just about every purpose imaginable, hence the designation "utility helicopter." It evacuated the wounded, carried troops on combat assaults, served as a command-and-control platform, and resupplied the troops in the field. It was the helicopter all pilots were trained to fly. The army acquired its first Hueys in 1959. A total of 15,000 were produced, over half of which saw service in Vietnam. The Huey was retired from active service in 2009 after fifty years of service.

Five army UH-1 models were introduced into Vietnam, in addition to USAF models. The UH-1A, the earliest model UH-1, served primarily as a medical evacuation helicopter. The UH-1B was configured as a gunship. B-model UH-1s were later modified, given a more powerful engine and improved rotor system, and were subsequently identified as UH-1C, then as UH-1M when the power plant was again upgraded. The tenure of the UH-1A was relatively brief; it was replaced by the UH-1D, which featured an extended fuselage and a more powerful engine. By February of 1971 most UH-1Ds had been replaced by the UH-1H, which featured another engine upgrade. Whether it was a D-model or an H-model, the absence of weapons attached to the external hard points, as shown on the Charley Models in figure 7, resulted in the slang designation of the UH-1D and UH-1H as a "slick."

Figure 7. UH-1C Charley Model gunship of the 174th AHC "Sharks" gun platoon. Photograph provided by Joe Kline, a crew chief in Operation Lam Son 719.

Equipped with the older and less powerful Lycoming L-11 engines, the UH-1C simply did not have the power required by Operation Lam Son 719. While all types of helicopters suffered the effects of high density altitude, the underpowered Charley Model suffered the most.[1] In an after action review the 223rd CAB commander indicated that the Charley Models in his command had to be restricted to a 50 percent reduction in ammunition load and 950 pounds of fuel (approximately 65 percent of fuel capacity).[2] As the penetration into Laos progressed, the Charley Models barely had enough fuel for a round-trip flight into the area of operations. Given this reduced fuel load, the aircraft had little time to loiter. Charley Models lacked the airspeed required to be effective escort aircraft and had difficulty keeping up with the UH-1H lift-ships that were equipped with the more powerful Lycoming L-13 engine. In order to be effective, the escort guns had to have the speed to maneuver all along the intended flight path, engage targets, and then be able to resume a protective posture over the flight. With less power, the UH-1C's rate of climb, when coming out of gun runs, was low compared to the AH-1G Cobra, leaving the Charley Model and its crew vulnerable to enemy small-arms fire for a longer period of time and less capable of getting back into position for a second firing pass on targets. The fire control systems were obsolete compared to the Cobra. Still, the Charley Model did have some advantages. With a crew of four (a pilot or aircraft commander, a copilot, a crew chief who manned one of door guns, and a door gunner) the Charley Model had four sets of eyes to acquire targets. In the low-intensity combat operations characteristic of most operations in South Vietnam, the Charley Model was an adequate gunship. But Lam Son 719 was in Laos, not South Vietnam, and the threat environment was far from being "low intensity."

In order to have enough fuel to make the trip and enough ammunition to get the job done, Charley Model pilots frequently ignored weight limitations and overloaded their aircraft to the point that a normal helicopter takeoff was impossible. The pilots would apply maximum power to get the aircraft almost to a hover (this was called being "light on the skids"), apply forward cyclic, and start the aircraft bumping and sliding along the runway or sod taxiway, slowly gaining forward speed as the aircraft slid forward. On some occasions, in order to reduce the weight on the aircraft during this critical first phase of takeoff, the crew chief and door gunner would run alongside the aircraft, and then jump aboard as the aircraft gathered speed. Once reaching approximately fifteen to eighteen knots of forward airspeed, the aircraft, like all helicopters, would attain what is known as effective translational lift. At this point the rotor disk begins to acquire the aerodynamic characteristics of a solid airfoil and produces additional lift. The aircraft shudders slightly, and the nose tends to pitch up slightly. The pilot then applies a small amount of forward cyclic to continue gaining airspeed, is soon airborne, and can make a slight power reduction while continuing to climb. In some cases at Khe Sanh, if the aircraft was positioned near the southeast corner of the airfield, the pilots could take advantage of the plateau. They could waddle the helicopters over to the edge and dive off like fledgling eagles—betting that they could attain adequate lift to climb out before running out of air space, altitude, and ideas.

Aircraft performance made the Charley models more vulnerable to enemy fire, and constant operation at the upper end (or "red line") of the engine and power train systems led to premature wear, and sometimes failure, of critical power train components. As could be expected, Charley Model operational ready rates plummeted. The pilots who flew Charley Models during Lam Son 719 were a special breed of men, and many remain loyal to the virtues of the Charley Model, refusing to make any major concessions that the AH-1G Cobra is a superior gunship. Bob Hackett and P. J. Roths both flew Charley Models during Lam Son 719. Bob Hackett was assigned to the gun platoon of the 174th AHC stationed in southern I Corps when his company moved north for Lam Son on 29 January 1971. He recalled that:

The unit was stationed in Duc Pho in southern I Corp. We were the only AHC there and our primary mission was to support the 11th Brigade of the 23d Infantry Division. Since we were near the coast, having enough power to hover was generally not a problem. On the hottest days it could be a struggle getting out of the revetment and have to make a sliding takeoff thru the parking area. Unlike Laos, we almost always had the superior firepower in our AO [Area of Operations] and rarely lost either crews or aircraft due to hostile fire. For that matter, we always flew low level with an attitude that we wanted someone to take a shot at us. That sure changed in Laos. . . .

The thing I remember most about flying around Khe Sanh during this time was the lack of power. I distinctly remember one high DA [density altitude] day where I could not hover out of POL [the refueling point]. I had to bounce the aircraft over the fuel lines and up to the runway. I had to make a running take off from there. I'm not sure of the time involved, but by the time I finally got airborne, I had burned off about a quarter tank or more of fuel.[3]

Figure 8. AH-1G Cobra. This particular aircraft, affectionately known as "Balls Deuce," was shot down on 1 June 1971, as described in chapter 12. Photograph provided by Wayne Twiehaus.

The AH-1G Cobra, the only army helicopter not named after an Indian tribe, was the first helicopter designed strictly as a gunship. Like the Charley Model, it was equipped with a 540-rotor system and could be armed with a combination of rockets, mini-guns, and grenade launchers. But unlike the Charley Model, the Cobra featured a state-of-the-art fire control system, a stability control augmentation system (SCAS) of gyros and hydraulic actuators that automatically and instantly fed small control inputs, providing a stable and accurate firing platform, and a more powerful engine. The fuselage was only three feet wide, providing a smaller profile when inbound to the target. The more aerodynamic design gave the Cobra higher airspeed and greater maneuverability. The most common weapons configuration was a combination of nineteen-shot and seven-shot rocket pods on the port and starboard wing stores, and a 7.62mm mini-gun and an M-129 40mm grenade launcher in the chin turret.[4] The turret could traverse 115 degrees either side of center. The mini-gun could be selectively fired at either 2,000 or 4,000 rounds per minute, and the 40mm fired at a rate of approximately 350 shots per minute.

A variety of warheads could be attached to the MK-40 2.75-inch folding fin aerial rocket (FFAR). The selection included 10-pound and 17-pound high explosive rounds, smoke rounds, white phosphorus, and flechette warheads. The flechette was a small metal dart, approximately one eighth of an inch in diameter and an inch long. The sharp, pointed, stamped metal projectile had a tail to stabilize in flight similar to the feathers on an arrow. Each warhead contained 2,000 flechettes.

The warhead unleashed its deadly contents at a fixed time after launch, and simultaneously discharged a puff of red smoke so that the pilot would know the distance from the warhead to the target when the warhead opened up. If the pilot fired too soon, the effects of the round would be degraded by the constantly expanding impact pattern and loss of velocity of the flechettes. If the pilot fired too late, the warhead would simply plow into the ground. The high-explosive warheads could be armed with either proximity fuses that result in an airburst or point-detonating fuses. However, the proximity fuses were rarely used. The weakness of the 2.75 FFAR was that if rocket were fired at a target in a swamp or rice paddy, the result was a geyser of mud and a greatly reduced lethal bursting radius. If fired at a target in a canopied forest, there was a high likelihood that the warhead would detonate in the canopy. Depending on the density of the canopy, the result might be a lethal airburst, or the warhead could have no measureable result. The high explosive antitank (HEAT) warhead could penetrate enemy armor. But given the accuracy of the system, the pilot would normally have to be close to the target, within the range of the 12.7mm machinegun mounted on enemy tanks.

Rockets were usually fired in pairs. The pilot's armament control panel enabled him to select the inboard or outboard rocket pods and the number of pairs to be fired. Up to nineteen pairs could be selected. When multiple pairs were selected, an intervalometer automatically selected which tubes would be fired, and it separated the pairs by a fraction of a second to keep the rockets from colliding as they left the pod. The warhead fuse automatically armed when the rocket accelerated to 9.5 Gs.

Figure 9. Wayne Twiehaus (leader of 2nd Platoon, and later executive officer of D Company, 158th AHC, 101st Airborne Division) inspecting the turret weapons of an AH-1G. Photograph provided by Wayne Twiehaus.

The turret weapons were typically controlled by the copilot/gunner in the front seat. The mini-gun was lethal, but could be prone to failure if not meticulously maintained. The 40mm grenade had a bursting radius similar to that of a hand grenade, approximately five meters. Like the 2.75 FFAR equipped with the high explosive warheads, the terrain influenced the terminal effects. But the gunner could put down a steady stream of grenades and quickly adjust to the target. Often referred to as the "chunker" or "thumper," the M-129 grenade launcher was an excellent weapon for suppressing ground fire while the pilot was breaking out of his dive and the broad side of the aircraft was an inviting target for enemy gunners. The comparatively low velocity of the projectiles and the high volume of fire would ensure that rounds were still impacting on the enemy, even after the pilot had turned past the turret traverse limits. If the timing of the wingman's attack of the target was right, he was inbound to the target in time to continue the attack on the target by the time the last 40mm grenade impacted.

The "school solution" (the procedure taught during flight training) for target attack was to reduce power to 25 psi of torque, while raising the nose of the aircraft to zero out the airspeed. This was best accomplished if the pilot could align the aircraft so that the target was either to his left or right and then dive toward the target. The purpose of losing the airspeed prior to the dive was to allow more time on the target prior to reaching the VNE (velocity never exceeded) of 190 knots. Once inbound to the target, the pilot would push in the armament panel circuit breakers, arm up his switches, and start his gun run. At the bottom of the dive, the pilot of the lead aircraft would notify his wingman which direction he was breaking, and the copilot/gunner in the front seat would start firing on the target with his turret weapons while the pilot pulled out of the dive and came back around for another run on the target.

In late 1970 and early 1971 some Cobras were equipped with the M35 20mm cannon, providing greater standoff range and destruction of hard targets. Mounted on the inboard attaching points of the port wing, the M35 was both dependable and lethal. The ammunition was a mix of high explosive, armor-piercing, and armor-piercing incendiary

Figure 10. M35 20mm cannon. Photograph provided by Wayne Twiehaus.

rounds. It could penetrate the thickest of forest canopies, light armor, and some field fortifications. However, the positioning of the weapon on the wing stores, combined with recoil and muzzle blast, created issues with aircraft maintenance. The 20mm cannon was moved from the wing stores to the turret position in the follow-on gunship (the redesign of the AH-01G), the AH-1S.

Two types of light observation helicopters (LOH) were flown during Lam Son 719, the OH-6A and the OH-58A. It soon became apparent that the enemy strength and firepower in Laos placed these helicopters and their crews at an unacceptable risk in their traditional scout role.[5] But both continued service during Lam Son 719 in the critical role of securing northern I Corps and the DMZ. The importance of this mission increased as the NVA made a concerted effort to attack allied lines of communications and supply points. Cobras assumed the scout mission in Laos.

Figure 11. A OH-6A with blades removed being pushed out of the hangar at A Company, 5th Transportation Battalion, for installation of rotor blades following repair in February or March of 1971 at Camp Eagle, Vietnam. Photograph from author's collection.

One of the amazing characteristics of the OH-6 was the survivability of the crew compartment during a crash. When you saw one go
down while flying at a low level during scout missions, you would swear
that no one could have survived the crash. But the Hughes engineers
built the OH-6 around a system of programmed collapse: the skids, tail
boom, and rotor system would collapse, absorbing much of the impact,
enhancing crew survivability. The OH-6 was nimble and quick, the
ideal helicopter for flying below tree-top level and looking for signs of
the enemy.

Three different types of cargo helicopters supported Lam Son 719,
the CH-47, CH-54 and the marine version of the CH-53. The CH-47
"Chinook" carried large loads of fuel, ammunition, artillery pieces, and
supplies forward, and in a mission that assumed greater importance
as the operation proceeded, back-hauled damaged aircraft. Classified as a "medium-lift helicopter," the CH-47 could carry a payload

*Figure 12. The red dust at Khe Sanh boils as a CH-47 picks up a damaged Cobra
during Lam Son 719. The small parachute attached to the tail of the Cobra helped
to keep the aircraft from spinning during evacuation. Photograph provided by
Wayne Twiehaus.*

Figure 13. CH-54 Tarhe. Photograph provided by Wayne Twiehaus.

Figure 14. CH-53. Photograph provided by Joe Kline.

of approximately 15,900 pounds under ideal conditions. It was the prime mover for ARVN 105mm howitzers, fuel, and ammunition, but heavier loads required a "heavy-lift helicopter."

With a payload of 25,000 pounds, the CH-54 "Tarhe," also known as the "Sky Crane," was the army's heavy-lift helicopter. During Lam Son the CH-54s moved the heavier 155mm howitzers, the heavier pieces of engineer equipment, and bulldozers for the ARVN. The CH-54 was unique in that it had a position for a third pilot in a rear-facing seat. This pilot maneuvered the aircraft while sling loads were attached.

The CH-53 provided heavy lift for the navy and marine corps. Two USMC squadrons out of Da Nang supported Lam Son 719. The USMC CH-53D had a lift capacity in excess of 17,000 lbs. Twelve CH-53s were damaged by enemy fire, one was destroyed, and another crashed while en route back to Da Nang. The cause of the crash was suspected to be combat damage.

Regardless of how many aircraft were destroyed and damaged, helicopters proved to be resilient. In reality, considering the heavy volume of antiaircraft, small arms, mortar, and artillery fire, losses of aircraft and crewmembers were comparatively light. Helicopter crews flew 118,651 sorties in support of Operation Lam Son 719.[6] The aviators left a legacy of uncompromising professionalism and courage under fire.

Appendix B

THE BUTCHER'S BILL

NIXON: What were the casualties this week?

KISSINGER: Thirty-two.

NIXON: I thought they'd be down.

KISSINGER: Cut in half –

NIXON: I mean I thought they'd be lower than that.

KISSINGER: Thirty-two is pretty low. Once you get below –

NIXON: Fifty?

KISSINGER: Fifty, its really –

NIXON: Forty? [unclear]

KISSINGER: That's cut in half –

NIXON: There's still some carryovers from –

KISSINGER: Yes.

NIXON: – the helicopter pilots, the poor guys. That's one bit of good news isn't it?

KISSINGER: Yeah.

—A conversation between President Nixon and Henry Kissinger on 10 May 1971[1]

All of Vietnam suffered devastating casualties during the war. Available sources contain a wide assortment of casualty figures for Lam Son 719. Lewis Sorley states South Vietnamese casualties as 1,118 killed in action, more than 4,000 wounded, and 209 missing; he puts the number of NVA killed in action at 16,244.[2] General Hinh and General Davidson published higher figures for South Vietnamese losses: 1,764 killed, 6,632 wounded, and 689 missing for a total casualty figure of 9,065.[3] *Newsweek* stated that the South Vietnamese casualties were closer to 9,800.[4]

Every account of Lam Son 719 includes quotes on the numbers of U.S. casualties and the numbers of aircraft damaged and destroyed. But the numbers in these accounts vary, and the authors provide little information on how they verified their figures as accurate. Nor do the authors state the criteria they used for determining which events are attributable to the operation. Given the passage of time, the reporting system that was in place, and, in some cases, the subjective nature of the report's elements, it is unlikely that these differences can be resolved.

It is difficult to find consensus for the total number of U.S. casualties during Operation Lam Son 719. According to the U.S. Army's Center for Military History, the count is 215 killed in action, 1,149 wounded, and 38 missing.[5] Some authors do not include the casualties from the Lam Son rear area in South Vietnam, and it is sometimes difficult to make the philosophical decision as to whether some casualties were the result of accidents or enemy action. D Troop, 3rd Squadron, 5th Cavalry, was attached to the 1st Brigade, 5th Mechanized Division, and was an active participant in protecting the Lam Son rear area from Quang Tri to Khe Sanh. D Troop had a minimum of seven aircraft hit, including five OH-58s, one AH-1G, and one UH-1H, sustaining a total of fourteen pilots or crew members killed in action.[6] However, some sources fail to include these figures in their tally of Lam Son 719 losses.

Intense efforts to rescue downed aircrews greatly reduced the numbers of American soldiers that would have otherwise been killed. At the onset of Lam Son 719, aircrew recovery was an accepted function of the other crews involved in the mission, whose members would swoop in and pick up their brothers in arms. As the operation progressed, it became apparent that a more organized and disciplined approach was required. Chase ships, accompanied by gunships to provide cover for crew extractions, followed the lift ships and went into action as soon as an aircraft was downed. The hazards of rescue operations increased proportionately to the amount of time the crew was on the ground due to the enemy's ability to quickly converge on the downed aircraft. The crew had to be picked up almost immediately. The number of chase ships dedicated to the mission varied from one chase ship for every ten lift ships to one chase ship for every five lift ships. Gunships, which were always in short supply, were allocated at rates varying from one light fire team (two gunships) for each five chase ships to three teams for each ten chase ships. The 101st Airborne Division after action report lists ninety-four extraction operations that resulted in the rescue of 347 crew members. Nine attempts were unsuccessful, leading to 30 crew members being listed as MIA.[7] Some of these soldiers were able to evade the enemy until such time as ARVN soldiers rescued them and others were subsequently classified as killed in action. An effort to recover the remains of some of those killed in action continues still.

It is equally difficult to find consensus on the number of aircraft destroyed and damaged. Early sources state that 108 were destroyed and 618 were damaged. Later sources set the numbers at 107 destroyed and 544 damaged. Without exception the authors of these sources provide no source for their statements and no criteria for the determination of the numbers. Summing the combat damage and loss figures in the 101st Airborne Division after action report results in a total of 632 incidents of battle damage involving 441 aircraft with different tail numbers with 90 aircraft destroyed. Some aircraft were subjected to combat damage on multiple days, and some aircraft that were listed as damaged were destroyed in subsequent actions.[8] Some aircraft that were initially categorized as destroyed were later classified as repairable.[9]

The 101st Airborne Division statistics do not include aircraft losses or damage from actions occurring anywhere except places identified by map grid coordinates preceded by the 100,000-meter grid identifier "XD"—an area that included the area of operations in Laos and extended approximately ten kilometers east of Khe Sanh. The report excludes losses of the 1st Brigade, 5th Mechanized Division, even though it played a vital role in securing the Lam Son rear area. Including the losses of the 1st Brigade and its supporting aviation units increases aircraft losses by eight. In addition to the 632 incidents of damage inflicted by enemy fire, the division's aviation safety office reported fourteen aircraft damaged as the result of accidents in a nontactical environment and another twenty damaged or destroyed in a tactical setting.[10] It is an accounting conundrum beyond solution. These figures do not include six USAF aircraft and one navy aircraft lost during the operation.[11] James Williams, the historian for the Army Aviation Center from 1997 to 2005, states that, officially, 197 helicopters were "irrecoverably lost" during Lam Son 719, but he provides no number for damaged helicopters.[12] It could have been worse had there not been a dedicated effort to recover downed aircraft from Laos.

The Communists claim 496 aircraft were destroyed or captured during Lam Son 719.[13] It is impossible to lend any credibility to this claim. For example, the Communists assert that they shot down twenty-eight aircraft on 16 March. A review of the 101st Airborne Division's after action report indicates that a total of thirteen aircraft sustained combat damage on that date. Of those thirteen, five were on the ground at Khe Sanh and damaged by a rocket attack and therefore cannot be candidates for the designation "shot down." Of the remaining eight, only one was destroyed, and the damage sustained on the remaining seven was categorized as light to moderate. Only one other aircraft was lost on that date—a Cobra assigned to the 4th Battalion, 77th ARA, that was involved in a weather-related accident.

Philosophically, it is difficult to accept the idea of excluding all losses attributed to accidents from the count of aircraft and crews lost during Lam Son 719. For example, the 101st Airborne Division's after action report does not include UH-1H 67-19516 or UH-1C 65-09503. These two aircraft collided in midair during an insertion on 23 February. Eight men died and both aircraft were destroyed. But because the incident was an accident, these losses were not included in the statistics even though the combat environment was a contributing factor.

As you peel back the layers of Lam Son 719, if you dig deep enough, you will finally reach the mammoth effort of the aviation maintenance units that struggled, often in vain, to keep the fleet in the air. Twenty-four-hour operations and mind-numbing fatigue were the rule, not the exception. Approximately two thirds of all aircraft receiving combat damage were repaired within forty-eight hours.[14]

The concept for maintenance support was that any maintenance or repair effort that could be accomplished in one day would be performed by the direct support detachment assigned to each of the aviation companies. If aircraft damage triage indicated that repairs would take in excess of three days, the aircraft was evacuated to the 101st Airborne Division's 5th Transportation Battalion. The 5th consisted of two aircraft repair companies and the headquarters company. Company A was stationed at Camp Eagle, and Company B was stationed at Phu Bai. In addition, the 335th Aircraft Maintenance Company, stationed at Quang Tri, reinforced the 5th Transportation Battalion. If the extent of repairs indicated a repair time in excess of ten days (or one thousand man-hours) the aircraft was further evacuated to the 58th Aviation Maintenance Battalion (General Support), located at Red Beach in Da Nang. Depending on the extent of damage, the aircraft was either repaired at Red Beach or evacuated back to the states for repair at the depot level. To enhance the repair capability of the 58th Battalion, the 34th Support Group deployed the floating aircraft maintenance facility (FAMF), the USS *Corpus Christi Bay*, to Da Nang Bay where a limited number of depot-level repairs could be made.

Excluding hundreds of repairs on items such as avionics, radios, and electrical components, the three direct support maintenance companies repaired 1,072 aircraft and returned them to the owning units. But not all of these aircraft required repairs due to combat damage. Some were brought in for scheduled inspections and changes of major components. Two hundred fifty-two aircraft were evacuated for repair at the general support or depot level. These numbers do not include numerous aircraft determined damaged beyond repair. Such aircraft were turned in for salvage.[15] Author John Prados refers to a figure of 107 aircraft "lost" in Laos and claims that this figure is understated. James Gibson refers to an air force report that 200 were lost. Both claim aircraft were not counted as "lost" as long as they could be "recovered," and that aircraft were counted as "recovered" even if all that could be retrieved was a piece of metalwork with the aircraft number.[16] Even allowing for the semantic differences between "lost and recovered" and "damaged and destroyed," it is difficult to accept these statements as fact. The 101st Aviation Group duty log contains multiple entries where commanders on the scene advised the tactical operations center that an aircraft that had been shot down, was obviously destroyed, and no recovery attempt should be made.

The confusion may rest in the fact that some aircraft classified as destroyed were extracted from Laos for two reasons. First, the determination of "damaged" versus "destroyed" was made after inspection, and these inspections, for obvious reasons, were not performed on the ground in Laos. Second, even if the level of damage indicated destruction, the wreckage often included weapons, radios, and sometimes communications security systems, which could not be allowed to fall into enemy hands. I doubt that an accurate accounting exists.

Volume 2, annex C, of the 101st Airborne Division's final report on Lam Son 719 states that the division and its supporting aviation units flew 118,651 sorties involving 39,179 flight-hours in support of Lam Son 719. If the statistical data is expanded to include support of the rear area, the sortie total increases to 204,065 and the flying hours increase to 78,968. Given the intense combat environment, aircrew casualties and aircraft losses were comparatively light. These statistics are a testament to the durability of the aircraft and the stamina of the men who flew, maintained, and repaired them.

NOTES

Abbreviations

CHECO   J. F. Loye, G. K. St. Clair, L. J. Johson, and J. W. Dennison, Contemporary Historical Evaluation of Current Operations, Lam Son 719 (Washington, D.C.: Department of the Air Force, 1971).

101st Aviation Group Narrative   101st Aviation Group, Operation Lam Son 719, *February 8, 1971 to March 25, 1971: A Narrative Description of Air Support by the 101st Aviation Group* (Camp Eagle, Vietnam: 101st Aviation Group, 1971).

Final Report   Headquarters, 101st Airborne Division, "101st Airborne Division Final Report," *Airmobile Operations in Support of Lam Son 719 Report* (Camp Eagle, Vietnam: 101st Airborne Division, 1971).

FRUS   U.S. Department of State, Office of the Historian, *Foreign Relations of the United States*, Washington, D.C.: U.S. Government Printing Office, 1988–2010.

Preface

1. See appendix B for a full account of losses.
2. Lewis Sorley, *Vietnam Chronicles: The Abrams Tapes, 1968–1972* (Lubbock: Texas Tech University Press, 2004), 558.

Introduction

1. Stanley Karnow, *Vietnam: A History* (New York: Penguin, 1983), 253.
2. "Notes of Conversation Between President-Elect Kennedy and President Eisenhower," in *FRUS, 1961–1963, vol. 24, Laos Crisis*, doc. 7.
3. Merle L. Pribbenow, trans., *Victory in Vietnam* (Lawrence: University of Kansas Press, 2002), 88.
4. Ibid.
5. "Memorandum from the Deputy Secretary of Defense (Gilpatric) to the President," *FRUS, 1961–1963, vol. 1, Vietnam*, doc. 42.

6. "National Security Action Memorandum No. 52," *FRUS, 1961–1963, vol. 1, Vietnam,* doc. 52.

7. "NSAM No. 104," retrieved from www.fas.org/irp/offdocs/nsam-jfk/nsam104.htm July 9, 2009.

8. Bruce Palmer, Jr., *The 25-Year War: America's Role in Vietnam* (Lexington: University Press of Kentucky, 1984), 11–12.

9. "Memorandum of Conference with President Kennedy," *FRUS, 1961–1963, vol. 24, Laos Crisis,* doc. 25.

10. "Memorandum from the Under Secretary of State for Political Affairs' SpecialAssistant (Jorden) to the Assistant Secretary of State for Far Eastern Affairs (Harriman)," *FRUS, 1961–1963, vol. 3, Vietnam,* doc. 64.

11. For more on Diem's rise to power see *FRUS, 1955–1957, vol. 1, Vietnam;* and *FRUS, 1958–1960, vol. 1, Vietnam.*

12. "Telegram from the Embassy in Vietnam to the Department of State," *FRUS, 1961–1963, vol. 2, Vietnam,* doc. 102.

13. One conspirator was Col. (later, Gen.) Nguyen Van Thieu, the commander of the 5th ARVN Division. Thieu continued Diem's practice of selecting the military's commander on the basis of personal loyalty as part of his anti-coup defense. Throughout the war every diplomatic effort to end this practice failed until mid-1972, when the Thieu government was faced with the prospect of being overrun by the NVA during the 1972 Easter Offensive.

14. *FRUS, 1961–1963, vol. 3, Vietnam,* docs. 266 and 284.

15. "Memorandum from the Chairman of the Joint Chiefs of Staff (Taylor) and the Secretary of Defense (McNamara) to the President," *FRUS, 1961–1963, vol. 4, Vietnam,* doc. 167.

16. "National Security Action Memorandum 263," *FRUS, 1961–1963, vol. 4, Vietnam,* doc. 263.

17. *FRUS, 1961–1963, vol. 3, Vietnam,* docs. 284, 285, 299, and 300.

18. Maxwell D. Taylor, *Swords and Plowshares: A Memoir* (New York: W. W. Norton, 1972), 301. The demise of Diem did not end the Buddhist crisis. Turmoil continued until a 1965 Buddhist uprising that approached the dimensions of a civil war. It was crushed by the president of South Vietnam, Nguyen Cao Ky. Neither Diem's suitability to govern nor his removal were new topics of discussion in 1963. Gen. Joseph Collins, Eisenhower's Special Representative to Vietnam, raised the issue in 1955 in *FRUS, 1955–1957, vol. 1, Vietnam.* Gen. Maxwell Taylor addressed the same issues six years later in *FRUS, 1961–1963, vol. 1, Vietnam,* doc. 210.

19. Virginia Morris, introduction to *A History of the Ho Chi Minh Trail: The Road to Freedom* (Bangkok: Orchid Press, 2006).

20. Karnow, *Vietnam: A History,* 340.

Chapter 1

1. "Situation Report Prepared in the Department of State for the President," *FRUS, 1961–1963, vol. 4, Vietnam*, doc. 325.

2. "Memorandum for Record of the Meeting," *FRUS, 1961–1963, vol. 4, Vietnam*, doc. 330. McCone's view of Johnson's attitude toward "do-gooders" and social reforms, while perhaps not germane to the battle against infiltration, should not be dismissed. Stated in more precise terms, the issues were corruption and the failure of South Vietnam's government to win the support of its people. In April 1961 Theodore Sorenson, President Kennedy's special counsel sent a memorandum to the president that contained the following quote: "There is no clearer example of a country that cannot be saved unless it saves itself through increased popular support, governmental, economic and military reforms and reorganizations; and the encouragement of new political leaders." See *FRUS, 1961–1963, vol. 1, Vietnam*, doc. 37 for the full text. Corruption was endemic in the Diem government, and all the governments that followed. For more on the topic, refer to *FRUS, 1961–1963, vol. 1, Vietnam*, docs. 7, 36, 164, 210, and 298; *FRUS, 1961–1963, vol. 2, Vietnam*, docs. 35, 108, 282, and 302; and *FRUS, 1961–1963, vol. 4, Vietnam*, docs. 130, 155, and 319.

3. Graham A. Cosmas, *MACV: The Joint Staff in the Years of Escalation, 1962–1967*, (Washington: U.S. Army Center of Military History, 2006), 160.

4. Phillip Davidson, *Vietnam at War: The History 1946–1975*, (New York: Oxford University Press, 1988), 324.

5. Cosmas, *MACV*, 161–64.

6. Davidson, *Vietnam at War*, 336.

7. Michael Beschloss, *Reaching for Glory: Lyndon Johnson's Secret White House Tapes 1964–1965*, (New York: Simon and Schuster, 2001), 408.

8. Karnow, *Vietnam: A History*, 430.

9. George C. Herring, *America's Longest War: The United States and Vietnam 1950–1975*, (New York: McGraw-Hill, 1986), 190.

10. *FRUS, 1961–1963, vol. 1, Vietnam*, doc. 220; George Ball, *The Past Has Another Pattern*, (New York: W. W. Norton 1983), 366, 367.

11. "National Security Action Memorandum No. 238," *FRUS, 1961–1963, vol. 2, Vietnam*, doc. 242.

12. "Letter from Director of Central Intelligence McCone to President Johnson," *FRUS, 1964–1968, vol. 2, Vietnam*, doc. 234.

13. "Letter from Director of Central Intelligence McCone to President Johnson," *FRUS, 1964–1968, vol. 2, Vietnam*, doc. 279.

14. "Memorandum from Secretary of Defense McNamara to President Johnson," *FRUS, 1964–1968, vol. 3, Vietnam*, doc. 212.

15. See H. R. McMasters, *Dereliction of Duty: Johnson, McNamara, the Joint Chiefs of Staff, and the Lies that Led to Vietnam* (New York: Harper Collins, 1997). McMasters describes how the national political leadership in the executive

branch led the nation into an expanded role in the Vietnam War and how senior military leadership advice was not used in decision-making.

16. Charles G. Cooper with Richard E. Goodspeed, Cheers and Tears: *A Marine's Story of Combat in Peace and War*, (Reno: Wesley Press, 2002), 3–6.

17. "Telegram from the Embassy in Laos to the Department of State," *FRUS, 1964–1968, vol. 28, Laos*, doc. 182.

18. Cosmas, MACV, 378–79.

19. U.S. Army War College Strategic Studies Institute, *A Study of Strategic Lessons Learned in Vietnam* (Mclean, VA: BDM, 1982), 6:74.

20. *FRUS, 1964–1968, vol. 28, Laos*, docs. 286, 288, 292, and 295.

21. The North Vietnamese habitually used the same areas along the eastern borders of Laos and Cambodia as sanctuaries and supply depots. These areas were referred to as "base areas" and numbered for ease of identification. The shapes of different base areas vary in historical references but the general locale remains the same.

22. "Memorandum from the Joint Chiefs of Staff to Secretary of Defense McNamara," *FRUS, 1964–1968, vol. 5, Vietnam*, doc. 418.

23. "Notes of Meeting," *FRUS, 1964–1968, vol. 5, Vietnam*, doc. 428.

24. William Westmoreland, *A Soldier Reports* (New York: Da Capo Press, 1989), 272.

25. John M. Collins, *Military Geography for Professionals and the Public*, (Washington: Potomac Books, 2012), chap. 19.

26. Ibid.

27. In later discussions of proposed assaults through the Tchepone corridor, there are references to five or six divisions being required. The Collins account, ibid., does not specifically specify how many divisions the plan required and if the divisions in his plan would also be responsible for securing Route 9 in Vietnam. This issue will surface during the discussion of Operation Lam Son 719, which resembled El Paso.

28. Collins, *Military Geography*, chap. 19.

29. "Memorandum for the File by President Johnson," *FRUS, 1964–1968, vol. 5, Vietnam*, doc. 441.

30. Maitland T. McInerney, *A Contagion of War*, (Boston: Boston Publishing, 2000), 168.

31. Davidson, *Vietnam at War*, 496–505.

32. See ibid., 473–572 for a detailed discussion of the Tet Offensive and the impact of this offensive on President Johnson's subsequent actions.

33. The P2V-5 would later be designated as the OP-2E.

34. Robert C. Havens in discussion with the author, 21 November 2012. Havens served as a petty officer and photo intelligence specialist with VO-67 from the time the squadron was first organized until it was disbanded.

35. Pat Sweeney (former USAF captain and FAC assigned to the 23rd TASS in 1967–68) in discussion with the author, 1 February 2013.

36. Bernard C. Nalty, *The War Against Trucks: Aerial Interdiction in Southern Laos, 1968–1972*, Air Force History and Museums Program (Washington, D.C.: United States Air Force, 2005), 302, 303.

37. Davidson, *Vietnam at War,* 484–92.

38. Palmer, *The 25-Year War*, 107.

39. The "tickets" referred to having the troops needed or the authorization for a specific course of action. In this case, when President Johnson denied Westmoreland's request for additional troops and authorization to go into Laos, Westmoreland "did not have the tickets." See Collins, *Military Geography*, chap. 19.

40. "Memorandum for the Record," *FRUS, 1964–1968, vol. 7, Vietnam*, doc. 49.

41. For additional details on the negotiation of the 31 October bombing halt agreement, Thieu's refusal to accept the NLF as a co-equal, and the allegation that the Nixon campaign attempted to sabotage the negotiations refer to *FRUS, 1969–1976, vol. 7, Vietnam*, docs. 82, and 123-212.

42. "Memorandum for the Record: The President's Meeting with General William W. Momyer," *FRUS, 1964–1968, vol. 7, Vietnam*, doc. 110; in the same volume, see also "Notes of Meeting with the President," doc. 68.

43. Nalty, *War Against Trucks*, 16–48.

44. "Notes of Meeting," *FRUS, 1964–1968, vol. 7, Vietnam*, doc. 248.

Chapter 2

1. "Memorandum from the President's Military Representative (Taylor) to President Kennedy," *FRUS, 1961–1963, vol. 24, Laos Crisis*, doc. 187.

2. Christopher Robbins, *The Ravens: The Men Who Flew in America's Secret War in Laos* (New York: Crown Publishers, 1987), viii.

3. "Editorial Note," *FRUS, 1964–1968, vol. 1, Vietnam*, doc. 206.

4. "Memorandum from the Joint Chiefs of Staff to Secretary of Defense McNamara," *FRUS, 1964–1968, vol. 28, Laos*, doc. 151. Barrel Roll, like many air campaigns following it, was originally conceived as a short-term operation but continued for years.

5. Jacob Van Staaveren, *Interdiction in Southern Laos 1960–1968* (Washington: Center for Air Force History, 1993), 49.

6. Ibid., 67.

7. Ibid.

8. "Telegram from the Commander in Chief, Military Assistance Command, Vietnam (Westmoreland) to the Commander in Chief, Pacific (Sharp)," *FRUS, 1964–1968, vol. 27, Mainland Southeast Asia, Regional Affairs*, doc. 165.

9. "Action Memorandum from the Deputy Assistant Secretary of State for East Asian Affairs (Habib) to the Under Secretary of State (Katzenbach)," *FRUS,*

1964–1968, vol. 27, Mainland Southeast Asia, Regional Affairs, doc. 210; "Memorandum from Secretary of Defense McNamara to President Johnson," *FRUS, 1964–1968, vol. 4, Vietnam*, doc. 36.

10. A pilot cleansed of his military identity was called "sheep dipped."

11. Forward Air Controllers Association, *Cleared Hot: Forward Air Controller Stories from the Vietnam War*, ed. Alice Witterman, Peter Condon, and Charles Pocock (Fort Walton Beach: Forward Air Controllers Association, 2008), 338.

12. "Telegram from the Commander, Military Assistance Command, Vietnam (Westmoreland) to the Commander in Chief, Pacific (Sharp)," *FRUS, 1964–1968, vol. 28, Laos*, doc. 235.

13. Walter Want in discussion with the author, 3 June 2012.

14. A forward area navigator (FAN) later replaced the second pilot.

15. A starlight scope was a night-vision device that intensified the ambient light.

16. Don Brown (Retired Lt. Col., USAF captain and FAC assigned to the 23rd TASS in 1967–1968) in discussion with the author, January 2012.

17. Darrel Whitcomb (formerly of the Ravens, and later the Nails, author of *The Rescue of Bat 21*) in discussion with the author, 22 January 2012.

18. Staaveren, *Interdiction in Southern Laos*, vii.

19. "USAF Ops. from Thailand Jan 67–Jul 1968 (Part 1)," Bud Harton Collection, The Vietnam Center and Archive, Texas Tech University, accessed 10 January 2013, http://www.vietnam.ttu.edu/virtualarchive/items .php?item=168300010948.

20. "Intelligence Memorandum Prepared by the Directorate of Intelligence of the Central Intelligence Agency," *FRUS, 1964–1968, vol. 28, Laos*, doc. 363.

21. "Intelligence Memorandum Prepared by the Central Intelligence Agency," *FRUS, 1964–1968, vol. 28, Laos*, doc. 370.

22. "USAF 1965–73 Fixed Wing Gunships," Bud Harton Collection, The Vietnam Center and Archive, Texas Tech University, accessed 10 January 2013, http://www.vietnam.ttu.edu/virtualarchive/items.php?item=168300010903.

23. See Nalty, *War Against Trucks* for a detailed discussion.

24. John Plaster, *SOG: The Secret War of America's Commandos in Vietnam* (New York: Simon and Schuster, 1997), 11.

25. "Telegram from the Embassy in Vietnam to the Department of State," *FRUS, 1964–1968, vol. 1, Vietnam*, doc. 318.

26. Plaster, *SOG*, 1–16.

27. Plaster, *SOG*, 18.

28. "Memorandum from the Deputy Assistant Secretary of State for East Asian and Pacific Affairs (Unger) to the Under Secretary of State (Katzenbach)," *FRUS, 1964–1968, vol. 28, Laos*, doc. 270.

29. "Telegram from the Department of State to the Embassy in Laos," *FRUS, 1964–1968, vol. 28, Laos*, doc. 277.

30. *FRUS, 1964–1968, vol. 28, Laos*, docs. 282, 292, 302, and 395.

31. "Telegram from the Embassy in Laos to the Department of State," *FRUS, 1964–1968, vol. 28, Laos,* doc. 302.

32. "Memorandum from the Central Intelligence Agency to President Johnson," *FRUS, 1964–1968, vol. 28, Laos,* doc. 304.

33. "Memorandum from the President's Special Assistant (Rostow) to President Johnson," *FRUS, 1964–1968, vol. 28, Laos,* doc. 317.

34. "Telegram from the Embassy in Laos to the Department of State," *FRUS, 1964–1968, vol. 28, Laos,* doc. 302.

35. Cosmas, *MACV,* 327.

36. "Memorandum from the Director of the Office of Laos and Cambodia Affairs (Herz) to the Assistant Secretary of State for East Asian and Pacific Affairs (Bundy)," *FRUS, 1964–1968, vol. 28, Laos,* doc. 334. Another weakness of centralized control is that the most immediate aircraft available may not have the best ordnance on board for the mission, be the best type aircraft for the mission, or have adequate fuel reserves.

37. Plaster, *SOG,* 62–68.

38. Ibid., 171.

39. "Group Mobile" was a term held over from the time the French occupied Indochina. It is roughly equivalent to a brigade or regiment and, as the name implies, a mobile force.

40. Sar Phouthasack in discussion with the author, throughout 2011 and 2012.

41. "Memorandum from the Deputy Assistant Secretary of State for East Asian and Pacific Affairs (Unger) to the Under Secretary of State (Katzenbach)," *FRUS, 1964–1968, vol. 28, Laos,* doc. 270.

42. "Telegram from the Embassy in Laos to the Department of State," *FRUS, 1964–1968, vol. 28, Laos,* doc. 216.

43. Plaster, *SOG,* 67–68.

Chapter 3

1. Monthly casualties were extracted from the American War Library. Retrieved from www.americanwarlibrary.com/vietnam/vwc24.htm on 21 June 2008.

2. "Memorandum from President Nixon to his Assistant for National Security Affairs (Kissinger)," *FRUS, vol. 6, Vietnam,* doc. 15.

3. For ease of identification of specific geographic areas, the border areas where the Communists habitually stored supplies and marshaled their forces for attacks into South Vietnam were referred to as "base areas." Each base area was numbered for ease of reference. Key transportation nodes on the Ho Chi Minh Trail were also identified as base areas.

4. Kenneth Sams, *Project CHECO Report: The Fall of A Shau,* (Headquarters, PACAF Tactical Evaluation Center, 1966).

5. *CMH Publication 90-23, Part 2,* (Washington: Center of Military History, 1989), 93–94.

6. Mark D. Bernstein, "Vietnam War: Operation Dewey Canyon," *Vietnam Magazine* (June 2007), retrieved from http://www.historynet.com/vietnam-war-operation-dewey-canyon.htm.

7. Charles D. Melson, "Thirty Years Later," *Fortitudine: Bulletin of the Marine Corps Historical Program* 28, no. 2 (1999): 3–8.

8. Davidson, *Vietnam at War*, 590–91.

9. "Notes of Meeting," *FRUS, vol. 7, Vietnam*, doc. 140.

10. "Memorandum of a meeting between the President's Assistant for National Security Affairs, Secretary of Defense Laird, and the Chairman of the Joint Chiefs of Staff (Wheeler)," *FRUS, 1969–1976, vol. 6, Vietnam*, doc. 12.

11. Henry Kissinger, *Ending the War in Vietnam* (New York: Simon and Shuster, 2005), 61, 62.

12. Ibid.

13. "Memorandum from President Nixon to his Assistant for National Security Affairs (Kissinger)," *FRUS, 1969–1976, vol. 6, Vietnam*, doc. 15.

14. "Memorandum from the President's Assistant for National Security Affairs (Kissinger) to President Nixon," *FRUS, vol. 6, Vietnam*, doc. 29.

15. "Telegram from the Department of State to the Embassy in Vietnam," *FRUS, 1969–1976, vol. 6, Vietnam*, doc. 30.

16. Kissinger, *Ending the War*, 63.

17. "Memorandum for the Record," *FRUS, vol. 6, Vietnam*, doc. 39. In footnote 2 to doc. 39, the author of the *FRUS* volume states that in his discussions with Henry Kissinger, prior to issuing the order, President Nixon originally intended to extend the retaliatory strikes to North Vietnam. Nixon later relented on his order that Secretary Rogers not be informed and Rogers was included in a meeting to discuss what the president had already decided to do.

18. "Editor's Note," *FRUS, 1969–1976, vol. 6, Vietnam*, doc. 41.

19. Alexander Haig and Charles McCarry, *Inner Circles: How America Changed the World* (New York: Warner Books, 1992), 207–208.

20. Ibid.

21. H. R. Haldeman, *The Haldeman Diaries* (New York: G. P. Putnam's Sons, 1994), 51.

22. Kissinger, *Ending the War*, 67.

23. *FRUS, 1969–1976, vol. 6, Vietnam*, docs. 11, 17, 18, 38, 48, 202, and 246.

24. Kissinger, *Ending the War*, 68.

25. Samuel Zaffiri, *Hamburger Hill*, (Novato: Presidio Press, 1988), 273, 274.

26. Davidson, *Vietnam at War*, 614.

27. Kissinger, *Ending the War*, 81, 82.

28. "Editor's Note," *FRUS, 1969–1976, vol. 6, Vietnam*, doc. 80.

29. Davidson, *Vietnam at War*, 596, 597.

30. "Memorandum from the President's Assistant for National Security Affairs (Kissinger) to the President," *FRUS, 1969–1976, vol. 6, Vietnam*, doc. 87.

31. The brigade's size and composition is not mentioned in Robert Ginsburg's memorandum, but it is reasonable to assume that the strength would be approximately 5,000 men. "Memorandum from Robert Ginsburg of the National Security Council Staff to the President's Special Assistant (Rostow)," *FRUS, 1964–1968, vol. 17, Eastern Europe*, doc. 71; "Soviet Invasion of Czechoslovakia, 1968," U.S. Department of State, Office of the Historian, Milestones: 1961–1968, retrieved from http://history.state.gov/milestones/1961-1968/soviet-invasion -czechoslavkia.

32. Benjamin L. Harrison, *Hell on a Hill Top* (Lincoln: iUniverse, 2004), 26.

33. When the president made the statement that "it would encourage the Communists," the subsequent text makes it clear that he was referring to Communists worldwide, not just the Vietnamese Communists.

34. "Memorandum for Record," *FRUS, 1969–1976, Vietnam, vol. 6*, doc. 136.

35. Ibid.

36. "National Intelligence Estimate: The U.S.S.R and China," *FRUS, 1969–1976, vol. 17, China, vol. 17*, doc. 24.

37. For more information on Nixon's efforts to establish contact with China see "Beijing-Washington Back-Channel and Henry Kissinger's Secret Trip to China: September 1970–July 1971," National Security Archive Electronic Briefing Book No. 66, ed. William Burr, last modified February 27, 2002, retrieved from http://www.gwu.edu/~nsarchiv/NSAEBB/NSAEBB66/.

38. National Archives, Combat Area Casualty File of 11/93, and The Adjutant General's Center (TAGCEN) file of 1981.

Chapter 4

1. For more information on the coup in Cambodia and Nixon's decision to support the Lon Nol government refer to *FRUS,1969–1976, vol. 6, Vietnam*, docs. 2, 10, 18, 42, 164, 179, 180, 202–209, 217, 224, 225, 227, 232, 233, 235, 238, 239, and 240.

2. "Minutes of Washington Special Actions Group Meeting," *FRUS, 1969–1976, vol. 6, Vietnam*, doc. 203.

3. "Minutes of Washington Special Actions Group Meeting," *FRUS, 1969–1976, vol. 6, Vietnam*, doc. 211.

4. *FRUS, 1969–1976, vol. 6, Vietnam*, docs. 231 and 235.

5. "Memorandum by Director of Central Intelligence (Helms)," *FRUS, 1969–1976, Vietnam vol.6*, doc. 289.

6. "Memorandum from the Acting Chairman of the Joint Chiefs of Staff (Westmoreland) to the Secretary of Defense (Laird)," *FRUS, 1969–1976, vol. 6, Vietnam*, doc. 244.

7. "Memorandum from the Senior Military Assistant (Haig) to the President's Assistant for National Security Affairs," *FRUS, 1969–1976, vol. 6, Vietnam*, doc. 219.

8. "Memorandum from the Senior Military Assistant (Haig) to the President's Assistant for National Security Affairs (Kissinger)," *FRUS, 1969–1976, vol. 6, Vietnam*, doc. 235.

9. "Memorandum from the Director of Central Intelligence (Helms) to the President's Assistant for National Security Affairs (Kissinger)," *FRUS, 1969–1976, vol. 6, Vietnam*, doc. 242.

10. "Memorandum from the Director of Central Intelligence (Helms) to the President's Assistant for National Security Affairs (Kissinger)," *FRUS, 1969–1976, vol. 6, Vietnam*, doc. 242, footnote 2.

11. Davidson, *Vietnam at War*, 626.

12. Stewart, *American Military History*, vol. 2, chapter 11.

13. Davidson, *Vietnam at War*, 627.

14. Ibid., 630.

15. Ibid., 589, 637.

16. "Telegram from the Commander, Military Assistance Command, Vietnam (Westmoreland) to the Commander in Chief, Pacific (Sharp)," *FRUS, 1964–1968, vol. 27, Mainland Southeast Asia, Regional Affairs*, doc. 252.

17. "Memorandum for the Record, Meeting with the President, October 23, 1968," *FRUS, 1964–1968, vol. 7, Vietnam*, doc. 110.

18. "Telegram from the Department of State to the Embassy in Laos," *FRUS, 1964–1968, vol. 27, Mainland Southeast Asia, Regional Affairs*, doc. 263.

19. "Memorandum from the Secretary of the Air Force (Brown) to the Deputy Secretary of Defense (Nitze)," *FRUS, 1964–1968 vol. 28, Laos*, doc. 399. Dr. Brown's memorandum does not specify whether the numbers were monthly or weekly. But taken in context with other statistical reports, I believe he is comparing totals for the current month to totals for the same month in the previous year.

20. "Record of President's Meeting with the Foreign Intelligence Advisory Board," *FRUS, 1969–1976, vol. 6, Vietnam*, doc. 344.

21. "Memorandum from the President's Assistant for National Security Affairs (Kissinger) to President Nixon," *FRUS, January 1969–July 1976, vol. 7, Vietnam*, doc. 107.

22. *Review of the Resistance War Against the Americans to Save the Nation*, (Hanoi: National Political Press, 1995), 221c. The number of tons reported in the publication appears to be understated but the dollar amount could be correct. Another aspect of Cambodian cooperation with the North Vietnamese is rice sales. As a "neutral" country, Cambodia was under no obligation to restrict rice sales to the North Vietnamese. Rice was a significant percentage of the tons of supplies required to support North Vietnamese operations. Buying rice from Cambodia greatly reduced the total tonnage of supplies that had to be shipped from the North. The manner in which these transactions were completed condemns Sihanouk. He cooperated in the charade that the North Vietnamese did not have a military presence in Cambodia and he, as well as others, profited.

23. "Editorial Note," *FRUS, 1969–1976, vol. 6, Vietnam*, doc. 239.

24. "Memorandum of Conversation," *FRUS, 1969–1976, vol. 6, Vietnam*, doc. 313.

25. Davidson, *Vietnam at War*, 631–37.

26. Ibid., 628.

27. Harrison, *Hell on a Hill Top*, 30.

28. The pace of combat in and around the A Shau Valley was driven by the monsoon cycle. The wet season brought combat activities to a near halt. With no overland supply routes to support U.S. fire support bases on the eastern rim of the valley and weather that could shut down air support activities for long periods of time many fire support bases were shut down at the onset of the wet season and reestablished on or near the same location at the beginning of the following dry season.

29. Harrison, *Hell on a Hill Top*, 86.

30. Nalty, *The War Against Trucks*, 143, 144.

31. According to Bernard Nalty, *The War on Trucks*, Tailwind was part of the original Gauntlet plan. But according to John L. Plaster, *SOG*, 234–36, Tailwind was not conceived until after the Gauntlet force was in trouble and needed a diversionary action to help it break contact.

32. "Memorandum from John H. Holdridge and Richard T. Kennedy to the President's Assistant for National Security Affairs (Kissinger)," *FRUS, 1969–1976, vol. 7, Vietnam*, doc. 50.

33. Plaster, *SOG*, 239, 240.

34. Willard J. Webb and Walter S. Poole, *The Joint Chiefs of Staff and the War in Vietnam, 1971–1973* (Washington, D.C.: Office of Joint History, Office of the Chairman of the Joint Chiefs of Staff, 2007), 6–8.

35. "Notes of Conversation Between President-Elect Kennedy and President Eisenhower," *FRUS, 1961–1963, vol. 24, Laos Crisis*, doc. 7.

Chapter 5

1. "Memorandum from the President's Assistant for National Security Affairs (Kissinger) to President Nixon," *FRUS, 1969–1976, vol. 7, Vietnam*, doc. 59.

2. "Memorandum from John H. Holdridge and Richard T. Kennedy to the President's Assistant for National Security Affairs (Kissinger)," *FRUS, 1969–1976, vol. 7, Vietnam*, doc. 50.

3. "Memorandum from the President's Assistant for National Security (Kissinger) to President Nixon," *FRUS, 1969–1976, vol. 7, Vietnam*, doc. 63.

4. "Memorandum from the President's Assistant for National Security (Kissinger) to Secretary of State Rogers, Secretary of Defense Laird, and Director of Central Intelligence Helms," *FRUS, 1969–1976, vol. 7, Vietnam*, doc. 39.

5. *FRUS, July 1970–January 1972, vol. 6, Vietnam*, doc. 235 is a memorandum from Kissinger to Haig. In this memorandum Kissinger instructs Haig, "The President

mentioned that he had ordered attacks against SAM targets in North Vietnam. As you know, Laird is moving as slowly on this as he can short of refusing to obey the President's instructions. I recommend you call Laird directly and then have Jon Howe or Winston get Capt. Robinson to check out whatever answers are provided by Secretary Laird. . . . The President instructed you to prepare a directive immediately to Secretary Laird which would require that he maintain the current level of tactical and B-52 support of operations in Southeast Asia for the next four months. As you know, this is a tricky operation and if we give Laird any leeway he will reduce the sorties regardless of the instructions he is given." The problem grew worse with time, as demonstrated by a number of documents contained in *FRUS, 1969–1976, vol. 8, Vietnam.*

6. "Minutes of a Washington Special Actions Group Meeting," *FRUS, 1969–1976, vol. 19, Korea,* doc. 28.

7. For more information on Nixon's problems with Laird and Rogers and Kissinger's increasing influence see *FRUS, 1969–1976, vol. 6, Vietnam,* docs. 35, 57, 152, 194, 248, 254, 260, and 267.

8. "Memorandum from the President's Assistant for National Security Affairs (Kissinger) to President Nixon," *FRUS, 1969–1976, vol. 6, Vietnam,* doc. 261.

9. Haldeman, *The Haldeman Diaries,* 249.

10. "Memorandum from K. Wayne Smith of the National Security Council Staff to the President's Assistant for National Security Affairs (Kissinger)," *FRUS, 1969–1976, vol. 7, Vietnam,* doc. 65.

11. In addition to being the vice president, Ky was the air marshal of the South Vietnamese Air Force.

12. "Transcript of a Telephone Conversation Between President Nixon and his Deputy Assistant for National Security Affairs (Haig)," *FRUS, 1969–1976, vol. 7, Vietnam,* doc. 78.

13. "Summary of Conclusions of a Meeting of the Washington Special Actions Group," *FRUS, 1969–1976, vol. 7, Vietnam,* doc. 87.

14. "Backchannel Message from the President's Deputy Assistant for National Security Affairs (Haig) to the President's Assistant for National Security Affairs (Kissinger)," *FRUS, 1969–1976, vol. 7, Vietnam,* doc. 89.

15. "Memorandum Prepared by Admiral R. C. Robinson of the Office of the Chairman of the Joint Chiefs of Staff," *FRUS, 1969–1976, vol. 7, Vietnam,* doc. 93.

16. "Memorandum for the President's File by the President's Deputy Assistant for National Security Affairs (Haig)," *FRUS, 1969–1976, vol. 7, Vietnam,* doc. 104.

17. Secretary Rogers's concern about the "thinning" of the ARVN forces in I Corps is a reference to the fact that the 1st ARVN Division was normally used, along with the U.S. 101st Airborne Division, to defend I Corps. Once the ARVN division was committed to Laos, the defenders of northern I Corps would be "thinned," meaning there would be fewer forces available to defend northern Military Region I after the ARVN 1st Infantry Division deployed to Laos.

18. "Memorandum for the President's File by the President's Deputy Assistant for National Security Affairs (Haig)," *FRUS, 1969–1976, vol. 7, Vietnam*, doc. 104.

19. Ibid.

20. Ibid.

21. Mark Clodfelter, *The Limits of Air Power*, (New York: Macmillan, 1984), 168.

22. "Memorandum for the President's File by the President's Deputy Assistant for National Security Affairs (Haig)," *FRUS, 1969–1976, vol. 7, Vietnam*, doc. 109.

23. Webb and Poole, *Joint Chiefs of Staff*, 8, 9.

24. "Memorandum for Record," *FRUS, 1969–1976, vol. 7, Vietnam*, doc. 105.

25. "Memorandum for the President's File by the President's Deputy Assistant for National Security Affairs (Haig)," *FRUS, 1969–1976, vol. 7, Vietnam*, doc. 104.

26. "Memorandum for the President's File by the President's Deputy Assistant for National Security Affairs (Haig)," *FRUS, 1969–1976, vol. 7, Vietnam*, doc. 112. South Vietnam was preparing for elections, and Nixon was doing all that he could to insure that Thieu was reelected.

27. Haig, *Inner Circles*, 273.

28. "Memorandum for the Presidents File," *FRUS, 1969–1976, vol. 7, Vietnam*, doc. 112.

29. "Memorandum from the President's Assistant for Nation Security Affairs (Kissinger) to President Nixon," *FRUS, 1969–1976, vol. 7, Vietnam*, doc. 116.

30. "Memorandum for the President's File by the President's Deputy Assistant for National Security Affairs (Haig)," *FRUS, 1969–1976, Vietnam, vol. 7*, doc. 104.

31. *FRUS, 1969–1976, vol. 7, Vietnam* , docs. 104, 105, and 109.

32. "Minutes of the WSAG Meeting," *FRUS, 1969–1976, vol. 7, Vietnam*, doc. 105.

33. The SOG mission was scrubbed due to the Congressional prohibition of U.S. ground forces from conducting cross-border operations.

34. Maj. Gen. Nguyen Duy Hinh, *Lam Son 719*, (Washington: U.S. Army Center of Military History, 1979), 36–38.

35. Kissinger, *Ending the War*, 198.

Chapter 6

1. *Final Report*, vol. 2, I-2.

2. Gen. Donn A. Starry, *Mounted Combat in Vietnam*, Center for Military History Publication 90–17 (Washington: Center of Military History, 1978), 187–90.

3. Ibid.

4. Hinh, *Lam Son 719*, 63–64.

5. Ibid.

6. Ibid.

7. Vietnam Helicopter Pilots Association (VHPA) Killed in Action (KIA) File, entry for 5 February 1971. The VHPA KIA files contain a synopsis for each event. Each synopsis was extracted for Department of Defense casualty information

files. Some the files have few details and others, where witnesses were available or a crash site investigation was possible, include graphic detail. To access the VHPA KIA files go to www.vhpa.org/KIA/panel/panelind.htm; files are arranged by either date or name.

8. Hinh, *Lam Son 719*, 39.

9. Kissinger, 2003, *Ending the War*, 187.

10. "Editorial Note," *FRUS, 1969–1976, vol. 7, Vietnam*, doc. 117.

11. "Minutes of a Meeting of the Senior Washington Special Actions Group" *FRUS, Vietnam, 1969–1976, vol. 7*, doc. 115, footnote 2.

12. The UH-1 helicopter was, as noted by the designation, a utility helicopter. It was operated in a variety of equipment configurations. There were hard points on both the port and starboard sides where additional equipment could be mounted on the exterior. Typically, if anything was mounted it was armament system. In this configuration it was a gunship. If nothing was mounted on the hard points the UH-1 was referred to as a "slick."

13. P. J. Roths in conversation with the author, February 11, 2011.

14. *Final Report*, vol. 2, I-2. The Hia Van Pass is situated on National Highway 1, just north of Da Nang. It is a point where the Annamite Mountains extend to the coast, and it geographically segregates Northern I Corps from the rest of South Vietnam.

15. Army aviation battalions in Vietnam were classified as Combat Aviation Battalions (CAB) and Assault Helicopter Battalions (AHB). The practical differences between the types of organizations are relatively minor, but in general terms, CABs were typically assigned to the 1st Aviation Brigade, an administrative headquarters, and then further attached to army divisions throughout Vietnam. The battalion's companies, Combat Aviation Companies (CAC), were relatively self-contained and had their own gunship platoons. Aviation battalions in the airmobile divisions were organized as Assault Helicopter Battalions (AHB), and instead of each company having a gunship platoon, the gunships were organized in a separate company (AHC) identified as D Company.

16. Col. John A. G. Klose, briefing to the aviation battalion commander precommand course, Fort Rucker, Alabama, 24 April 2001, video. Copy provided by Col. (retired) Mike Sloniker.

17. Assault support aircraft companies were equipped with CH-47 helicopters and provided heavy lift support.

18. Hinh, *Lam Son 719*, 58. *Final Report*, vol. 2, I-2.

19. Plaster, *SOG*, 287.

20. Graham A. Cosmas and Terrence Murphy, *U.S. Marines in Vietnam: Vietnamization and Redeployment, 1970–1971*, (Washington: Department of the Navy, History and Museums Division, Headquarters, U.S. Marine Corps, 1986), 207–10.

21. *From Khe Sanh to Chepone* [Tchepone], (Hanoi: Foreign Languages Publishing House, 1971), 22.

22. Pribbenow, *Victory in Vietnam*, 272.

23. Dave R. Palmer, *Summons of the Trumpet: U.S.–Vietnam in Perspective*, (Novato: Presidio Press, 1978), chapter 27.

24. "Memorandum from the President's Assistant for National Security Affairs (Kissinger) to President Nixon," *FRUS, 1969–1976, vol. 7, Vietnam*, doc. 111.

25. "Memorandum for the President's File by the President's Deputy Assistant for National Security Affairs (Haig)," *FRUS, 1969–1976, vol. 7, Vietnam*, doc. 112.

26. Ibid.

27. "Memorandum for the President's File by the President's Deputy Assistant for National Security Affairs (Haig)," *FRUS, 1969–1976, vol. 7, Vietnam*, doc. 109.

28. Plaster, *SOG*, 286–87.

29. Ibid.

Chapter 7

1. Hinh, *Lam Son 719*, 40–41.

2. Ibid., 39–42.

3. "Arc-light" was the code name for B-52 bombing strikes, after Operation Arc Light in 1965. The units planned to cross the border at 0700 hours, but early morning ground fog shut down flight operations.

4. Hinh, *Lam Son 719*, 64.

5. Sorley, *Vietnam Chronicles*, 543. States that the NVA was credited with having an estimated 140 antiaircraft weapons of 23-mm or greater size in the area of operations at the beginning of the operation. Hinh, *Lam Son 719*, 57, states that the NVA was "credited with having 170–200 antiaircraft weapons of mixed calibers in the operational area."

6. Sorley, *Vietnam Chronicles*, 533. General Southerland reported that "some of those weather cuts on Route 9 were 20 feet deep" and that the ARVN planners had misread aerial photographs and assumed that the cuts were two feet deep.

7. 101st Aviation Group, *Operation Lam Son 719, February 8, 1971 to March 25, 1971: A Narrative Description of Air Support by the 101st Aviation Group* (Camp Eagle, Vietnam: 101st Aviation Group, 1971). Events for 8 February, hereafter referred to as "101st Aviation Group Narrative."

8. In an aircraft intended to have two trained aviators at the controls, the crew positions of the pilot and copilot were titled "aircraft commander" and pilot. Aircraft commanders were selected based on experience and demonstrated skills regardless of rank. "Pilots" were normally pilots with less experience. It was not uncommon for the "pilot" to be senior in rank to the "aircraft commander."

9. Details of aircraft lost and damaged were extracted from the 101st Aviation Group operations duty log, available at the National Archives. The names of the aircrew killed in action (KIA) and wounded in action (WIA) were extracted from the history files of the Vietnam helicopter Pilots Association (VHPA), http://www.VHPA.org.

10. Hinh, *Lam Son 719*, 67.

11. Ibid., 68.

12. *CHECO*, 42.

13. 101st Aviation Group duty log, 8–11 February.

14. 101st Airborne Division, *Airmobile Operations in Support of Operation Lam Son 719*, (1 May 1971), annex D, Summary of Combat Damage.

15. 101st Aviation Group Narrative, 8 February, 29. In his June 1971 debriefing report, Lt. Gen. James Sutherland, upon conclusion of his tenure as the Commanding General, XXIV Corps, described the Communist antiaircraft as "a well integrated, sophisticated, highly mobile" system. He could have also added "resilient." The best efforts of the allied forces failed to eliminate or even significantly suppress the threat except on a localized, temporary basis.

16. 101st Aviation Group duty log, 9 February.

17. VHPA KIA Files, 9 February 1971.

18. In looking at the dates and times of the meetings in Washington, remember that an international date line separates Washington and Vietnam and that the time in Saigon is eleven hours ahead of Washington.

19. "Minutes of a Meeting of the Washington Special Actions Group," *FRUS, 1969–1976, vol. 7, Vietnam*, doc. 123.

20. "Minutes of a Meeting of the Washington Special Actions Group," *FRUS, 1969–1976, vol. 7, Vietnam*, doc. 124.

21. "Minutes of a Meeting of the Washington Special Actions Group," *FRUS, 1969–1976, vol. 7, Vietnam*, doc. 125.

22. Collins, *Military Geography*, chap. 19.

23. Sorley, *Vietnam Chronicles*, 532.

24. 101st Aviation Group Narrative, 10 February.

25. 101st Aviation Group duty log, 10 February.

26. 101st Aviation Group Narrative, 10 February.

27. VHPA KIA files, 10 February 1971.

28. 101st Aviation Group duty log, 10 February.

29. Ibid. A subsequent investigation of this incident is recorded in Richard Pyle and Horst Faas, *Lost Over Laos*, (Cambridge, Mass.: Da Capo Press, 2003), 143–55. This book laments the loss of four photojournalists who ignored warnings and were apparently on one of the two helicopters.

30. Hinh, *Lam Son 719*, 69.

31. 101st Aviation Group Narrative, 11 February.

32. Hinh, *Lam Son 719*, 69–71.

33. Ibid., 77.

34. 101st Aviation Group duty log, 11 February.

35. Ibid.

36. Hinh, *Lam Son 719*, 70.

37. Ibid., 74.

38. Ibid.

39. "Minutes of a Meeting of the Washington Special Actions Group," *FRUS, 1969–1976, vol. 7, Vietnam,* doc. 126.

40. The engine oil cooler was external to the turbine engine and connected to the engine by oil lines. Both the oil cooler and the lines were vulnerable to combat damage. If there was a sudden drop in oil pressure or the oil level, a sensor immediately shut off flow to the cooler and illuminated a caution light in the cockpit. Once this light was illuminated, the pilot's emergency procedure was to immediately monitor engine oil pressure and temperature and land "as soon as practical."

41. VHPA KIA files, 11 February 1971.

42. *CHECO,* 50.

43. VHPA KIA files, 12 February 1971.

44. 101st Aviation Group duty log, 12 February. Hinh, *Lam Son 719,* states that the combat assault into LZ Delta 1 happened on 11 February, but the duty log states that combat assault was launched at 1100 hours on 12 February and completed at 1205 hours. Duty log entries are recorded as the events are reported.

45. 101st Aviation Group Narrative, 11 February.

46. Ibid., 12 February.

47. Ibid., 1910 hours.

48. Refer to appendix A, "The Helicopters of Lam Son 719," for photographs and a detailed description of all types of helicopters involved in Lam Son 719.

49. Gen. John J. Tolson, *Vietnam Studies: Airmobility: 1961–1971,* (Washington: Center of Military History, 1989), 9.

50. Hinh, *Lam Son 719,* 81, 82.

51. 101st Aviation Group Narrative, 13 February.

52. Hinh, *Lam Son 719,* 74.

53. Davidson, *Vietnam at War,* 646. The term "casualties" is not confined to KIA. It includes WIA and missing in action (MIA).

54. Lewis Sorley, *A Better War,* (Orlando: Harcourt, Inc., 1999), 247.

55. Kissinger, *Ending the War,* 200.

56. In reading *FRUS 1969–1976, vol. 7, Vietnam,* doc. 156, there is strong evidence that the CIA had either a listening device in Thieu's office or agents that reported his conversations. The footnote refers to an unpublished CIA report (CS 317/09016/71). See "Intelligence Report Prepared in the Central Intelligence Agency," *FRUS, 1969–1976, Volume 7, Vietnam,* doc. 17 as an example. Inasmuch as the CIA report mentioned in document 156 was not published, the source of the information and the reason why there was a delay in providing this information to the White House are unknown.

57. Pribbenow, *Victory in Vietnam,* 274.

58. "Minutes Meetings of the Washington Special Actions Group," *FRUS, 1969–1976, vol. 7, Vietnam,* docs. 126 and 131.

Chapter 8

1. "Backchannel Message from the President's Assistant for National Security Affairs (Kissinger) to the Ambassador to Vietnam (Bunker)," *FRUS, 1969–1976, Vietnam, vol. 7,* doc. 156.

2. *Final Report,* vol. 1, I-9 and I-10.

3. Hinh, *Lam Son 719,* 79.

4. "Summary of Conclusions of a Meeting of the Washington Special Actions Group," *FRUS, 1969–1976, vol. 7, Vietnam,* doc. 130.

5. Sorley, *Vietnam Chronicles,* 535; Earle H. Tilford Jr., Crosswinds: *The Air Force's Setup in Vietnam,* (College Station: Texas A&M University Press, 2009), 133.

6. Plaster, *SOG,* 289; Robert M. Gillespie, *Black OPS Vietnam: The Operational History of MACVSOG,* (Annapolis: Naval Institute Press, 2011), 226–27.

7. Hinh, *Lam Son 719,* 46.

8. *CHECO,* 50.

9. Ibid., 51.

10. Hinh, *Lam Son 719,* 74–77.

11. Dennis Fuji in conversation with Lt. Col. (Retired) Mike Sloniker (VHPA Historian), 2 December 2001.

12. Pribbenow, *Victory in Vietnam,* 275.

13. *CHECO,* 51.

14. Hinh, *Lam Son 719,* 76.

15. *CHECO,* 52.

16. 101st Aviation Group duty log, 20 February.

17. An autorotation is a power-off landing. This was an emergency procedure all helicopter pilots practiced until they were proficient. In this maneuver the pilot lowers the collective pitch control reducing the pitch of the main rotor blades. The airflow through the main rotor is reversed, and this reversed airflow continues to turn the blades in much the same manner as a windmill. The aircraft comes down in a high rate of descent. Just prior to impact the pilot applies pitch, again reversing the airflow and the kinetic energy in the blades keeps the blades turning long enough for the pilot to cushion the landing—if everything goes as planned. In this case, the pilot intentionally shut off the fuel flow to the engine in an attempt to decrease the possibility of a catastrophic fire before the aircraft landed.

18. Maj. Henry Jeffery, senior advisor, 1st ARVN Ranger Group, Combat After Action Report, Headquarters, U.S. Army Advisory Group, I Corps and Military Region I, APO SF 96349, (undated), retrieved from http://research.archives.gov /description/305340 on 30 December 2012.

19. Pribbenow, *Victory in Vietnam,* 275.

20. Hinh, *Lam Son 719,* 79, reports that 639 NVA soldiers were killed during the action at Ranger North. Considering the outcome and the fact that the NVA held the ground after the battle was over, a precise body count was most likely impossible.

21. 101st Aviation Group Narrative, 21 February, states that aircraft commanders encountered a new problem when they reached the LZ. Aircraft were being overloaded by healthy troops trying to fight their way onto the on to the ships, often to the exclusion of the wounded. Colonel Davis was forced to issue the order that resupply ships would no longer land on the LZ. They would come to a high hover, out of reach of the ARVN soldiers, and drop the supplies.

22. Hinh, *Lam Son 719*, 80.

23. 101st Aviation Group duty log, 21 February.

24. 101st Aviation Group Narrative, 19 February.

25. Sorley, *Vietnam Chronicles*, 539.

26. The 101st Aviation Group duty log contains five entries between 18 February and 2 March reporting operations that had to be cancelled due to gunship shortages. Another eight entries are aircraft status reports referring to units that have few or no operational gunship remaining. Four entries during the same period are reports of units that were limited in the number of sorties they could fly by crew rest regulations. Regulations stated that a pilot could not accumulate more than 140 hours in a 30-day period. The solution was to declare a tactical emergency and waive the regulation.

27. The expected OR rate for aviation units in Vietnam was 80 percent of the assigned aircraft. It was expected that, given the ratio of flying hours to maintenance hours, 20 percent of the aircraft would be in maintenance at any given time for a combination of scheduled inspections, replacement of components that were required to be changed after a given number of flying hours, minor repairs, and combat damage.

28. 223rd CAB Operations duty Log entry 1700 hours, 24 February 1971.

29. Rick Freeman in conversation with the author, 4 March 2011.

30. Raw data for the statistical analysis was extracted from *Final Report*, vol. 2, annex D.

Chapter 9

1. 101st Aviation Group duty log, 22 February.

2. Hinh, *Lam Son 719*, 78, 79.

3. "Transcript of a conversation between President Nixon and Chairman of the Joint Chiefs of Staff (Moorer)," *FRUS, 1969–1976, vol. 7, Vietnam*, doc. 134.

4. Davidson, Vietnam at War, 606–607, 207. "Meeting of the Senior Review Group," *FRUS, 1969–1976, vol. 7, Vietnam*, doc. 103; Kissinger, *The White House Years*, 989.

5. Hinh, *Lam Son 719*, 126.

6. "Transcript of a conversation between President Nixon and Chairman of the Joint Chiefs of Staff (Moorer)," *FRUS, 1969–1976, vol. 7, Vietnam*, doc. 134.

7. Sorley, *Vietnam Chronicles*, 548.

8. According the 101st Aviation Group Narrative, 365 rangers were inserted at Ranger North on 11 February. After Ranger North was overrun, 200 rangers were able to make back to Ranger South. General Hinh stated that only 107 of the 200 were able to "continue to fight." If none of the 107 were wounded, which is unlikely, the casualty rate was 70 percent. The USMC historical account of Lam Son 719, Cosmas and Murphy, U.S. Marines in Vietnam, states that the 39th Ranger Battalion had losses of 178 men killed or missing and 148 wounded. Based on these figures and the 101st Group figures of 365 inserted, you have a KIA rate of 51.2 percent and a WIA rate of 40.5 percent, and the combined casualty rate was 91.7 percent.

9. Lt. Col. (Retired) Allen "Skip" Butler in conversation with the author, July 2011.

10. Hugging involved staying as close as possible to the opposing force reduced the opportunity for the Americans or South Vietnamese to come to the aid of their ground force with artillery or airstrikes. The Communists frequently employed this tactic on American or South Vietnamese forces.

11. Hinh, *Lam Son 719*, 80.

12. Sorley, *Vietnam Chronicles*, 544–46.

13. Ibid., 544–46.

14. 101st Aviation Group duty log, 24 February.

15. Howard K. Butler, *Army Aviation Logistics and Vietnam, 1961–1975* (St. Louis: History Office, United States Army Aviation Systems Command, 1985), 460–61.

16. Pribbenow, *Victory in Vietnam*, 275, 276.

17. David Fulghum and Terrance Maitland, *South Vietnam on Trial*, (Boston: Boston Publishing, 1984), 80–82.

18. The sources include Hinh, *Lam Son 719*; Starry, *Mounted Combat in Vietnam*; Fulghum and Maitland, *South Vietnam on Trial*; *CHECO*; and the 101st Aviation Group duty log.

19. At this point the sources are still in agreement with the exception of the location of the two companies patrolling outside the FSB.

20. Hinh, *Lam Son 719*, 82, provides no further details concerning the relief column.

21. Starry, *Mounted Combat in Vietnam*, 192.

22. Hinh, *Lam Son 719*, 85.

23. Ibid., 86, 87.

24. *CHECO*, 57, 58.

25. The apparent conflict in the time lines does not pose a problem. The air cavalry was not a subordinate unit of the 101st Aviation Group, and it is reasonable to assume that 1625 hours is time the report was relayed to the 101st Group, not the time that the air cavalry observed the parachutes.

26. 101st Aviation Group duty log, 25 February.

27. Ibid.

28. Maj. Gen. Benjamin L. Harrison, (Senior Army Advisor to the ARVN 1st Infantry and Airborne Divisions) in conversation with the author, 28 May 2013.

29. Hinh, *Lam Son 719*, 98; Fulghum and Maitland, *South Vietnam on Trial*, 83.

30. George Galdorisi and Tom Phillips, *Leave No Man Behind*, (Minneapolis: Zenith Press, 2008), 365, 356.

31. Starry, *Mounted Combat in Vietnam*, 193, 194.

32. Hinh, *Lam Son 719*, 88.

33. 101st Aviation Group duty log, 26 February, 27 February.

34. 101st Aviation Group duty log, 28 February–1 March.

35. Ibid.

36. *CHECO*, 60.

37. 101st Aviation Group duty log, 2 March.

38. Ibid.

39. Hinh, *Lam Son 719*, 73.

40. 101st Aviation Group duty log, 2 March–4 March.

Chapter 10

1. 101st Aviation Group duty log, 1 March.

2. Ibid.

3. Hinh, *Lam Son 719*, 91.

4. In his position as aviation officer for Lam Son 719, General Berry served as the senior staff assistant in all army aviation matters for the XXIV Corps commander and assumed responsibility for directing the activities of all aviation units.

5. Hinh, *Lam Son 719*, 78.

6. "Backchannel Message from the President's Assistant for National Security Affairs (Kissinger) to the Ambassador to Vietnam (Bunker)," *FRUS, 1969–1976, vol. 7, Vietnam*, doc. 142.

7. Kissinger, *Ending the War*, 203.

8. By definition, the direct support mission required the 223rd to support the 1st ARVN Division and authorized the battalion to answer directly to the ARVN division's request for assistance, without clearing the mission with the group headquarters. Assigning this mission to the 223rd, a battalion headquarters with no experience in air assault operations, was a preventable mistake. Other options were available.

9. 14th CAB duty log, 2 March.

10. Ibid.

11. Mike Sloniker, "Lam Son 719 with Pictures," Vietnam Helicopter Pilots Association, (unpublished collection of veteran interviews and photographs).

12. *CHECO*, 94–95.

13. Sloniker, "Lam Son 719 with Pictures."

14. Ibid. Dize's narrative in "Lam Son 719 with Pictures" expresses a degree of uncertainty as to whether or not this incident happened during the assault on Lolo. However, a 101st Group duty log entry matches the details of tail number, location, and the number of MIA and WIA that Dize provided to the Vietnam Helicopter Pilots Association.

15. Doug Womack (Aircraft Commander, 71st CAC) in conversation with the author, 4–7 January 2012.

16. *Final Report*, vol. 2, annex D, appendix 3, p. 2.

17. 101st Aviation Group duty log, 3 March.

18. Doug Womack conversation.

19. *Final Report*, vol. 2, annex D, appendix 4, pp. 3 and 4.

20. Doug Womack conversation.

21. Letter from Bob Clewell, 27 December 1991, Vietnam Helicopter Pilots Association (VHPA) Collection: Lam Son 719, The Vietnam Center and Archive, Texas Tech University, folder 10, box 1. http://www.vietnam.ttu.edu /virtualarchive/items.php?item=2960110001, accessed 3 January 2013.

22. 101st Aviation Group duty log, 3 March.

23. Ibid.

24. *Final Report*, vol. 2, annex D, appendix 3, p. 2, and appendix 4, pp. 3 and 4.

25. Headquarters, XXIV Corps, "Lam Son 719 After Action Report 30 Jan–6 Apr." (Da Nang: Headquarters, XXIV Corps, 1971.) Retrieved from http://www .vietnam.ttu.edu/virtualarchive/items.php?item=8850509001 on 28 May 2013.

26. 101st Aviation Group Duty Log, 26 February, 2 March, 3 March, 8 March, and 9 March. Ironically, those Charley Models were shot down. After the UH-1H with the press aboard landed at Delta 1 and the press disembarked, it lifted off to orbit the area until the press was ready to leave, because remaining on the ground would have invited a mortar attack. While the last lift was en route to Lolo, the aircraft commander of one of the lift ships fell for the NVA ruse of popping a smoke grenade to mark a false LZ. He started his approach and was immediately shot down west of Delta 1. The escort team was monitoring the radios and went to the aid of the downed crew. Both escort Charley Models were also shot down, and one of the door gunners was critically wounded. The UH-1H assigned to the press detail was able to rescue the Charley Model crews and sprint the wounded door gunner back to Khe Sanh for medical assistance, but the press was now stranded at Delta 1. Near the end of the day, Maj. Bob Clewell monitored the radio transmissions concerning the reporter's dilemma and flew into Delta 1 to retrieve them. Quite naturally, the reporters were appreciative and published an article in the 15 March edition of Newsweek entitled, "Just Say it Was the Comancheros," referring to the administrative call sign of Clewell's A Company, 101st AHB.

27. Hinh, *Lam Son 719*, 89.

28. *CHECO*, 117.

29. Ibid., 117.

30. 101st Aviation Group duty log, 3 March.

31. Ibid.

32. *CHECO*, 99, 100.

33. 101st Aviation Group duty log, 5 March.

34. VHPA KIA Files, 5 March.

35. 223rd Combat Aviation Battalion After Action Review, Lam Son 719. Copy provided by Mike Sloniker.

36. *Final Report*, vol. 2, annex D.

37. The Hac Bao was the elite ARVN 1st Infantry Division Reconnaissance Company. Each air cavalry troop had a platoon of infantry that could be used for dismounted reconnaissance or, if needed, search and rescue operations. Because the Cooper-Church amendment prohibited American ground soldiers from entering Laos, the Hac Bao was attached to the 2nd Squadron, 17th Cavalry, to assist in search-and–rescue operations. 101st Aviation Group duty log, 5 March.

38. "17th Cavalry Intelligence Summary 67-71," 2nd Squadron, annex I, Texas Tech Vietnam Virtual Archive.

39. Ibid.

40. *Final Report*, vol. 2, annex D.

41. Sorley, *Vietnam Chronicles*, 567.

42. Davidson, *Vietnam at War*, 648.

43. Hinh, *Lam Son 719*, 104. CHECO, 67, reports that the new FSB was established at Sophia East. Sophia East, Brick, and Brown were all located in close proximity to each other, and the conflict was minor.

44. Hinh, *Lam Son 719*, 101–104.

Chapter 11

1. "Memorandum from the President's Assistant for National Security Affairs (Kissinger) to President Nixon," *FRUS, 1969–1976, vol. 7, Vietnam*, doc. 150.

2. 101st Aviation Group duty log, 8–9 March.

3. Ibid.

4. Hinh, *Lam Son 719*, 107.

5. "Transcription of a Telephone Conversation between President Nixon and the Chairman of the Joint Chiefs of Staff (Moorer)," *FRUS, 1969–1976, vol. 7, Vietnam*, doc. 152.

6. 101st Aviation Group duty log, 17–18 March. GCA, meaning "ground controlled approach," was a radar system designed to guide an aircraft to the airfield. The radar operator continuously monitored the aircraft's heading and altitude, keeping the aircraft at a safe altitude and clear of the terrain. Once the pilot was in the airfield approach area, the operator vectored the aircraft to the runway and gave the pilot the appropriate instructions for beginning his descent, keeping the pilot informed as to his position relative to the glideslope and the appropriate airspeed. Once the pilot had the airfield in sight, he took over and landed visually.

7. "Quebec Whiskey" is the phonetic alphabet designation for the letters Q and W.

8. Zero ceiling and zero visibility was often referred to as "0–0."

9. 101st Aviation Group duty log, 18 March.

10. "Fixer Alpha" is believed to be the call sign of Maj. Gen. Benjamin Harrison, the U.S. Senior Advisor to the 1st ARVN Division.

11. Aerial rocket artillery units retained artillery terminology. A "section" is two aircraft, the same as a light fire team in escort gun companies. ARA Cobras were normally equipped with four 19-shot rocket pods, whereas the normal configuration for escort Cobras was two 19-shot pods and two 7-shot pods. The increased armament load meant that, while the ARA may have greater firepower, the fuel load would have to be reduced in order to compensate for the additional weight of the rockets.

12. 101st Aviation Group duty log entries, 18 March.

13. Klose, briefing to the Fort Rucker aviation commanders precommand course, 2001.

14. "Backchannel Message from the President's Deputy Assistant for National Security Affairs (Haig) to the President's Assistant for National Security Affairs (Kissinger)," *FRUS, 1969–1976, vol. 7, Vietnam*, doc. 151.

15. Hinh, *Lam Son 719*, 109–10.

16. Ibid., 111.

17. "Backchannel Message from the President's Assistant for National Security Affairs (Kissinger) to the Ambassador to Vietnam (Bunker)," *FRUS, 1969–1976, vol. 7, Vietnam*, doc. 156.

18. "Backchannel Message from the President's Deputy Assistant for National Security Affairs (Haig) to the President's Assistant for National Security Affairs (Kissinger)," *FRUS, 1969–1976, vol. 7, Vietnam*, doc. 158.

19. Hinh, *Lam Son 719*, 112.

20. Ibid., 114.

21. Klose, Briefing to the Fort Rucker aviation commanders precommand course, 2001.

22. Earle Swift, *Where They Lay: A Forensic Expedition in the Jungles of Laos*, (New York: Houghton Mifflin Harcourt, 2005), 16.

23. Dale Spratt (Commander of the 174th AHC during Lam Son 719) in conversation with the author, June 2012.

24. Andrew Wiest, *Vietnam's Forgotten Army, Heroism and Betrayal in the ARVN*, (New York: New York University Press, 2008), 220, 221.

25. *Final Report*, vol. 2, annex D.

26. 101st Aviation Group duty log, 21 March.

27. Starry, *Mounted Combat in Vietnam*, 194–96.

28. Ibid.

29. 101st Aviation Group duty log, 21 March.

30. *CHECO*, 74.

31. Starry, *Mounted Combat in Vietnam*, 196.

32. Ibid., 24.

33. Sorley, *Vietnam Chronicles*, 566.

34. Cosmas and Murphy, *U.S. Marines in Vietnam*, 199.

35. 101st Aviation Group duty log, 12 March.

36. Cosmas and Murphy, *U.S. Marines in Vietnam*, 377.

37. *Final Report*, vol. 2, annex D. A mortar firing through a small opening in a forest canopy is difficult to detect, and the NVA mortar crews typically prepared alternate positions and moved frequently.

38. Maj. Dale Spratt (Commander, 174th CAC) in conversation with the author, 11 May, 2011.

39. VHPA KIA files, 22 March. The USMC account states that two helicopters were shot down during the air drop attempt, but this cannot be confirmed. The "fog of war" was thick on 22 March 1971.

40. Cosmas and Murphy, *U.S. Marines in Vietnam*, 377.

41. Hoang Tich Thong, "Operation Lam Son 719 in 1971," VNAFMAMN, retrieved from http://vnafmamn.com/lamson_719.html 4 April 2012.

42. Cosmas and Murphy, *U.S. Marines in Vietnam*, 377.

43. Ibid., 387.

44. 101st Aviation Group duty log, 23 March.

45. Pribbenow, *Victory in Vietnam*, 276.

46. Hinh, *Lam Son 719*, 120.

47. 101st Aviation Group duty log, 24 and 25 March.

48. Hinh, *Lam Son 719*, 120.

49. 101st Aviation Group duty log, 24 March.

50. Hinh, *Lam Son 719*, 121–25.

51. Davidson, Vietnam at War, 651.

52. Hinh, *Lam Son 719*, 8, 52–53.

Chapter 12

1. Wiest, *Vietnam's Forgotten Army*, 226, 227.

2. "Editorial Note," *FRUS, 1969–1976, vol. 7, Vietnam*, doc. 174.

3. Davidson, *Vietnam at War*, 654, 655.

4. Sorley, *Vietnam Chronicles*, 568. Liar's Dice is a barroom game of chance. Two people place their bets then take turns shaking a leather cup containing six dice. After one shakes the dice, he turns the cup over and peeks at the dice and announces the results. If the opponent doubts the claim he can "call" and the cup is lifted to reveal the hand. If it was a bluff, the person who shook the dice loses the bet. If it was not a bluff the person who called loses the bet. Each claim of the results must be higher than the last—hence it is Liar's Dice.

5. *FRUS, 1969–1976, vol. 7, Vietnam*, docs. 188, 201, and 220.

6. "Transcript of a Conversation Between President Nixon and His Assistant for National Security Affairs (Kissinger)," *FRUS, 1969–1976, vol. 7, Vietnam*, doc. 218. In Alexander Haig's memoir, Inner Circles, 275, Haig wrote, "On the third day [presumably 11 February—the day the ARVN advance came to an inexplicable halt] the president called me to his office. Secretary of the Treasury John B. Connally, the conservative Democrat from Texas on whose advice and moral support Nixon increasingly relied during this period was present. The President was in a cold rage. Without preamble, he told me that he was relieving General Abrams from command in Vietnam immediately. 'Go home and pack your bag,' he said. 'Then get on the first available airplane and fly to Saigon. You are taking command.'" There is either a flaw in Haig's recollection, or this conversation happened twice. In the volume covering the 1972 Easter Offensive, *FRUS, 1969–1976, vol. 8, Vietnam*, doc. 120 indicates that this conversation took place over a year later, on 4 May 1972 while ARVN forces were buckling under the pressure of the North Vietnamese attack.

7. Harrison, *Hell on a Hill Top*, 31.

8. Sorley, *Vietnam Chronicles*, 574.

9. Davidson, *Vietnam at War*, 645.

10. Sorley, *Vietnam Chronicles*, 531.

11. "Transcript of a Telephone Conversation Between the President's Assistant for National Security Affairs (Kissinger) and the U.S. Army Chief of Staff (Westmoreland)," *FRUS, 1969–1976, vol. 7, Vietnam*, doc. 178.

12. "Editorial Note," *FRUS, 1969–1976, vol. 7, Vietnam*, doc. 239.

13. "Memorandum of Conversation," *FRUS, 1969–1976, vol. 7, Vietnam*, doc. 313.

14. Gen. Cao Van Vien, *Indochina Monographs: Leadership*, (Washington: U.S. Army Center of Military History, 1981), 105–106.

15. CINCPAC message 150236Z. "Backchannel Message from the President's Deputy Assistant for National Security Affairs (Kissinger)," *FRUS, 1969–1976, vol. 7, Vietnam*, doc. 89.

16. *FRUS, 1969–1976, vol. 7, Vietnam*, docs. 89, 91, and 96.

17. Henry Kissinger, *The White House Years*, (Boston: Little, Brown and Company), 979–81.

18. Webb and Poole, *Joint Chiefs of Staff*, 12, 13.

19. "Summary of Conclusions of a Meeting of the Washington Special Actions Group," *FRUS, 1969–1976, vol. 7, Vietnam*, doc. 87.

20. Webb and Poole, *Joint Chiefs of Staff*, 3.

21. Kissinger, *The White House Years*, 996.

22. "Memorandum for the Record," *FRUS, 1969–1976, vol. 7, Vietnam*, doc. 105. It is possible that Johnson's description of "six divisions" may not have registered in Kissinger's mind as "two corps." An army corps does not have a fixed number divisions assigned. A corps is a command-and-control headquarters, and divisions are assigned as required for the mission. However, six divisions can generally be equated to two corps.

23. Kissinger, *The White House Years*, 994–97.

24. "Memorandum from the President's Assistant for National Security Affairs (Kissinger) to President Nixon," *FRUS, 1969–1976, vol. 7, Vietnam*, doc. 95. For additional reading on the deliberate effort to keep Secretary Rogers uninformed see docs. 96 and 98. For Rogers's reaction during the 18 January meeting, see doc. 104.

25. Palmer, *The 25-Year War*, 111.

26. Sorley, *A Better War*, 249.

27. U.S. Army War College Strategic Studies Institute, A *Study of Strategic Lessons Learned in Vietnam*, 6:4–56.

28. An Cheng Guan, *Ending the Vietnam War, The Vietnamese Communist Perspective*, (New York: Routledge Curzon, 2004), 62.

29. Hinh, *Lam Son 719*, 74.

30. Sorley, *Vietnam Chronicles*, 557. Henry Jeffery, "1st ARVN Ranger Group, Combat After Action Report, Headquarters, U.S. Army Advisory Group, I Corps and Military Region I, APO SF 96349," (undated), retrieved from http://research. archives,gov/description/305340 30 December 2012.

31. The Howze Board evaluated the concept of airmobility, and the results of this study led to the creation of the army's first airmobile division.

32. John A. Bonin, "Army Aviation Becomes an Essential Arm: From the Howze Board to the Modular Force," (PhD diss., Temple University Graduate Board, 2006).

33. Klose, briefing to the aviation battalion commander precommand course, 2001.

34. Webb and Poole, *Joint Chiefs of Staff*, 15, 16.

35. Davidson, *Vietnam at War*, 654, 655.

36. Cosmas, *MACV*, 328. The C-7 "Caribou" was a small twin-engine transport designed for operations on short, unimproved runways.

37. Webb and Poole, *Joint Chiefs of Staff*, 15, 16.

38. Ibid., 6.

39. Kissinger, *The White House Years*, 1181.

40. Cao Van Vien, *The Final Collapse*, (Washington: United States Army Center of Military History, 1985), 13.

41. Darrel D. Whitcomb, *The Rescue of Bat 21*, (Annapolis: Naval Institute Press, 1998), 42–44.

42. G. H. Turley, *The Easter Offensive*, (Novato: Presidio Press 1985), 202, 203.

43. XXIV Corps Lam Son 719 after Action Report, 33.

44. Davidson, *Vietnam at War*, 654.

45. Hinh, *Lam Son 719*, 87.

46. Robert F. Broyles, Interviewed by Lt. Gen. Sidney B. Berry, Jr. (U.S. Army Retired), U.S. Army Military History Institute, Senior Officer Oral History Program, Carlisle Barracks, 1983.

47. Hinh, *Lam Son 719*, 158.

48. "Task Organization, ARVN I Corps for Lam Son 719," in Hinh, *Lam Son 719*, appendix A.

49. John Grider Miller, *The Co-Vans: U.S. Marine Advisors in Vietnam*, (Annapolis: Naval Institute Press, 2000), 132, 147, and 148.

50. Ibid., 377.

51. Field artillery doctrine dictates that the supporting artillery has the inherent task to position its batteries within range of the supported force. The U.S. artillery was prohibited from crossing the border and it was approximately ten kilometers from Delta to the border. In order to support Delta, the artillery would need to be able engage targets two kilometers beyond Delta. It's unlikely that there were suitable, defensible firing positions on the border and that these positions could be as many as four kilometers east of the border. Given these distances, FSB Delta was probably never within range of U.S. 155mm artillery and would have been on the outer limits of U.S. 8-inch artillery under the best of circumstances. However, Delta was well within the range of the VNMC artillery at FSB Hotel.

52. Haig, *Inner Circles*, 276.

53. Cosmas and Murphy, *U.S. Marines in Vietnam*, 377.

54. "Memorandum for Henry Kissinger from Tom Latimer, CIA and Lam Son Intelligence Failures, (12 April 1971)," retrieved from http://www.nixonlibrary .gov/virtuallibrary/11nov/declass04.pdf 3 July 2012.

55. If this report was not forwarded until 3 February, it would be speculative to assume that it could have arrived in time to alter the early days of the operation.

56. "Minutes of a Meeting of the Washington Special Actions Group," *FRUS, 1969–1976, vol. 7, Vietnam*, doc. 126.

57. Harry Reasoner, "ABC News, February 1971," retrieved from http://www .nixwebs.com/SearchK9/helitac/harryreasoner.htm 1 June 2012.

58. "From Enemy to Friend, Questions and Answers on the Vietnam War," folder 39, box 01, James Ridgeway Collection, The Vietnam Center and Archive, Texas Tech University, 1998, retrieved from http://www.vietnam.ttu.edu /virtualarchive/items.php?item=2560139001 3 January 2013.

59. Sorley, *Vietnam Chronicles*, 583, 584.

60. "Conversation between President Nixon and his Assistant for National Security Affairs (Kissinger)," *FRUS, 1969–1976, vol. 7, Vietnam*, doc. 210.

61. James Sutherland, "Senior Officer Debriefing Report: LTG James Sutherland Jr., Commanding General XXIV Corps, Period 18 June 1970 thru 9 June 1971," 15, copy provided by USAF historian Deborah Kidwell at the Defense Technical Information Center, Fort Belvoir, Virginia.

62. The events at FSBs Hickory and Fuller, as well as the deaths of Wann, Magers, and Carden, are as recalled by the author, a participant in the battle at Fuller and a member of D Company, 158th Aviation Battalion.

63. VPHA KIA files, 31 March–3 July 1971.

64. While some historians may disagree with the characterization of Abrams being "kicked upstairs," *FRUS, 1969–1976, vol. 7, Vietnam,* doc. 123, a transcription of a taped conversation between Nixon and Kissinger, confirms that this is an accurate description, regardless of whether or not it was justified.

Appendix A

1. "Density altitude" is a term that refers to the capability of air to produce lift. Hot, humid air is thinner, and an airfoil produces less lift in this environment.
2. 223rd CAB after action review, Lam Son 719.
3. Bob Hacket, in discussion with the author 10–11 February 2011.
4. Like a Gatling gun, the mini-gun had multiple barrels and fired when each barrel reached top dead center in the rotation.
5. *Final Report*, vol. 2, IV-13 and IV-14.
6. Ibid., vol. 2, figure C-8a.

Appendix B

1. "Conversation between President Nixon and his Assistant for National Security Affairs (Kissinger)," *FRUS, 1969–1976, vol. 7, Vietnam,* doc. 200.
2. Sorley, *A Better War,* 255–61.
3. Hinh, *Lam Son 719,* 137; Davidson, Vietnam at War, 650.
4. A. J. Langguth, *Our Vietnam: The War 1954–1955,* (New York: Simon and Schuster, 2000), 579.
5. *The United States Army is a Global Era, 1917–2005,* vol. 2 of *American Military History,* ed. Richard W. Stewart (Washington, D.C.: U.S. Army Center for Military History, 2005), 358. A memorandum from Kissinger to Nixon reports U.S. KIA as 180 in *FRUS, 1969–1976, vol. 2, Vietnam,* doc. 182.
6. VHPA KIA files, 30 January 1971–25 March 1971.
7. *Final Report*, vol. 2, IV-98–IV-101.
8. Ibid., annex C.
9. Sorley, Vietnam Chronicles, 585.
10. *Final Report*, vol. 2, figs. IV-34 and IV-35.
11. *CHECO*, fig. 17.
12. James W. Williams, *A History of Army Aviation,* (New York: iUniverse, 2005), 166.
13. *From Khe Sanh to Chepone,* (Hanoi: Foreign Languages Publishing House, 1971), 37.
14. Sorley, *Vietnam Chronicles,* 608.
15. *Final Report*, vol. 2, section IV, parts L and M.
16. John Prados, *The Blood Road, The Ho Chi Minh Trail and the Vietnam War,* (Hoboken: John Wiley and Sons, Inc., 1999) 354; James W. Gibson, *The Perfect War: Technowar in Vietnam,* (New York: Grove Atlantic Inc., 1986), 400.

Glossary

AAA Anti-aircraft artillery.

ADF Automatic direction finder; an aircraft navigation radio receiver that indicates the course to, or bearing from, a navigational beacon transmitting on the prescribed frequency.

Air Assault Also called Combat Assault. A helicopter movement of combat troops in an attack, a type of airmobile operations.

Aircraft Commander Also called AC. The aircrew member designated by competent authority as being in command of an aircraft and responsible for its safe operation and accomplishment of the assigned mission.

Airmobile Operation An operation in which combat forces and their equipment move about the battlefield by helicopters to engage in ground combat.

AHB Assault Helicopter Battalion.

AHC Assault Helicopter Company.

AMC Air Mission Commander.

ARA Aerial rocket artillery; later referred to as AFA (aerial field artillery).

Arc Light The code name for U.S. B–52 bombing missions in Vietnam, Laos, and Cambodia.

ARVN Army of the Republic of (South) Vietnam.

ASHB Assault Support Helicopter Battalion.

ASHC Assault Support Helicopter Company.

Autorotation An unpowered helicopter emergency landing.

Avenue of Approach Also called AA. An air or ground route of an attacking force of a given size leading to its objective or to key terrain in its path.

Battery   An artillery unit corresponding to a company or similar unit in other branches of the army.

Battle-Damage Assessment   Also called BDA. The assessment of damage resulting from the application of military force.

Base Area   Areas used by the Communists to resupply and stage their forces for attack, these areas were normally located along the borders of Laos and Cambodia, base areas were assigned numbers for ease of reference.

B–52   An all-weather, intercontinental, strategic heavy bomber.

Binh Tram   A military way station on the Ho Chi Minh Trail. This also refers to the North Vietnamese unit that operated the way station.

Breakfast   Code name for the initial secret U.S. bombing operation in Cambodia.

CAB   Combat Aviation Battalion. The internal organization of a CAB is different from that of an Assault Helicopter Battalion (AHB) in that each subordinate company had its own gunship platoon, whereas in an AHB all gunships were organized in a separate company.

CAC   Combat Aviation Company.

Cache   A source of subsistence and supplies, typically containing items such as food, water, medical items, and/or communications equipment, packaged to prevent damage from exposure and hidden in isolated locations by such methods as burial, concealment, and/or submersion, to support isolated personnel.

Call sign   Any combination of characters or pronounceable words, which identifies a communication facility, a command, an authority, an activity, or a unit; used primarily for establishing and maintaining communications.

Casualty   Any person who is lost to the organization by having been declared dead, duty status—whereabouts unknown, missing, ill, or injured.

CEOI   Communications and Electronics Operating Instructions.

Chalk number   The number given to a complete load and to the transporting carrier.

CIA   Central Intelligence Agency.

CIDG   Civilian irregular defense group.

CINCPAC   Commander-in-Chief Pacific Command; a U.S. military joint services command headquartered in Hawaii.

Close air support   Also called CAS. Air action by fixed and rotary-wing aircraft against hostile targets that are in close proximity to friendly forces and that require detailed integration of each air mission with the fire and movement of those forces.

Commando Hunt   A series of air interdiction campaigns conducted over the infiltration routes in southern Laos from November 1968 to April 1972.

COMUSMACV   Commander, U.S. Military Assistance Command, Vietnam.

Concept of operations   A verbal or graphic statement that clearly and concisely expresses what the joint force commander intends to accomplish and how it will be done using available resources.

COSVN   Central Office of South Vietnam; the Communist political and military headquarters for the southern half of South Vietnam.

D-Day   The unnamed day on which a particular operation commences or is scheduled to commence.

Density Altitude   Atmospheric density as affected by heat and humidity compared to altitude above sea level on a "standard day."

DIA   Defense Intelligence Agency.

Diversion   The act of drawing the attention and forces of an enemy from the point of the principal operation; an attack, alarm, or feint that diverts attention.

DMZ   Demilitarized zone; established roughly at Vietnam's 17th parallel, the demarcation line separating North and South Vietnam. The DMZ was established on recognizable terrain located within five kilometers each side of the demarcation line.

Duty log   A daily record of events as they transpired, normally recorded on Department of the Army Form 1594, signed and authenticated by the responsible officer at the end of the day.

EC–121   An unarmed, four-engine propeller-driven reconnaissance aircraft.

FAC   Forward air controller; a pilot who searches for and marks targets for strike aircraft, directs the airstrike, and when possible, provides a bomb damage assessment.

FAN   Forward area navigator.

Forward arming and refueling point   Also called FARP or FARRP (forward area rearming and refueling point). A temporary facility organized, equipped and deployed by an aviation commander and deployed closer to the area where operations are being conducted to provide fuel and ammunition.

FSB   Fire support base; typically beginning as a landing zone. Once secured by infantry, supporting artillery and headquarters elements are brought in to support continuing operations in the surrounding area.

G-3   Operations staff officer at division and corps level.

G-4   Logistics staff officer at division and corps level

GVN   Government of Vietnam (South Vietnam).

Group   A controlling headquarters for two or more subordinate units.

HEAT   High explosive antitank.

Hue   A major city in northern South Vietnam and capital of former Vietnamese empire.

ICC   International Control Commission; established under the 1954 Geneva Accords and incorporated into the 1962 Geneva agreement on Laos.

JGS   Joint General Staff of South Vietnam.

J-2   Intelligence Directorate of a Joint Staff.

J-3   Operations Directorate of a Joint Staff.

Kha   A tribal minority indigenous to the Laotian panhandle.

Khe Sanh   A Vietnamese hamlet located in western Quang Tri Province, the northernmost province of South Vietnam, and also the name given to a U.S. combat base located near the hamlet.

KIA   Killed in action.

Lam Son 719   A February–March 1971 operation in Laos by South Vietnamese forces to interdict the Ho Chi Minh Trail.

Lang Vei   A South Vietnamese hamlet located along Route 9, adjacent to the Laotian border; the site of a forward area refueling and rearming point established to support helicopter operations in Laos.

LAW   Light antitank weapon.

LFT   Light fire team, two helicopter gunships.

LNO   Liaison Officer.

LOH   Light observation helicopter.

LZ   Landing zone; the intended landing site for helicopter operations.

MAAG   Military Assistance Advisory Group.

MACV   Military Assistance Command, Vietnam.

MACV-SOG   Often called SOG. Military Assistance Command, Vietnam, Studies and Observation Group; the organization that planned and carried out covert operations against North Vietnam.

Meeting engagement   A combat action that occurs when a moving force, incompletely deployed for battle, engages an enemy at an unexpected time and place.

Menu   The code name for a series of bombing raids targeting NVA positions in Cambodia during 1969.

MIA   Missing in action.

Military Region   The government of Vietnam divided the country into four zones for military and administrative purposes; Military Region 1 contained the five northernmost provinces of South Vietnam; Military Region 2 included provinces in the central and north central sections; Military Region 3 was made up of the south central part of the country and included Saigon; Military Region 4 in the Mekong Delta held the rest of the country; sometimes a Military Region was also called a Corps Tactical Zone, and the regions were referred to as I Corps, II Corps, III Corps, and IV Corps.

NCO   Noncommissioned officer.

NLF   National Liberation Front; the political arm of South Vietnamese Communists.

NSAM   National Security Action Memorandum.

NSDM   National Security Decision Memorandum.

NSC   National Security Council.

NVA   North Vietnamese Army.

NVN   North Vietnam.

OPCON   Operational Control.

OPLAN   Operation Plan.

OPSEC   Operations Security.

OR   Operationally ready.

Phu Bai   A South Vietnamese city located in Thau Thien Province, southwest of Hue.

POW   Prisoner of war.

Prairie Fire   The code name for a program of American-led cross-border reconnaissance and exploitation patrols into eastern Laos; this replaced the code name "Shining Brass."

Preparation   "Prepped" in slang terminology. When used in discussion of a landing a force on enemy-held terrain, preparation refers to the practice of bombarding the area prior to the landing to soften up enemy defenses.

PZ   Pick-up zone; the location at which troops and/or supplies are loaded into helicopters for movement to the landing zone.

Quang Tri   The northernmost province of South Vietnam. It also refers to Quang Tri City, the provincial capital, located near the coast of the South China Sea and immediately south of the DMZ.

Range probable error   Error in range that is exceeded as often as not; a known error to be considered in selecting artillery systems for engaging targets in close proximity to friendly forces.

RPG   Rocket-powered grenade.

RVN   Republic of Vietnam.

SAM   Surface-to-air missiles.

SAR   Search-and-rescue.

SEATO   Southeast Asia Treaty Organization.

SGU   Special Guerrilla Unit.

Shining Brass   A program of American-led covert cross-border reconnaissance and exploitation patrols into eastern Laos; the program was later re-named "Prairie Fire."

Silver Buckle   Guerilla operations to interdict, mine, and disrupt enemy lines of communication in an area of the Ho Chi Minh Trail south of Tchepone.

SOG   Short form of MACV-SOG. Studies and Observation Group.

Squadron   A cavalry unit corresponding to a battalion or similar unit in other branches of the army.

Steel Tiger   United States air operations over the northern portion of the Laotian panhandle designed to interdict the Ho Chi Minh Trail.

S-3   Operations staff officer at battalion and brigade level.

SVN   South Vietnam.

TACAIR   Tactical air support; air operations carried out in coordination with surface forces and which directly assist land or maritime operations.

Task force   A temporary grouping of units under one commander, formed for the purpose of carrying out a specific mission or operation.

TASS   Tactical air support squadrons.

Tchepone   Alternate spellings include Sepone, Xe Pone, Xe Pon, and Chepone. A city in the Laotian panhandle that was the terrain objective for Operation Lam Son 719.

Troop   A cavalry unit corresponding to a company or similar unit in other branches of the army.

TOC   Tactical operations center.

USAF   United States Air Force.

USARV   United States Army, Vietnam; the army headquarters in Vietnam.

USMC   United States Marine Corps.

Vandergrift   A fire support and logistical support base located along Route 9, midway between Dong Ha and Khe Sanh.

VC   Vietcong.

Vietnamization   A program intended train, equip and pass the burden of combat from U.S. forces to South Vietnamese forces.

VNAF   Vietnamese Air Force.

VNE   Velocity never exceeded.

VNMC   Vietnamese Marine Division.

WIA   Wounded in action.

WSAG   Washington Special Actions Group.

Commonly Used Slang Terms

AC   Aircraft Commander. It was also used as an abbreviation for "aircraft."

ASAP   As soon as possible.

Cav   Cavalry.

Charley Model   UH-1C helicopter gunship.

Cold   Refers to the status of enemy activity at a landing zone or pick up zone. If the LZ is "cold," there is no enemy activity.

Final   The last and "final" phase of a prescribed landing pattern. An aircraft approaching the landing threshold was on "short final."

Friendlies   Refers to the force on the ground as being either U.S. or South Vietnamese.

Gun run   The aerobatic maneuvers associated an attack by a helicopter gunship.

Hootch   A slang term for a small building or hut.

Hot   Refers to the status of enemy activity at a landing zone or pick up zone. If the LZ is "hot," the enemy is present and firing.

Liar's Dice   A barroom game of chance and deception wherein each player is given a cup and five dice to roll and hide. Players make successively higher declarations regarding the results (e.g. "I have four 5's") until someone contests the declaration. When the declaration is called or contested, the dice are revealed. If the declarer was bluffing, he loses the bet. If he was not, the person who contested the declaration loses the bet.

Lift ship   A UH-1H helicopter transporting soldiers en route to a landing zone.

Slick   A UH-1 helicopter not equipped with armament systems on its external hard points.

BIBLIOGRAPHY

Primary Sources and Interviews

Berry, Lieutenant General Retired Sidney B., interviewed by Lieutenant Colonel Robert F. Broyles. Carlisle Barracks, PA: U.S. Army Military History Institute, Senior Officer Oral History Program, 1983.

Brown, Don (Retired USAF Lieutenant Colonel), interviewed by the author. Edmond, OK, 22 January 2012.

Butler, Allen "Skip" (Retired Lieutenant Colonel and former Aircraft Commander assigned to the D Company, 158th Aviation Battalion), interviewed by the author. 17 January 2012.

Davidson, Phillip. Vietnam at War: The History 1946–1975. New York: Oxford University Press, 1988.

Dize, Jesse (Former member of the 48th Assault Helicopter Company during Lam Son 719), interviewed by Mike Sloniker. Philadelphia, 4 July 1994.

Freeman, Rick (Retired Chief Warrant Officer, Aircraft Commander, 4th Battalion, 77th Aerial Rocket Artillery), interviewed by the author. 29–30 April 2011.

Fuji, Dennis (Former Specialist 5th Class), interviewed by Mike Sloniker. 2 December 2001.

Harrison, Benjamin L. (Senior Army Advisor to the ARVN 1st Infantry and Airborne Divisions), interviewed by the author. 28 May 2013.

Havens, Robert (Veteran, VO-676), interviewed by the author. 21 November 2012.

Headquarters, 101st Airborne Division. "101st Airborne Division Final Report," Airmobile Operations in Support of Lam Son 719 Report, Camp Eagle, Vietnam: 101st Airborne Division, 1971.

Headquarters, XXIV Corps. "Lam Son 719 After Action Report 30 January–6 April." Da Nang: Headquarters, XXIV Corps, 1971.

Hinh, Maj. Gen. Nguyen Duy. Lam Son 719. Washington, D.C.: U.S. Army Center of Military History, 1979.

Kissinger, Henry. Ending the War in Vietnam. New York: Simon and Schuster, 2005.

——. The White House Years. 1st. Boston: Little, Brown, 1979.

Lukens, Richard C. "Rick" (Retired Chief Warrant Officer), interviewed by the author. 3 October 2010.

101st Aviation Group. 101st Aviation Group Staff Duty Journal, 8 February 1971–25 March 1971. Khe Sanh, Vietnam: 101st Aviation Group.

Phouthasack, S. A. R. (Retired Major Special Guerilla Unit, Laos), interviewed by the author. 30 June 2012.

Review of the Resistance War Against the Americans to Save the Nation. Hanoi: National Political Press, 1995.

Roths, P. J. (Former Chief Warrant Officer and Aircraft Commander, 174th Assault Helicopter Company), interviewed by the author. 12 February 2011.

Sorley, Lewis. Vietnam Chronicles: The Abrams Tapes, 1968–1972. Lubbock: Texas Tech University Press, 2004.

Spratt, Dale (Retired U.S. Army Major, Commander, 174th Combat Aviation Company), interviewed by the author. 15 March 2011.

Sutherland, James. "Senior Officer Debriefing Report: LTG James Sutherland, Commanding General XXIV Corps, Period 18 June 1970 thru 9 June 1971." Washington: Department of the Army, 1971.

Sweeney, Patrick (Former USAF Captain and Forward Air Controller assigned to the 23rd TASS), interviewed by the author. 1February 2013.

U.S. Department of State, Office of the Historian. *Foreign Relations of the United States, 1961–1963, Vol. 1, Vietnam, 1961.* Washington, D.C.: Unites States Government Printing Office, 1988.

———. *Foreign Relations of The United States, 1961–1963, Vol. 2, Vietnam, 1962.* Washington, D.C.: U.S. Government Printing Office, 1990.

———. *Foreign Relations of the United States, 1961–1963, Vol. 3, Vietnam, January–August 1963.* Washington, D.C.: U.S. Government Printing Office, 1991.

———. *Foreign Relations of the United States, 1961–1963,Vol. 4, Vietnam, August–September 1963.* Washington, D.C.: U.S. Government Printing Office, 1991.

———. *Foreign Relations of the United States, 1961–1963, Vol. 23, Southeast Asia.* Washington, D.C.: U.S. Government Printing Office, 1994.

———. *Foreign Relations of the United States, 1961–1963, Vol. 24, Laos Crisis.* Washington, D.C.: U.S. Government Printing Office, 1994.

———. *Foreign Relations of the United States, 1964–1968, Vol. 1, Vietnam, 1964.* Washington, D.C.: U.S. Government Printing Office, 1992.

———. *Foreign Relations of the United States, 1964–1968, Vol. 2, Vietnam, January–June 1965.* Washington, D.C.: U.S. Government Printing Office, 1996.

———. *Foreign Relations of the United States, 1964–1968, Vol. 3, Vietnam, June–December 1965.* Washington, D.C.: U.S. Government Printing Office, 1996.

———. *Foreign Relations of the United States, 1964–1968, Vol. 4, Vietnam, 1966.* Washington, D.C.: U.S. Government Printing Office, 1998.

———. *Foreign Relations of the United States, 1964–1968, Vol. 5, Vietnam, 1967.* Washington, D.C.: U.S. Government Printing Office, 2002.

———. *Foreign Relations of the United States, 1964–1968, Vol. 6, Vietnam, January–August 1968*. Washington, D.C.: U.S. Government Printing Office, 2002.

———. *Foreign Relations of the United States, 1964–1968, Vol. 7, Vietnam, September 1968–January 1969*. Washington, D.C.: U.S. Government Printing Office, 2003.

———. *Foreign Relations of the United States, 1964–1968, Vol. 17, Eastern Europe*. Washington, D.C.: U.S. Government Printing Office, 1996.

———. *Foreign Relations of the United States, 1964–1968, Vol. 23, Laos*. Washington, D.C.: U.S. Government Printing Office, 1998.

———. *Foreign Relations of the United States, 1969–1976, Vol. 3 Vietnam, January–October 1972*. Washington, D.C.: U.S. Government Printing Office, 2010.

———. *Foreign Relations of the United States, 1969–1976, Vol. 6, Vietnam, January 1969–July 1970*. Washington, D.C.: U.S. Government Printing Office, 2006.

———. *Foreign Relations of the United States, 1969–1976, Vol. 7, Vietnam, July 1970–January 1972*. Washington, D.C.: U.S. Government Printing Office, 2010.

———. *Foreign Relations of the United States, 1969–1976, Vol. 17, China, 1969–1972*. Washington, D.C.: U.S. Government Printing Office, 2006.

———. *Foreign Relations of the United States, 1969–1976, Vol. 19, Part 1, Korea, 1969–1972*. Washington, D.C.: U.S. Government Printing Office, 2010.

———. *Foreign Relations of the United States, 1969–1976, Vol. 20, Southeast Asia, 1969–1972*. Washington, D.C.: U.S. Government Printing Office, 2006.

Veterans of the 71st Combat Aviation Company, interviewed by Mike Sloniker. Philadelphia, 4 July 1994.

Want, Walter W. (Former USAF Captain and Forward Aircraft Controller, 23rd TASS), interviewed by the author. 3 June 2012.

Womack, Doug (Former Chief Warrant Officer and Aircraft Commander, 71st CAC), interviewed by the author. 4–7 January 2012.

Secondary Sources

Ball, George. *The Past Has Another Pattern*. New York: W. W. Norton, 1983.

Bernstein, Mark D. "Vietnam War: Operation Dewey Canyon." *Vietnam Magazine* (June 2007). http://www.historynet.com/vietnam-war-operation-dewey-canyon.htm.

Beschloss, Michael. *Reaching for Glory: Lyndon Johnson's Secret White House Tapes 1964–1965*. New York: Simon and Schuster, 2001.

Bonin, John A. "Army Aviation Becomes an Essential Arm: From Howze Board to the Modular Force." PhD Dissertation. Temple University, 2006.

Butler, Howard K. *Army Aviation Logistics and Vietnam, 1961–1975*. St. Louis: History Office, United States Army Aviation Systems Command, 1985.

Clodfelter, Mark. *The Limits of Air Power*. New York: Macmillan, 1984.

Collins, John. *Military Geography for Professionals and the Public*. Kindle Edition. Washington, D.C.: Potomac Books, 2012.

Cooper, Charles, and Richard Goodspeed. Cheers and Tears: *A Marine's Story of Combat in Peace and War.* Edited by Richard Goodspeed. Reno: Wesley Press, 2002.

Cosmas, Graham A. *MACV: The Joint Staff in the Years of Escalation, 1962–1967.* Washington, D.C.: U.S. Army Center of Military History, 2006.

Cosmas, Graham A., and Terrence Murphy. *U.S. Marines in Vietnam: Vietnamization and Redeployment, 1970–1971.* Washington, D.C.: Department of the Navy, History and Museums Division, U.S. Marine Corps, 1986.

Forward Air Controllers Association. *Cleared Hot: Forward Air Controller Stories from the Vietnam War.* Edited by Alice Witterman, Peter Condon, and Charles Pocock. Fort Walton Beach, FL: Forward Air Controller Association, 2008.

14th Combat Aviation Battalion. "The Vietnam Center and Archive." The Vietnam Center and Archive, Texas Tech University. January 1, 2013. http://www.vietnam.ttu.edu/virtualarchive/items.php?item=168300010620. Accessed 13 January 2013.

From Khe Sanh to Chepone [Tchepone]. Hanoi: Foreign Languages Publishing House, 1971.

Fulghum, David, and Terrance Maitland. *South Vietnam on Trial.* Boston: Boston Publishing, 1984.

Galdorisi, George, and Tom Phillips. *Leave No Man Behind.* Minneapolis: Zenith Press, 2008.

Gibson, James W. *The Perfect War: Technowar in Vietnam.* New York: Grove Atlantic, 1986.

Gillespie, Robert M. *Black Ops Vietnam: The Operational History of MACVSOG.* Annapolis, MD: Naval Institute Press, 2011.

Haig, Alexander, and Charles McCarry. Inner Circles: *How America Changed the World.* New York: Warner Books, 1992.

Haldeman, H. R. *The Haldeman Diaries.* New York: G. P. Putman's Sons, 1994.

Harrison, Benjamin L. *Hell on a Hill Top.* Lincoln: iUniverse, 2004.

Hay, John J. Vietnam Studies, *Tactical and Materiel Innovations.* Washington, D.C.: United States Army Center for Military History, 1974.

Herring, George C. *America's Longest War: The United States and Vietnam 1950–1975.* New York: McGraw-Hill, 1986.

Karnow, Stanley. *Vietnam: A History.* New York: Penguin Group, 1984.

Klose, John A. G. "Briefing for the Aviation Battalion Commander's Precommand Course." Briefing. Fort Rucker, AL: Historian, United States Army Aviation School, 2001.

Langguth, A. J. *Our Vietnam: The War 1954–1975.* New York: Simon and Schuster, 2000.

Loye, J. F., G. K. St. Clair, L. J. Johnson, and J. W. Dennison. *Contemporary Historical Evaluation of Current Operations, Lam Son 719.* Washington, D.C.: Department of the Air Force, 1971.

McInerney, Maitland T. *A Contagion of War*. Boston: Boston Publishing, 2000.

McMasters, H. R. *Dereliction of Duty: Johnson, McNamara, the Joint Chiefs of Staff, and the Lies that Led to Vietnam*. New York: Harper Collins, 1997.

Melson, Charles D. "Thirty Years Later." *Fortitudine: Bulletin of the Marine Corps Historical Program* 28, no. 2 (1999): 3–8.

Miller, John Grider. *The Co-Vans: U.S. Marine Advisors in Vietnam*. Annapolis, MD: Naval Institute Press, 2000.

Morris, Virginia. *A History of the Ho Chi Minh Trail: The Road to Freedom*. Bangkok: Orchid Press, 2006.

Nalty, Bernard C. *The War Against Trucks: Aerial Interdiction in Southern Laos, 1968–1972*. Washington, D.C.: Air Force History and Museums Program, 2005.

101st Aviation Group. *Operation Lam Son 719, February 8, 1971 to March 25, 1971: A Narrative Description of Air Support by the 101st Aviation Group*. Camp Eagle, Vietnam: 101st Aviation Group, 1971.

Palmer, Bruce. *The 25-Year War: America's Role in Vietnam*. Lexington: University of Kentucky Press, 1984.

Palmer, Dave R. *Summons of the Trumpet: U.S.–Vietnam in Perspective*. Novato: Presidio Press, 1978.

Plaster, John L. *SOG: The Secret War of America's Commandos in Vietnam*. New York: New American Library, 1997.

Prados, John. *The Blood Road, The Ho Chi Minh Trail, and the Vietnam War*. New York: John Wiley and Sons, 1999.

Pribbenow, Merle L., trans. *Victory in Vietnam*. Lawrence: University of Kansas Press, 2002.

Pyle, Richard, and Horst Fass. *Lost Over Laos*. Cambridge, Mass.: Da Capo Press, 2003.

Robbins, Christopher. *The Ravens: The Men Who Flew in America's Secret War in Laos*. New York: Crown Publishers, 1987.

Sams, Kenneth. *Project CHECO Report: The Fall of A Shau*. Headquarters, Pacific Air Force, 1966.

Sloniker, Mike. "Lam Son 719 With Pictures." Vietnam Helicopter Pilots Association. Unpublished, 2007.

Sorley, Lewis. *A Better War*. Orlando: Harcourt Books, 1999.

Staaveren, Jacob Van. *Interdiction in Southern Laos 1960–1968*. Washington, D.C.: Center for Air Force History, 1993.

Starry, General Donn. "Mounted Combat in Vietnam," Center for Military History Publication 90–17. Washington, D.C.: U.S. Army Center for Military History, 1978.

S-2, 2nd Squadron, 17th Air Cavalry. Intelligence Summary 67–71. Camp Eagle, Vietnam: 2nd Squadron, 17th Air Cavalry, 1971.

Swift, Earle. *Where They Lay: A Forensic Expedition in the Jungles of Laos*. New York: Houghton Mifflin Harcourt, 2005.

Taylor, Maxwell D. *Swords and Plowshares: A Memoir.* New York: W.W. Norton, 1972.

Tilford, Earle H. Jr. *Crosswinds: The Air Force's Setup in Vietnam.* College Station: Texas A&M University Press, 2009.

Tolson, John J. *Vietnam Studies: Airmobility 1961–1971.* Washington, D.C.: United States Government Printing Office, 1989.

Turley, G. H. *The Easter Offensive.* Novato, CA: Presidio Press, 1985.

223rd Combat Aviation Battalion. After Action Report, Lam Son 719. Quang Tri, Vietnam: 223rd Combat Aviation Battalion, 1971.

223rd Combat Aviation Battalion. Staff Duty Journal, February 1971. Quang Tri, Vietnam: 223rd Combat Aviation Battalion, 1971.

U.S. Air Force Museum. "National Museum of the US Air Force." National Museum of the USAF, Media Search. www.nationalmuseum.af.mil/shared/media/photodb/photos. Accessed 17 December 2012.

U.S. Army Center for Military History. *American Military History.* Edited by Richard W Stewart. Volume 2. Washington, D.C.: U.S. Army Center for Military History, 2005.

———. *Vietnam Studies, U.S. Army Special Forces 1961–1971.* Washington, D.C.: U.S. Army Center of Military History, 1973.

U.S. Army War College Strategic Studies Institute. *A Study of Strategic Lessons Learned in Vietnam.* Mclean, VA: BDM, 1982.

Valentiny, Capt. Edward. *Project CHECO Report Operations From Thailand January 1967–July 1968.* CHECO Division, HQ PACAF.

Vien, Gen. Cao Van. *Leadership.* Washington, D.C.: U.S. Army Center of Military History, 1981.

———. *The Final Collapse.* Washington, D.C.: United States Army Center of Military History, 1985.

Vietnam Helicopter Pilots Association. Killed in Action File. *Vietnam Helicopter Pilots Association.* www.vhpa.org/KIA/panel/panelind.htm. Accessed 17 December 2012.

Webb, Willard J., and Walter S. Poole. *The Joint Chiefs of Staff and the War in Vietnam 1971–1973.* Washington, D.C.: Office of Joint History, Office of the Chairman of the Joint Chiefs of Staff, 2007.

Westmoreland, William. *A Soldier Reports.* New York: Grove Atlantic, 1989.

Wiest, Andrew. *Vietnam's Forgotten Army, Heroism and Betrayal in the ARVN.* New York: New York University Press, 2008.

Williams, James W. *A History of Army Aviation.* New York: iUniverse, 2005.

Zaffiri, Samuel. *Hamburger Hill.* Novato: Presidio Press, Inc., 1988.

Acknowledgements

Invasion of Laos, 1971 is the product of the gracious assistance of a host of Vietnam veterans and scholars. First among them is Lt. Col. (retired) Mike Sloniker, the long-time historian for the Vietnam Helicopter Pilots Association, who provided documents and introductions to other veterans who were the subjects of my interviews. I found a friend in every interview as we shared our common experiences and was personally enriched by the individual perspectives each veteran brought to the discussion. I was reminded of the special brotherhood we shared during a time when much of America shunned its warriors. I undertook this project in hopes that the families of the men who died might understand the greatness of their gift.

I am not a writer, as many scholars who reviewed my constantly evolving manuscript can attest. I am indebted to Charles E. Rankin, editor-in-chief of Oklahoma University Press, for his patience, encouragement, and introductions to historians Deborah Kidwell and Dale Wilson, who gave freely of their time and expertise.

The inspiration to take on this task came from many sources. Native Americans, perhaps more than any other segment of our society, respect their veterans. A large portion of Citizen Potawatomi Nation's Cultural Heritage Center is dedicated to veterans. On the wall, above the photographs is the following inscription by an unknown author: "Poor is the nation that has no heroes, but disgraceful are those who having them, forget." Uncommon valor was common during Lam Son 719. Pilots, crew chiefs, door gunners, and South Vietnamese soldiers boarded helicopters bound for hell. They were not heroes for what they did, but rather for why they did it. Few were without fear, but their shared sense of brotherhood allowed them to do little else.

My family was the greatest source of inspiration. My wife and best friend, Jan, was a constant source of encouragement, just as she was during our twenty-five years in the army. My final source of inspiration was my grandsons. Boys, this was for you.

INDEX

Italicized page numbers indicate figures.

Stewart, Clark, 112

Studies and Observation Group (SOG), 43, 46, 49. *See also* Operation Shining Brass

Sullivan, William, 22, 34–35, 44, 45, 46, 48–49

Sutherland, James, 95, 103, 108, 127, 135, 143, 145, 147, 151, 201, 202

Sweeney, Pat, 237n35

Tactical air support squadron (TASS), 36

Tactical air support (TACAIR), 115

Tank forces, 152–53, 184

Taylor, Maxwell, 9, 18, 43

Tchepone, Laos, 3, 6, 91

Tchepone operation: Air Force in landing zone preparation, 161–62; air support in, 160–61; aircraft lost in LZ Lolo insertions, 164; Kissinger briefing on, 159–60

Tet Offensive, 25–28, 58, 197

Thailand, 67, 165

Thau Thien Province, South Vietnam, 62, 119, 192

Thieu, Nguyen Van, 30, 60, 85, 124, 129, 140, 159, 173, 174, 180, 191, 195, 197, 208, 234n13

Thompson, Robert, 193, 194

Thong, Hoang Tich, 186

Tin, Bui, 209

Tonkin Gulf incident, 15

Trail-watch party system, 45

Tri, Do Cao, 74, 199

Twiehaus, Wayne, *220*

UH-1C Charley Model gunship, 122, 148, *215*; average altitude of hits on, 139; at LZ Lolo, 162, 165; operational ready rate of, 137, 145–48; vulnerabilities of, 215–17

UH-1H, 214–17

United States: 1964 presidential elections, 15; 1968 presidential elections, 30; anti-war protests in, 74–75

U.S. Air Force: air power doctrine of, 46; aircraft losses, 230; in fall of FSB 31, 150–51; forward air controllers and, 35–36; in landing zone preparation, 161–62; rivalry with army aviation, 201–203

U.S. counterinsurgency campaign, 15

U.S. Marines in Vietnam, 1970–1971, 206

U.S. Military Assistance and Advisory Group (MAAG), 5

U.S. Military Assistance Command, Vietnam (MACV), 14, 29, 43, 45, 46, 114, 146

U.S. 1st Battalion, 77th Armor, 100

U.S. 1st Brigade, 5th Mechanized Infantry Division, 87, 99, 118, 119, 144, 158

U.S. 1st Cavalry Division, 19, 53, 69

U.S. 1st Cavalry Regiment, 100

U.S. 1st Infantry Division, 19, 128

U.S. 1st Squadron, 1st Cavalry Regiment, 100

U.S. 2nd Airborne Battalion, 154

U.S. 2nd Squadron, 17th Air Cavalry, 110, 113, 116, 117, 121, 143, 144, 156, 172

U.S. 3rd Battalion, 187th Infantry, 58–60

U.S. 3rd Brigade, 9th Infantry Division, 69, 76

U.S. 3rd Infantry Regiment, 159

U.S. 3rd Marine Division, 54, 61

U.S. 3rd Squadron, 5th Cavalry, 99, 228

U.S. 4th Infantry Division, 19, 26, 69

U.S. 5th Cavalry, 99, 228

U.S. 5th Infantry Division, 158

U.S. 5th Mechanized Division, 87, 99, 230